Transforming Writing Instruction
in the Digital Age

TEACHING PRACTICES THAT WORK
Diane Lapp and Douglas Fisher, Series Editors

Designed specifically for busy teachers who value evidence-based instructional practices, books in this series offer ready-to-implement strategies and tools to promote student engagement, improve teaching and learning across the curriculum, and support the academic growth of all students in our increasingly diverse schools. Written by expert authors with extensive experience in "real-time" classrooms, each concise and accessible volume provides useful explanations and examples to guide instruction, as well as step-by-step methods and reproducible materials, all in a convenient large-size format for ease of photocopying.

Transforming Writing Instruction in the Digital Age

Techniques for Grades 5–12

Thomas DeVere Wolsey
Dana L. Grisham

Series Editors' Note by Diane Lapp and Douglas Fisher
Foreword by Bridget Dalton

THE GUILFORD PRESS
New York   London

© 2012 The Guilford Press
A Division of Guilford Publications, Inc.
72 Spring Street, New York, NY 10012
www.guilford.com

Printed in the United States of America

This book is printed on acid-free paper.

Last digit is print number: 9 8 7 6 5 4 3 2 1

Library of Congress Cataloging-in-Publication Data

Wolsey, Thomas DeVere.
    Transforming writing instruction in the digital age : techniques for grades
5–12 / Thomas DeVere Wolsey and Dana L. Grisham.
        p.   cm. — (Teaching practices that work)
    Includes bibliographical references and index.
    ISBN 978-1-4625-0465-7 (pbk.)
    1. English language—Composition and exercises—Study and
teaching (Secondary)—Computer-assisted instruction.   2. Internet in
education.   I. Grisham, Dana L., 1945– II. Title.
    LB1631.3.W65 2012
    428.0071′2—dc23
                                                            2011052461

About the Authors

Thomas DeVere Wolsey, EdD, is Specialization Coordinator for the literacy graduate degree programs for teachers at Walden University and an affiliate researcher at the National Center for the Twenty-First Century Schoolhouse at San Diego State University. He worked in public schools for 20 years teaching English and social studies. Dr. Wolsey is interested in how school spaces affect learning, how technology changes and intersects with literacy instruction, and how writing in the disciplines is best taught.

Dana L. Grisham, PhD, is a member of the Core Adjunct Faculty at National University, where she teaches courses online in the master of arts program in reading for teachers. A retired professor from The California State University, she also coordinated the Graduate Reading Program at San Diego State University and served as Faculty Coordinator of the Center for the Advancement of Reading for the Office of the Chancellor. Her research focuses on the intersection of literacy and technology. Dr. Grisham is Associate Editor of *Reading and Writing Quarterly*.

Series Editors' Note

As our schools continue to grow in linguistic, cultural, and socioeconomic diversity, educators are committed to implementing instruction that supports both individual and collective growth within their classrooms. In tandem with teacher commitment, schools recognize the need to support teacher collaboration on issues related to implementing, evaluating, and expanding instruction to ensure that all students will graduate from high school with the skills needed to succeed in the workforce. Through our work with teachers across the country, we've become aware of the need for books that can be used to support professional collaboration by grade level and subject area. With these teachers' questions in mind, we decided that a series of books was needed that modeled "real-time" teaching and learning within classroom instruction. Thus the series *Teaching Practices That Work* was born.

Books in this series are distinguished by offering instructional examples that have been studied and refined within authentic classroom settings. Each book is written by one or more educators who are well connected to everyday classroom instruction. Because the series editors are themselves classroom teachers as well as professors, each instructional suggestion has been closely scrutinized for its validity.

In *Transforming Writing Instruction in the Digital Age: Techniques for Grades 5–12*, Thomas DeVere Wolsey and Dana L. Grisham share examples of intentional and engaging instructional ideas that incorporate technology to promote writing development. While "intentional and engaging" is sometimes believed to be an oxymoron when referring to classroom teaching and learning, these authors have accomplished this dual purpose. They provide examples of instruction designed to help teachers support their students' continuous growth as writers who can create and share their ideas in ways that transform their thinking and the thinking of their readers.

This book's examples and scenarios illustrate how to engage students with writing by bringing into the classroom many forms of social networking that both students and teachers normally expect to use only outside of school. Organized by the use of hashtags, the book is enjoyable to read not just for the new teaching ideas but also for its clever way of enabling the reader to gain more insights about the "digital learners" inhabiting contemporary classrooms.

We invite you into the "real-time" teaching offered in this book and hope you'll find this series useful as you validate and expand your teaching repertoire. And if you have an idea for a book, please contact us!

DIANE LAPP
DOUGLAS FISHER

Foreword

My friend calls out, "The water's amazing! Jump in!" I hesitate. "Hmmmnn, shall I? It looks cold. Are those clouds on the horizon? I like to swim, but snorkeling is relatively new to me." I stand at the edge of the dock, watching my friend enjoy herself. I know she is an experienced snorkeler and this is one of her favorite spots. I grab hold of my gear and step off the edge. "Okay, here goes, I'm JUMPING! Wow, this feels great!" And away we go, my friend and I, swimming over the coral reef, ready for an adventure together.

Thomas DeVere Wolsey and Dana L. Grisham have written a book about technology and writing that invites us to "Jump in!" and join them in the adventure of integrating technology into the teaching and learning of the millennial generation. They invite us to jump (or step, if you are feeling a bit more cautious) into the exciting and sometimes turbulent waters of teaching writing in today's schools. They guide us to focus on what's important about writing, learning, and the role that technology and media can play in improving the quality of our students' compositions, their use of writing to transform learning, and their engagement with academic literacy.

Leaders in the scholarship and practice of digital literacies, DeVere and Dana are expert guides who share the wealth of their knowledge and experience in this book, which is designed to help teachers take the next step forward in using technology to engage students in writing that is *worth doing*. The book artfully combines theory and practice, presenting numerous examples and vignettes to offer a vision of what is possible, along with the concrete suggestions and practical tips that are essential to success. I had barely started reading the manuscript and taking notes to prepare me for writing this foreword when I found myself opening a second document file to take note of teaching ideas, digital tools, and resources that I knew would be useful to me in my own work. The book had a larger effect on me, however, stimulating my thinking about our underlying models of composition in a digital world and the urgent need to improve both theory and practice. It also reinvigorated me. The status quo is not working for too many of our students. It's not working for many of us who are teachers. Using technology to help students create, communicate, connect, and learn is one way to change things. I believe that teachers, literacy coaches, teacher educators, and curriculum specialists will find this book to be a valuable resource, one that provides multiple entry points and pathways to follow in accordance with their individual goals, subject areas, and levels of technology expertise. In the following section, I highlight some of the key features of the book that I think make it a particularly valuable resource.

 ♦ *Student learning and writing pedagogy drive technology integration, not the other way around.* I love "cool tools." In fact, my colleague Debbie Rowe and I lead a multimodal composition research group for doctoral students that begins each session with one of the members sharing a digital tool that has interesting implications for research and practice. DeVere and Dana offer a rich array of digital tools and resources throughout their book. However, it is abundantly clear from the Introduction through to the last page that their book is about writing, is about learning, and is about engagement. Technology and media are essential to making that happen. We need the nuts and bolts to build something, but we also need to have a vision for what we're building, to understand why it's important, and to know how we go about constructing it. Before we begin, we want some evidence that what we're doing is supported by previous experience and success.

Dana and DeVere set their vision in the Introduction and then extend and apply it in each chapter. They draw on Bereiter and Scardamalia's (1987) models of writing as either "knowledge telling" or "knowledge transformation." While they acknowledge the role of "writing to tell," their passion is in helping students use writing for knowledge transformation. I appreciate the way they structure each chapter to open with sections on "What is it?" and "Why is it important?" before moving on to how technology can help. Theory and research are embedded throughout (and where the research is limited, they suggest practices that are promising). The continuing message is that technology is both medium and message, and that it is their particular use by knowledgeable teachers and their students that will move us forward.

 ♦ *Writing is not just for English; writing is discipline specific.* Often there is a divide between folks who love to teach writing for literary purposes and those who love to teach their content and view writing as a vehicle to communicate learning. DeVere and Dana offer a more integrative perspective. They make a strong case for why writing is part of academic literacy. Writing is not just a matter of genre and text structure; rather it's a way of thinking and using language and symbol systems to communicate within our community. A real strength of this book is the range and depth of examples from English, social studies, and science classrooms that illustrate how technology and media can transform the learning process and offer new opportunities for students' creative expression, social interaction, and learning. Students compose to grapple with challenging content and accomplish purposes specific to the subject matter. While composing tools might be considered somewhat generic, Dana and DeVere illustrate how it is what you do with them in relation to particular academic content and skills that can make all the difference between a "just okay" and an "amazing" student-learning experience and outcome.

◆ *We're all in this together, or teachers and students are making it happen.* In public speeches about educational reform and in professional development efforts, we often hear that teachers are leaders and that our notion of "what works" should expand to include practitioners' expertise and experience. The democratization of publishing on the Internet has offered many teachers the opportunity to communicate directly with an audience that is interested in learning from and with them as they go about the daily work of teaching in schools. Blogs, websites, and wikis are just a few of their online venues. However, teachers' voices are less well represented in published textbooks. One of my favorite features in this book is the inclusion of in-depth classroom examples in each chapter. Some examples are written by teachers, whereas others are written by DeVere and Dana at a level of detail that shows their intimate knowledge of the teacher, his or her classroom, and students. It is the combination of Dana and DeVere's expertise with the expertise of some amazing classroom teachers that give this book depth and credibility.

◆ *Affect matters—for students and for us.* Have you ever taken a course or a workshop because of the *way* the instructor teaches, as much as the content of the course? The importance of affect and the social basis of learning is just as true for adults as it is for children—perhaps even more so, since we bring firmly entrenched beliefs and dispositions along with vast stores of knowledge and skills to each learning encounter. Clearly, DeVere and Dana are highly expert and experienced in the field of writing and technology and there is much to be learned from the information in this book. They are somewhat unusual, I think, in the way that they have shared some of who they are through their writing of this book. Their writing style and tone are conversational as they think out loud, conjecture, joke, and share strong feelings and convictions. They respect teachers and children. They understand and have experienced the realities of real teaching, real kids, and the unpredictability and promise of teaching with technology. They are resilient and hopeful about the future of students in our schools and the role of technology and writing in making change happen. By the end of the book, I was very glad to have had Dana and DeVere's guidance and to know that they are continuing their adventures in writing and technology. Jump in and try an adventure of your own—I know I will.

BRIDGET DALTON, EdD
Vanderbilt University

Postscript: An alternative representation of this foreword, communicated through a word cloud (*http://www.wordle.net*).

Introduction
Writing for and with the Millennial Generation

We note that writing represents the most intellectually complex form of human communication, deserving much more extensive and skilled instruction in our schools and universities (Graham & Perrin, 2007). The millennial generation's intrinsic involvement with technologies, which we will refer to in this book as new or online literacies, add another complex layer to the issue, particularly for teachers and professors who may not view recent technological innovations in such a positive light.

The millennials—the age cohort we call Gen-Y—are just like us, only different. The authors of this book are baby boomers. If a television show comes on we want to watch, we sit down at the appointed time and do so. If we miss it, it will come around again in reruns. But those in the millennial generation customize the show's schedule to their liking. The show is on at 8 o'clock on Tuesday, but the work schedule conflicts? No problem—set the digital video recorder (DVR) or catch it on the Internet and watch it later.

Those born in the post-World War II era share some characteristics in general that are different from the characteristics of the following generation, popularly known as Gen-X. In turn, the millennials (or Gen-Y) differ in important ways from Gen-X. One thing you may notice is that we never use the term "digital native" (Prensky, 2001) to refer to the millennial generation; it is a metaphor we find problematic. Generational trends are determined, in part, by lifespan and age or chronology, but also by defining events and trends. For example, the end of World War II defined differences in how many Americans lived their lives, thus signaling the demarcation between the "Greatest Generation" and the baby boomers. The generation Strauss and Howe (1991) call the G. I. generation confronted the problem of nuclear weapons, the atrocities of Nazi Germany, and the contradiction of the Japanese American internment at home. The baby boomer generation faced the era of nuclear weapons and the Cold War and the promise of education and civil rights for all. Age cohorts, or generations, reach across time to impact the present and change the future.

Rapidly evolving digital technologies during the last two decades present new opportunities and new challenges for our millennial-generation writers. Adolescents form personal and social identities throughout middle and high school, and the millennial generation illustrates this through the social networking tools they use. Middle and high school students may partially construct these identities in a writing community. More important, technology can help with content-learning tasks and identity construction.

Development toward adulthood also involves a "decentering" process (Chandler, 1977). As children grow toward maturity, they become less self-centered and egoistic, learning to consider themselves as part of family groups, then social groups, then part of the larger world around them. One of the goals of schooling is to aid in this process; to socialize students into ever-larger community contexts. Although adolescents in recent times have always attempted to socialize themselves outside adult contexts, today's students often socialize with each other using technology (Williams, 2008). Social networking is pervasive and provides a new and exciting kind of community for adolescents. In talking with young adults, we have learned that the rapid pace of technology changes how adolescents interact with each other, what they value as they form their identities, and the forms of literacy that they use.

What Is Writing and Composing?

Each generation values written communication differently. In our grandparents' generation, handwritten letters to friends and families were the norm. In examining today's mail, the vestigial remains of this practice include holiday letters, cards for birthdays, thank you notes, and so on. Neither of the authors can remember a time in the current century when we have received a handwritten friendly letter. Yet, this literacy form is still taught in all our elementary schools (though often not learned).

Each technological innovation shrinks the world and brings us into contact with people different from ourselves. Through the Internet we may come into contact with communities and cultures much different from our own. One must be able to command multiple media (pictures, text, audio, video, hypertext links) to construct a space for one's persona to be revealed strategically.

Writing instruction in the United States is a neglected instructional area (Graham & Perrin, 2007). This book proposes the idea that writing should and can be a transformative learning experience in grades 5–12 and within and across the many disciplines or content areas students encounter in their careers as students in those grades.

How to Use This Book

In addition to this Introduction, we have divided this book into seven parts. Each part addresses a different aspect of writing with technology in the disciplines and is divided up into several smaller chapters. Each part and each chapter can be read alone, or you may choose to read from page one straight through the end of the book. In Part One, we explain some of the ideas about technology and pedagogy that we have found to be useful. Part Two explores the idea that writing in the disciplines is a complex task that encourages student writers to use writing to think of themselves as creators of ideas and transformative thinkers, an idea you will see again in Technique 6. Composing, as we have noted, is a good way to foster thinking about the disciplines. Social studies teachers often tell students to think like historians; science teachers suggest that students will find thinking like a scientist exciting. We agree, and writing with technology is one important route to thinking about content. Some ideas for content-area learning through writing and technology are found in Part Three and Part Four, respectively. English language arts presents certain challenges that are different in some ways as students explore works of fiction—the focus of Part Five. Never before have young writers had access to other modalities for composing, such as creating a podcast or movie; thus a few ideas are presented for putting language, images, video, and audio together in Part Six with a wrap-up of special topics in Part Seven.

To make reading easier and to help you put the ideas into practice in your own classroom, we have added a couple of features we think you'll like. First, we use Twitter-style hashtags to help you find ideas and cross-reference them. We avoided organizing the techniques by the type of technology—you know, a technique on blogs, a technique on wikis, and so on. Writers choose the format that meets their needs rather than composing to fit the tool. The hashtags will help you find content (for example, #science), tools (for example, #wikis), and ideas (for example, #revising, #advocacy). A list of all the hashtags can be found on page xx.

Most chapters in Parts Three through Six are written in the format below, with some variation depending on the topic:

- ◆ What is it?
- ◆ Why is it important?
- ◆ How will technology help?
- ◆ What do I do?

- ◆ Differentiation possibilities
- ◆ Additional resources
- ◆ Examples
  - ◆ Real-time teaching examples from teachers we know
  - ◆ Online examples
  - ◆ Scenarios from the fictional Metro High School and Community Middle School

We welcome you to our own transformative experience in writing this book for you and for your students.

Contents

······················· **PART SIX** ·······················

Composing with Multimedia 185

······················· **PART SEVEN** ·······················

Wrapping It Up 195

Hashtags by Technique

PART ONE

Getting Started with Tools and Teaching

Often, students are told that writing is the opposite, or mirror, of reading. However, it might be argued that composing tasks are much more than a simple reflection of reading (Berninger & Richards, 2002). As cognitively demanding as reading is, composing thoughts in a way that others might read and value requires more than just recognition of what others have thought and how they have organized their work; composition taxes the brain (Kellogg & Whiteford, 2009) in ways that include planning ideas and attending to the needs of those who might read the piece, considering multiple sources along with the similarities and contrasts found in such sources, creating new ideas drawn from those sources, reviewing the feedback on many drafts, revising ideas, and attending to the conventions of English that make any written work comprehensible. Writing well is a complex cognitive task, and when young writers are asked to make sense from equally complex knowledge of disciplines such as science and history, the task may seem overwhelming. But it does not have to be overwhelming. With expert planning by skilled teachers, writing tasks can become challenging and engaging work for students in middle and high schools. More important, those writing tasks are learning opportunities for students who are learning to think like mathematicians, scientists, historians, and musicians. For the teacher, getting started means knowing what resources are available, understanding how to manage the technology-friendly classroom, and embracing writing as a means of learning discipline-specific content.

Resources
Anytime, Anywhere

Cross-reference hashtags: #access, #advocacy, #definitions

What Is It?

Before teachers can integrate 21st-century technologies into their instruction, they need a clear picture of what technologies are available and what technologies they can obtain. Once a basic inventory of resources is complete, the next step is to plan how students might store electronic files and move them from one computer to another (or to a cell phone, television, or the Internet). For students where and when they can access technology might be summed up as anytime and anywhere. Imagine Elena, a seventh-grade student, asking her teacher, "I read about some animals scientists cloned. Is cloning related to meiosis?" Then imagine the teacher replying, "That is a really great question, Elena. I signed up for the computer lab at the end of the month. When we are there in a couple of weeks, why don't you look it up on the Internet?"

As you can see, having digital access as close to the point of learning when the need arises is a critical component of effective technology integration that brings students and their teachers to the 21st century. To drive home this point, consider a scenario explained by our colleague, Nancy Frey, who uses a caricature to explain the importance of having technology readily available. Once again, imagine a teacher saying, "Let's write about the influence of the Gutenberg printing press on our society today. I have signed us up for the pencil lab, and we'll go there to use the pencils and paper on Thursday."

Why Is It Important?

Two key criteria for technology in education that prepares students to be effective citizens, to be successful in the workplace, and to be lifelong learners are the following:

◆ Communication, connectivity, and collaboration are integral to the learning process.

◆ Students can learn from any place at any time (Software and Information Industry Association, 2010, p. 17).

In a study conducted when computers were not generally available in public school classrooms, the researchers found that students in first grade used computers three times more often if the computers were in their classrooms rather than in a computer lab (Beckenstein & Staunton, 1998). Zandvliet (2006) took the argument further by proposing that computer labs were designed at a time when computers were highly sophisticated devices that only rocket scientists (quite literally) might be able to access. He suggests that though the computers are more sophisticated than ever, they are also tools that need not be confined to a single space in schools. While computer labs are sometimes good uses of space in a school building, several considerations are worth the attention of students and teachers that make computers and other digital technologies available anytime and anywhere.

Another consideration is the degree to which students are permitted to use school and personal technologies. Many schools ban iPods and cell phones, yet these tools may be powerful learning devices when students are taught how and when to use them. Fisher and Frey (2008) argue that rather than ban such technologies as an MP3 player or cell phone outright that school policies should promote concepts of courtesy and appropriate educational use of those tools. More applications become available over the Internet every day, sometimes referred to as cloud computing. Recently, the Kentucky Department of Education made numerous software applications available to over 700,000 Kentucky students that are accessible online (eSchool News, 2010). Other schools are using Google Apps to provide applications such as spreadsheets, word processors, document sharing, and e-mail to students at no or low cost (Google, 2011). The cost savings are huge, but the potential for students to access software they need not buy themselves is relevant because students often work from multiple computers at home and at school.

What Do I Do?

If your school has an inventory of computer equipment, obtain it. If not, work with your administrators to find out where all the technology is located and who has access. Next, use Form 1.1 at the end of this chapter to make some determinations about anytime, anywhere access. This survey may be used by an individual teacher or given to all teachers at a site to gain a broader picture of technology use at the school.

Examples: Access Technology Three Ways

Besides the traditional computer lab, we propose three other approaches to putting technology into students' hands. First, there are several one-to-one initiatives that put one computer in students' backpacks. One of the most publicized is Maine's Learning Technology Initiative (Maine Department of Education, 2009). A goal for the Maine initiative is to ensure relevant technology for all secondary students; that is, equitable access to the tools of the 21st century. Some schools secure grants to provide one computer or similar technology for each student. Second, as we explored above, reasonable access to the Internet can be had by schools that choose to equip each classroom with some computers. Such an approach may mean that students have to work at different times. As well, whole-class instruction with every student's fingers on a keyboard will not be possible. Third, many forward-thinking school systems are exploring how best to implement bring-your-own-technology (BYOT) initiatives. The principle here is that many students have powerful computers in their cell phones, iPads, and netbooks. They should be permitted, within reason, to use these tools they already have (Ullman, 2011). Of course, care must be taken to ensure access, so combining these approaches to varying degrees may be the most useful in the long run.

Anytime, Anywhere Digital Technology Access Survey

Availability

1 How many computers in the school are potentially available to students (do not include administration computers or teachers' desk computers that are off-limits to students).

2 How many students are enrolled at the school?

3 Calculate the ratio of student-access computers to students (divide line 1 by line 2):

4 How many computer labs are available in the school?

5 How many computers are available to students in the school library or another common area?

6 How many computers are available in classrooms?

7 Are students able to check out laptop or other portable computing devices for school use?

8 Are students able to check out laptop or other portable computing devices for home use?

9 Divide the number of computers in classrooms by the number of total classrooms:

Are students able to use computer stations by

a Obtaining a pass to a lab or the library when the need arises?

b Working in small groups at a classroom computer station when the need arises?

c Working in small groups at a computer lab or library when the need arises?

d Working individually at a computer lab or library when the need arises?

e Working individually or in small groups when the teacher takes the entire class to a lab or uses a portable laptop cart?

f Working as a whole class with teacher direction?

(cont.)

Additional Technologies

What other technologies might students use at school? (Consider cell phones, music or podcast players, LAN cards, e-books, etc.)

Responsiveness of Internet Filtering

1   Are teachers permitted to work with instructional technology administrators to unblock content on the Internet?

2   To what degree can teachers override Internet filters to access appropriate content for their classes including videos, blogs, and wikis? Rate 1 to 5.

3   To what degree do instructional technology administrators respond quickly to the requests of teachers to access sites that are otherwise blocked? Rate 1 to 5.

Applications

1   Are appropriate software applications available on student-use computers in classrooms, in the library, and in computer labs? Rate 1 to 5.

2   Do students have access to web-based or cloud computing applications in school?

3   Does the school or district use a course management system (for example, Moodle, eCollege, BlackBoard).

4   Do information systems work together seamlessly (for example, do scores posted in an instructor gradebook post easily or automatically to the student information system [SIS] that generates grades available to students, administrators, and parents)?

5   May parents access student work and scores via the Internet?

Management
Computers in the Classroom

Cross-reference hashtags: #access, #advocacy,
#classroommanagement

What Is It?

Whether you have a computer center with four or five computers, you sign out a cart full of netbooks, or you go to a lab, managing computers in the classroom requires teachers to think about classroom management. Students may or may not be savvy users of computers, but like all classroom tasks teachers should consider what students can do, what they may not be able to do, and what they might do if left to their own devices. Before the Internet was available in classrooms, the authors used simulations (and still do) that required students to use knives, rubber bands, small plastic pieces that might serve as projectiles, and paper cut into small pieces. It was no miracle that students did not shoot the rubber bands, cut themselves or their peers to ribbons, or shoot small plastic game pieces across the room. Rather, we found success simply because we took the time to make sure students knew what the appropriate uses of these tools were and what they were to do should a mishap occur.

Why Is It Important?

When students work with technology to compose their thinking about content, management of the technology automatically comes into play. Effective management of the technology not only improves the opportunities for students to learn but they also become increasingly responsible users of technology. How students use technology impacts others, a concept worth reinforcing constantly and with increasing sophistication as they progress through the grade levels.

How Will Technology Help?

Most school districts and educational agencies have an acceptable-use agreement based on their acceptable-use policies (AUPs) that students and their parents must sign before students are permitted to use many digital technologies at school. However, tech-ready teachers know that just because students (and their parents) signed an acceptable-use agreement does not mean that they understand the implications of those policies and rules. Acceptable-use agreements cover a broad range of topics and are intended for many grade levels. Like the dense documents written in tiny fonts that accompany credit cards adults use, the acceptable-use agreement is often signed but not read. Teachers can reinforce the key principles that apply when students use classroom technology by being familiar with the acceptable-use agreement or policy themselves.

What Do I Do?

Several steps can help teachers manage students' use of digital technology when they write in their content areas. First, and most important, be aware of the acceptable-use policy in the school. Use the classroom technology management checklist (see Figure 2.1) to determine the demands of the task and the students' needs.

Example: Metro High Scenario

Mrs. Gabriel, at Metro High, knew her students were eager to use the computers, but she wanted to make sure that students used their time on the computers wisely

---

- ☐ The teacher practiced the task using digital technology to determine about how long it would take and any pitfalls that might occur. A student might try out the task, as well (Bourgeois, n.d.) and report to the teacher any difficulties or background knowledge other students might need.

- ☐ The teacher reviewed the software and websites students might need to complete the writing task. Help files or task cards were created or available for any tasks for which students might require help.

- ☐ Students know what to do and how to obtain help from a teacher or student computer expert if they encounter a problem.

- ☐ Students have earned a classroom digital expectations chit.

- ☐ The teacher has made clear what software and online tools students may use. The teacher has provided clear directions to students about what sites are permissible for Internet searches.

FIGURE 2.1. Classroom technology management checklist.

and responsibly. First, because students were to post blog entries, she asked them to type them out in the school's word processing program, then save them on their flash drives. She remembered the first time students posted work to a blog and they had to write it out by hand before retyping it into the blog; now, with netbooks, all the students could work directly on a word processor. Though Mrs. Gabriel had been working with technology for many years in her ninth-grade science class, she reviewed her technology management plan (see Figure 2.1) to make sure she did not forget anything. Right away, Mrs. Gabriel recognized that her students had never embedded links into their blog posts before. So, she asked one of her students to create a test post that included a link to the classroom webpage, then let her know of any difficulties with using the linking tools in the blog site. She also knew that the test student would become the class expert on embedding links. Next, she checked the blog site to make sure there were no changes since the last time her students posted their work. In case students struggled with this, she posted the following link to the classroom webpage under the topic "help" to a help file students could consult if they needed it: *http://www.google.com/support/blogger/bin/answer. py?hl=en&answer=41379*. Mrs. Gabriel kept a list of help files on her shared bookmark site for different types of tasks (see Technique 8).

Mrs. Gabriel knew that students sometimes needed assistance that the help file did not provide, so she reminded students to place a small, brightly colored sticky note on the top of the monitor so she could see it. Students, she reminded them, should consult a neighbor for help before putting up the sticky note flag. When she first had computers in the classroom, she asked students to place a red, plastic cup on the monitor if they needed help. Now that monitors were slim and flat, the sticky notes worked better. Near the computer stations, she kept a stack students could use as needed.

Earlier in the year, Mrs. Gabriel used a survey tool (see Figure 2.2) to prepare students for using digital technology in her classroom. She knew that every teacher had different expectations based on the acceptable-use agreement. So, students were not allowed to use digital technology until they had passed the digital expectations quiz and earned a chit allowing them to work on the computers or use other technology. Her quiz was simple but direct; each student viewed a video she posted to a hosting site (for example, YouTube, TeacherTube) about her classroom technology procedures, then clicked a link to take a short quiz to remind them of the important aspects of working on computers in Mrs. Gabriel's classroom (see Figure 2.3 for an example quiz). Before students started their blogging task, she reminded them of the login procedure for the blogging site and the types of links they were to embed in their posts.

Additional Resource

Learn more about the laws regarding online safety and public schools.

Nielsen, L. (2011). World's simplest online safety policy. *TL Advisor Blog.* Available at *http://techlearning.com/blogs/39012.*

◆ FreeOnlineSurveys: *http://freeonlinesurveys.com*
   As the name implies, this site offers free surveys.

◆ Pollanywhere: *http://www.pollanywhere.com*
   Students can respond to polls or questions using their cell phones.

◆ SurveyMonkey: *http://www.surveymonkey.com*
   Create free surveys using SurveyMonkey. Paid subscriptions have more options.

◆ Survey Pirate: *http://www.surveypirate.com*
   Create free surveys.

◆ Zoomerang: *http://www.zoomerang.com*
   Create free surveys using Zoomerang. Paid subscriptions have more options.

FIGURE 2.2. Survey tools.

1. I may touch the monitor, keyboard, or mouse of a computer another student is using . . .
   a. If I can help
   b. Never*
   c. When I see another student make a mistake

2. If I accidentally end up on a website that is not appropriate for school,
   a. I should close the browser and hope no one saw
   b. Notify the teacher right away*
   c. Keep browsing to see if anything else is interesting

3. If something goes wrong with the computer,
   a. I should shut down the computer
   b. Notify the teacher or class computer expert*
   c. Smack the monitor and hope it works after that

4. I may post my classwork online . . .
   a. If the teacher approves it
   b. If I want my peers to help me evaluate it
   c. Both of the above*

5. I want to use my cell phone to e-mail a photo of today's homework to a sick friend, so . . .
   a. I hide the phone under my desk and hope the teacher does not see me
   b. I get permission from the teacher*
   c. Keep my cell phone in my backpack and tell my friend I'm not allowed to use personal technology at school

Using this format, develop five to ten questions that are reminders to students about class expectations for digital technology use. Post them to an online survey tool students should complete before they use classroom technology.

FIGURE 2.3. Earn the digital tools chit. *Correct answers.

Management
The Hardware

Cross-reference hashtags: #access, #classroommanagement, #hardware

What Is It?

In previous sections, we explored access to computers and classroom management issues related to student behavior. A few considerations about hardware should be noted, as well.

Why Is It Important?

Students must take responsibility for the care and maintenance of the equipment they access in the classroom. Recently, researchers in Virginia (Ruiling & Overbaugh, 2009) reported that teachers were often frustrated when they were unable to obtain technical support in a timely way. While technical support may be problematic for teachers and students, one way to cut down on the need for support is to help students learn to care for the hardware they must share with other students in the classroom.

How Will Technology Help?

From the basics of not abusing technology by banging on it or otherwise dismantling parts to caring for computers, students should learn to respect the learning environment by making sure that the hardware is cared for and available for the next person who uses it. Taking care of technology evolves as technology evolves, as well. For example, in 2004, Starr recommended that students turn their mouses over so that the teacher can see that the students have not removed the track balls. In 2011, most computer mice use an optical system and no longer rely on a track ball. (We recommend that you check out the other classroom computer management suggestions in the Starr article, however: *http://www.educationworld.com/a_tech/tech/tech116.shtml*.) Instead, students must remember to notify the teacher if the battery needs to be replaced or if a mouse button no longer works. By the way, did you know that the plural of mouse (when it refers to a computer-user interface device) is correct as mouses or mice? We used it both ways in this paragraph, but in general, we recommend choosing either mouses or mice and sticking to that.

What Do I Do?

Effective teachers know that students are motivated, in large part, when they feel they are part of a classroom community of learners. The sense of community is built in many ways; however, like Glasser (1986) we found in our own teaching that students could buy into two basic principles:

1 Learning in this classroom is both challenging and fun; in short, we like learning.

2 Tools such as computers help to make learning challenging and fun.

When students develop a sense of collaboration in the classroom, they are more likely to care for the tools that make collaboration and learning possible. Teachers can make these two ideas explicit to students; after all, while students implicitly know these ideas, they don't always act on them because they are not at the forefront of their thoughts. Once students begin to realize that how they treat the computer mouse and keyboard affects how others might learn, they start to think about how their actions improve both the challenge and the fun of learning in the classroom when everyone works together. It is not the computer technician's job to keep the keyboards clean, rather, that's a job for everyone who uses the keyboards, for example.

Direct Instruction

Cross-reference hashtags: #differentiate, #directinstruction, #instruction, #model, #podcasts

What Is It?

What do writing instruction and direct instruction have in common? A good question, and one we attempt to answer in this section. However, before we explore how direct instruction can help young writers, we had better define the terms we are using. "Direct instruction" is a term used quite often in many educational environments. But what it means may be interpreted in many ways. Cobern and his colleagues (2010) explored inquiry models of science learning compared to direct instruction models and identified advantages for each approach. In their research, they were careful to define direct instruction (which they termed "direct active"). They defined direction instruction as the teacher explaining and presenting concepts, which could include a traditional lecture approach, but they also included hands-on practical work and application of concepts under teacher supervision as part of their definition of direct instruction.

Lectures have a bad reputation, as Hunter (1982) asserts, but this need not be the case. In one study (Covill, 2011) at the college level, students indicated they learned a great deal from the lectures they attended. Hunter proposes that lecture information be organized and clear, and that it include models of the information or processes. Lectures can be an important part of effective direct instruction. Notice where we are headed with this line of thinking. Direct instruction and lecture are not synonyms, but both can be helpful tools for assisting student authors to become more proficient.

Why Is It Important?

Teachers know things. They are experts in their content areas and they know how to communicate with others about that content. What teachers can share and how they guide students' work is critically important. One idea that has taken root in many classrooms is the idea of the "mini-lesson" (Atwell, 1987) in which the teacher shares a skill or a solution to a particular problem in writing. Mini-lessons are the place in the classroom routine where teachers share things they know. The term "mini-lesson" is a bit problematic because it isolates the idea of a lesson in terms of what teachers say and do without attending rigorously to the features of a lesson that emphasize what students say, write, or do.

We tend to call a teacher presentation, well, a teacher presentation. While lectures are a form of teacher presentation, we stick to the latter term because lectures tend to be oriented to the entire class and conjure images of a teacher at the front of the room with chalk dust everywhere. A presentation need not be conducted in this way and can be done with small groups or even individuals. Teachers are valuable sources of information, a kind of text (see Barthes, 1967) on which students can rely as they construct their own understanding of the world and subsequently write about it. Teacher presentation is an integral component of direct instruction when it is well designed, prepared with the needs of the audience in mind, and includes useful models of writing in and across disciplines that highlight the skills, strategies, and thinking characteristic of the discipline (thinking like a scientist, a mathematician, writer of fiction, and so on). Durkin (1990) suggests that instruction, in a larger sense, "refers to what someone or something does or says that has the potential to teach one or more individuals what they do not know, do not understand, or cannot do" (p. 472). She elaborates that direct instruction can be planned or unplanned; that is, it can be part of a lesson plan or small-group instructional plan, or it can be something the teacher does on the spot when an unanticipated learning situation arises.

Direct instruction regarding writing tasks can include topics related to features of language specific to a given discipline (see Technique 18), expectations regarding format and style (see Technique 9), working with sources (see Technique 8), using vocabulary specific to the discipline or that improves precision in writing (see Technique 15), and so on.

How Will Technology Help?

The Internet makes some writing models available on demand. Any number of models, presented as graphic organizers, are available online simply by going to an image search engine (such as *images.google.com*) and typing in "writing process," for example. However, digital technology can improve direct instruction, and we highlight the presentation aspect of direct instruction here. First, teacher presentations no longer need to be a one-time event. Screen capture, podcasts, and video all make it possible for teachers to record their lectures so that they become a kind of resource to which students can return when they need clarification just as they might reread sections of a textbook to check a fact. For the first time, the media makes the teacher available when the student needs it, not just when the lecture is scheduled or the demonstration shown. In Technique 33, directions for creating podcasts (#podcasts) may be found.

What Do I Do?

There are numerous possibilities as to how technology can enhance direct instruction including teacher presentation. We focus on four aspects that can help students improve their writing proficiencies.

Model

When learning is complex, models can be very useful ways to add context, increase complexity without overwhelming learners, and show students what instructional expectations look like. Models may be found in many places, and technology makes them easier to find, easier to create, and easier to archive for later use. First, as students write, keep samples of their writing in folders on your computer that correlate with the instructional units you have planned. Of course, these works are the intellectual property of the students who created them, so ask permission to keep and use the work for instructional purposes. Second, word processing programs make it possible to highlight and annotate models to indicate key features of the written work. Third, keep multiple models available. When students have multiple representations (Rose & Meyer, 2002) of a concept or product they are likely to notice common attributes and also find the differences where they may work creative magic in their academic writing.

Differentiate and Flip Your Classroom

In the next section, the notion of differentiation is further explored as it relates to instructional activities. Differentiated instruction, when it comes to teacher presentation, can be enhanced through technology. If teachers keep archives as podcasts, vidcasts, or screencasts, students with hearing difficulties can access these sources with headphones at their convenience. Captioning and transcripts can add access possibilities for students who prefer to read rather than listen. Students may pause a digital lecture and look something up, and hyperlinks to online sources can be included for students to further explore ideas from the presentation. Consider flipping your classroom (Techpudding, 2011) by creating videos, podcasts, and screencasts students can view at home. They can listen to your lecture for homework and use class time for meaningful work on projects, in collaborative groups, and to write with guidance from peers and teachers.

Expand Conception of Direct Instruction

Teachers are thinkers, and naturally, they like to talk about and explain what they understand. Teacher presentation can be a useful pedagogical tool if it is well planned and used judiciously without squeezing out other important classroom tasks where other types of learning might be more effective. As we noted above, direct instruction is more than just lecture and demonstration. It also means the hands-on work students do and the applications to which they apply the concepts learned from presentation of information.

Plan Direct Instruction

As content teachers, we have rich understandings of our disciplines. We can help students understand the discipline more thoroughly when we help them not just with the topics we want them to learn but with how they use language to shape their own understanding. In the next chapters, we explore a variety of ways teachers can use technology to shape disciplinary learning through writing. These can become the foundation for direct instruction in content-area writing.

A Word about Differentiation

Cross-reference hashtags: #assistivetech, #differentiate

What Is It?

Differentiation means that students get assignments that match their capabilities and interests, and that also challenge them beyond their current capabilities and interests at times. Although Mr. Coley, a fifth-grade teacher you will meet again in Part Three, updates his classroom Website on a daily basis, teachers might choose to do this on a weekly basis and distribute the work to multiple students. One student might report on each content area or section throughout the week or the teacher might rotate the students in pairs to prepare the posts and each class as a whole can assist in editing the post for the classroom website. Mr. Coley edits and posts to the classroom website, but teachers could also work with their students to accomplish this.

Why Is It Important?

Internet writing practices can be as simple or complex as the teacher chooses (Karchmer-Klein, 2007). Karchmer-Klein asserts that Internet writing practices support required curriculum standards, encourage students to think about the social implications of their work, and help prepare students with the literacy skills necessary to be successful in the 21st century. We also strongly agree with Frey, Fisher, and Gonzalez (2010) that "while technological tools present new opportunities for learners to engage with one another, they should not be the tail that wags the dog but instead need to be continually considered against the backdrop of 'old' literacies: reading, writing, speaking and listening" (p. 72).

What Do I Do?

Examine your teaching first. Where do you currently differentiate your lessons? What are students' needs, and what does the curriculum demand?

Differentiation Possibilities

There are a number of ways to differentiate instruction and much has been written to suggest that differentiation is essential to student learning. Tomlinson and Allan (2000) provide this definition:

> By definition, differentiation is wary of approaches to teaching and learning that standardize. Standard-issue students are rare, and educational approaches that ignore academic diversity in favor of standardization are likely to be counterproductive in reaching the full range of learners. (p. 2)

In a standards-based teaching world, where accountability is high stakes not only for students but also for teachers, administrators, schools, and districts, we all need to remember that it is our students—that collection of highly individual persons—that we need to think about when we plan for instruction. We can generally divide differentiation into three components: content, process, and products (Tomlinson, 2001).

Content

How do we provide access to the content? Our diverse student population provides us with a challenge to see how content may be provided—not just through lectures and reading of texts, but in other ways. Technology provides us with some tools for doing that. We have already mentioned the podcast. Teachers can record and post their lectures to a website, where students can download them and listen to them on their MP3 players. Textbooks, so dense and often reader "unfriendly," can likewise be recorded for struggling readers to listen to on MP3 players. Pairing struggling readers with a more accomplished reader (peer tutors) can assist those who have reading difficulties or those English learners who need a language broker. Finally, rushing to "cover" the curriculum shorts our students because the covered curriculum does not provide for deeper learning and application of the knowledge in new ways. We need to align our tasks/objectives to learning goals for our students, make sure that we teach to concepts and principles, adjusting the complexity to the needs of our diverse learners. Because digital technologies make a much wider range of current materials available to us, content is enhanced by making additional possibilities available as students write to learn.

Process

There are at least two ways to vary process in the secondary classroom. The first is by using grouping techniques. By flexibly grouping your students, you can think about discussion and interactions between groups that promote deeper learning. We mentioned the use of learning buddies/peer tutors, but we also recommend team learning of all kinds (Grisham & Molinelli, 1995; Johnson, Johnson, & Holubec, 1994; Kagan's online magazine [*http://www.kaganonline.com/online_magazine/teacher_&_trainer_tips.php*]). CAST (2011) has a Universal Design for Learning (UDL) resource posted on their website at *http://aim.cast.org/learn/historyarchive/backgroundpapers/differentiated_instruction_udl* that provides the teacher with many resources, primarily online. As we noted earlier in this technique, students deepen their learning when they discuss topics and produce products collaboratively. Technology has the potential to improve collaboration and to improve writing processes.

When using collaborative groups it is important to think about classroom management. Tomlinson (2001) identifies 17 essential strategies to manage differentiated instruction. Having used collaborative teams extensively in our secondary and university classrooms, we can state unequivocally that it can be done, but requires a tolerance for elevated noise levels and unstinting vigilance.

Products

The way that students demonstrate their learning is through the products they create (testing, of course, is one way, but not necessarily the most effective way in all circumstances). Products can vary widely from lab reports to oral presentations to artwork to podcasts and to presentations of different sorts. Is it the best use of our instructional time to ask every student to present exactly the same product? Probably not, and in some cases, wherever we are able, we should allow some choice of demonstration of knowledge. Should everyone produce at the same level? Probably not. Whenever we can, we need to take into consideration the achievement levels of our students and what represents their best efforts. This is often challenging at the secondary level, but that doesn't mean it is impossible. As with processes, technology can improve the range of products available for teaching and learning.

Universal Design for Learning

Developed at CAST (2011) and based on principles of design from architecture, UDL has become a useful framework for providing access to content for all learners (Rose & Meyer, 2002). These principles inform how teachers might differentiate learning activities.

Principles of the Universal Design for Learning Framework

Principle 1: To support recognition learning, provide multiple, flexible methods of presentation.

Principle 2: To support strategic learning, provide multiple, flexible methods of expression and apprenticeship.

Principle 3: To support affective learning, provide multiple, flexible options for engagement (CAST, 2011).

We recommend that you explore the resources on the CAST website (*http://www. cast.org*). Everything there is free and can provide you with many ideas and tools to enhance the differentiation of your instruction and the integration of technology.

How Will Technology Help?

Nancy Frey and colleagues (2010) present a scenario in a high school class where one student sits in a corner with earbuds, eight classmates work on computers, a small group meets with the teacher, and another group of students are engaged in discussion around a table. All are working on the same assignment—the Industrial Revolution (p. 72). The teacher has designed the class such that students are working on a variety of activities to deepen their understanding of the topic. The single student in the corner is listening to a draft of a podcast that her group has made. The differentiation here supports varying learning modalities, technology integration, small groups, and teacher support.

Assistive Technology

Assistive technologies for struggling writers include such technology supports as outlining/mapping programs like *Inspiration* (2008; see also Karchmer-Klein, MacArthur, & Najera, 2008), *Draft: Builder* (Don Johnston Inc., 2008), and *Visual Thesaurus* (ThinkMap Inc., 2011), which can assist students with disabilities to store and organize what they generate during the brainstorming and data-collection steps of the writing process. Finally, text readers may help struggling readers access complex texts (see Dalton & Strangman, 2006).

Text-to-speech software can provide auditory feedback for prewriting and composing. Commercially available programs like *Write-Out-Loud* (Don Johnston Inc., 2008) or utilities built into the operating system such as *Narrator* (Microsoft Inc., 2011) or *VoiceOver* (Apple Inc., 2012) can scaffold writing with oral reading feedback that fosters metacognition and allows students who struggle with reading and writing to monitor their composing. We need to learn about and teach students to use these features and we need to seek funding for the commercially available products that can help us differentiate instruction for struggling readers of all kinds.

Most students can use pencils and paper or keyboards and screens with varying degrees of proficiency. Young writers should be encouraged to use these as much as they can. However, writing tasks present challenges for students with learning and physical disabilities because of the physical nature of most writing tasks, as well. Transcription, the act of putting language onto the page (MacArthur, 2006) or screen, presents particular difficulties for some students.

Assistive technologies can be helpful; however, care must be taken, according to MacArthur (2006), to ensure that the cognitive burden of one technology does not impose a new burden that is not helpful. For example, holding a pencil and creating letters with it imposes certain cognitive demands on a writer; typing imposes different demands on the writer that may or may not actually assist the student with written expression. King-Sears, Swanson, and Mainzer (2011) suggest that teachers use a framework for selecting technology placed in service of students who face disabilities. Their framework proposes that students' needs and the learning objectives or outcomes form the foundation of the technology choice. Next, the teacher examines the technology that is available while creating opportunities to integrate assistive technologies with other instructional activities. Implementation and monitoring of student learning, they assert, is equally critical. In Table 5.1, we present several assistive technologies that may be useful based on the King-Sears et al. framework and drawn from the work of MacArthur and others.

In Parts Three, Four, and Five, several suggestions for differentiating curriculum are included with each technique. Because differentiation is founded on the needs of the students and the standards addressed through curriculum, the suggestions we present in subsequent chapters are not exhaustive. Rather, they are a way to begin thinking about how you can help students meet learning goals and standards while their own needs are met, as well. As often as students need differentiated lessons and activities to meet their learning profiles, readiness levels, interests, and the prior knowledge they bring to any given learning activity (Hall, Strangman, & Meyer, 2003), students need gentle nudges to expand their capacities. This is the heart of differentiation—moving forward from where the student is at present to where the student might take the next step on the educational journey.

Additional Resources

CAST (Universal Design for Learning, or UDL): *http://www.cast.org.*
Katie Wood Ray on building writers' stamina:
   http://www.youtube.com/watch?v=y4KIcbOe5kQ.
Stenhouse Blog on writers' stamina: *http://blog.stenhouse.com/archives/2010/01/19/quick-tip-tuesday-short-bursts-to-build-stamina.*

TABLE 5.1. Assistive Technologies

	Description	Applications and limitations
Word processors	As ubiquitous as word processors may seem, they can be important assistive technologies that reduce the cognitive load of tasks such as revising and transcription of thoughts to paper or screen.	Limited skills in typing may be a hindrance for some students. General effects for students with a learning disability are positive for use of word processors. Adapted keyboard with larger keys and so on may be helpful for some writers.
Spell checkers	Built into many word processors and other digital applications, spell checkers let the writer know when potential errors occur.	While spell checkers do have positive effects on the ability of writers to correct their errors, there are limitations. Students whose spelling is so poor that the spell checker may not recognize the word and realize smaller benefits, for example. Students can be taught strategies for using spell checkers, such as generating alternative spellings or looking for homonyms.
Speech synthesis	Speech-synthesis software reads the work students have already created (and other texts, as well) so that students might hear how their words sound aloud (compare Davis & McGrail, 2009)	There are few studies to support the use of speech-synthesis software to read back to students what they have written. However, as speech-synthesis technology evolves, there may be increasing possibilities for this tool.
Word prediction	Word-prediction tools differ from spell checkers in that they predict possible words the writer may intend and present them to the author. In typing the sentence "I am going to the p ... ," the software may present choices such as "patio," or "pool" and eliminates choices as new letters are added.	For some students, word-prediction software eliminates keystrokes thus reducing the physical demands of typing. Word-prediction software may serve as a spelling aid, as well.
Speech recognition	Speech-recognition software listens to the oral ideas of the author and transcribes them. This technology is evolving, and for students with severe problems in transcription, this may be a useful alternative.	Speech-recognition software may be confused by background noise, incorrect pronunciation on the part of the speaker, or speech patterns that the software does not easily recognize. The software may introduce errors that the author will have to correct.

PART TWO

Writing and Thinking

Writing, as an act of composing one's thinking and making sense of the world, is generally accepted as a useful tool for demonstrating learning and even for learning as a result of writing. In Part One, we explored the nuts and bolts of working with technology; in Part Two, we turn our attention to why we ask students to write and what benefits accrue to them when they do so in service of learning in academic disciplines.

Embracing Writing
Knowledge-Transforming Writing

Cross-reference hashtags: #access, #feedback,
#protocols, #writingprocess

What Is It?

More than 30 years ago, two writers participated in a panel discussion about writing nonfiction. One said writing was fun and easy; the other said it was hard and lonely (Zinsser, 1980). Both were published writers, and one made his living writing essays, columns, nonfiction books, and novels and teaching writing. The other was an accomplished professional in another field who also wrote as an avocation. What could make the difference between these two views of writing? Why are their characterizations of writing so vastly different? There is, of course, no single answer to this question. At times, most readers of this book have found writing an easy task and at others a difficult or even lonely task. The same can be said for the authors of this book. Sometimes the words just pour from the keyboard and at other times each letter has to be coaxed out one by one.

It is at times like this that the work of researchers who have come before can be very helpful. For those who wish to teach others to write as a way to learn and as a way to communicate with others effectively about complex ideas and in challenging disciplines, we turn to the work of Bereiter and Scardamalia (1987) who wondered about many of the same conundrums about composing that Zinsser (1980) noted. Why is it that writing comes naturally at times and seems cognitively demanding at others? Bereiter and Scardamalia proposed two models of writing that can help us think about this difficult question. More important, their models may help us think about how we can help our students to be more effective writers, more effective learners in our content areas, and more precise thinkers. If you stick with us for just a few paragraphs, we think you will see why these two models of writing can be useful ways to think about writing tasks in fifth- through twelfth-grade classrooms.

The first model describes the idea of writing as something that just flows as the fingers hit the keyboard keys; the other is more difficult and studied. The first model Bereiter and Scardamalia (1987) suggested was based on the very basic premise that at times, writing tasks flow from the natural tendencies of human beings to communicate, abilities common to almost every student who walks through our doors on the first day of class. To describe the other model, we turn to Bereiter and Scardamalia themselves to describe what they term the more studied ability to write that is often much more difficult. They wrote, "What distinguishes the more studied abilities is that they involve deliberate, strategic control over parts of the process that are unattended to in the more naturally developed ability" (p. 6). It is important to note that the line between easy writing and more difficult writing tasks is not as clear as the models make it seem; however, what is clear from the work of Bereiter and Scardamalia is that often difficult writing is a composing process that is trying to get at a challenging cognitive problem in some way. They term the two models "knowledge telling" and "knowledge transforming."

Here, we are not suggesting a hierarchy with knowledge telling on the low side and knowledge transforming on the upper side. There are certainly times when knowledge telling approaches are appropriate and sensible. Perhaps this is why teachers try to bridge the difficulty novice writers face by employing the aphorism that if students can think it or say it, they can write it. Sometimes the most interesting story is the one that just flows from the pen. At the same time, we agree with Bereiter and Scardamalia (1987) that knowledge-transforming tasks present certain cognitive challenges that may not be apparent in knowledge-telling tasks.

Why Is It Important?

The problem that students face is often they are asked to write as if they are already masters of the subject. They are telling what they know, or at least what they should know according to the curriculum guide, standards, and the teachers' edition of the approved textbook. However, inspired writing is often more than telling; rather, the author takes the reader on a journey of discovery and wonder. So, while we may assign our students to write an essay to explore the causes of the American Revolutionary War, students can view this as a simple retelling of the information from the class lecture and what was read in the textbook. The prompt or direction to write about the causes of the Revolution is just retelling. In a way, it is a version of the input–response–evaluate format identified as characteristic of oral classroom discussion (Mehan, 1979) where the teacher asks a question to which the teacher already has an answer in mind. The student responds and the teacher then evaluates the degree of correctness. Some writing tasks students are asked to complete are just like that, only protracted over longer periods of time, compared to a class discussion, from the point where the student is given the direction to write until the time the composition is turned in.

One strength of the knowledge-transforming model Bereiter and Scardamalia

(1987) propose is that it explicitly suggests that writers consciously exercise control over the written work even when, perhaps especially when, that writing presents a challenging problem. For teachers, that is really good news. Good news? Right, good news because if accomplished writers can exercise control over and shape the written output, then it is likely that those control processes can be identified and they can be taught to novice writers. There is even better news, though; digital technologies can help students apply strategies to their writing, give them access to the writing processes of others, and help them notice the strategies they are using.

How Will Technology Help?

While numerous technologies exist to help students with the difficult, knowledge-transforming tasks found in many disciplines, we focus on four of them. Knowledge-transforming writing requires access to resources, command of the writing tools, effective models of written work students can consult, and feedback from teachers knowledgeable about writing in their specific disciplines. Digital technologies are just the thing for all four of these purposes. First, technology improves access to resources and reference materials students need as they write. It can also cut down the time needed to access those resources. In times past, a book or article might arrive from a cooperating but distant library via interlibrary loan in a good 6 or 7 weeks. Now, many articles and books, even difficult to obtain texts, can be located in minutes and delivered right to the computer screen in seconds. An entire chapter (see Technique 8) is devoted to how teachers can help students manage the sources on which they draw when they write.

Technology can make writing processes visible (for example, Word formatting symbols, Wiki/Google Docs history function). From the very small functions of writing on a computer to keeping track of revisions and editing, students benefit when they know what the technology is doing and how they can manipulate their words and sentences. Being able to see the formatting symbols in a word processor can help writers overcome the challenges of making their work look good on the screen or on paper when the document is printed. See Figure 6.1 for an example of what formatting marks look like when these normally hidden items are made visible. When writers can see the effect of their keystrokes on the appearance of the document, they can control them and correct them as necessary. In Figure 6.1, the ·· is a place where the space bar has been hit, twice. The ¶ is the pilcrow or paragraph marker, and it shows the places where the enter key has been struck.

As important, perhaps more so, the grammar and spell-check functions can be enabled to automatically highlight potential errors. If students are taught to attend to what the spelling and grammar functions are telling them, many errors can be avoided. Figure 6.2 shows how a squiggly underline indicates a misspelled word, a signal that students often ignore if they are not aware the words they have typed are misspelled or used incorrectly.

We call tasks such as attending to spelling and grammar or formatting a docu-

1. Paragraph marker should appear at the end of a paragraph and is usually inserted when the enter key is struck. The nonprinting character that indicates the end of a paragraph looks like this: ¶

2. Sometimes an author wants to insert a line break without starting a new paragraph. Do this by pressing shift+enter. The nonprinting character looks like this: ↵

3. Space characters indicate where the space bar has been struck. They are just a series of raised dots. They look like this ······ and knowing how many times the space bar has been struck can help solve some formatting problems. Some fonts do not have a space character (as odd as that sounds), and a series of small squares shows up, instead.

4. A degree symbol ° is created by pressing the control (Ctrl), shift, and space bar together. A nonbreaking space keeps words or initials from being separated at the end of a line (phrases, initials, and proper names are examples when words or letters should not be broken up at the end of a line). The degree symbol can also be found around en and em dashes.

5. If you press the tab key, the cursor will move over the same amount of space each time you press it. The nonprinting character for a tab space looks like this: → Normally, one tab space is enough. However, notice that the paragraph dialog box can also automatically format paragraph indents.

6. Breaks indicate where sections, pages, and columns break. A page break, for example, is useful when writers want to ensure that text, such as a reference list, appear on a separate page. If text won't move where you want it, look for a break using the nonprinting characters hide/show tool. A page break looks like this:
   ·····················Page Break····················· ¶

7. There are other formatting marks, but the list here represents the most common. To learn more about some features of Word, navigate to *http://www.delicious.com/TDWolsey/Word*.

Finally, the paragraph dialog box is a useful tool for writers using Word. It can do many tasks such as eliminate the annoying space between paragraphs that is Word's default, create hanging indents in a reference list, double-space text, or automatically create paragraph indents. It is not a nonprinting character, but it is a useful tool. It is found on the paragraph group in Word 2007 and 2010. Click the little arrow in the lower-right corner of the paragraph group on the "Home" menu to access this dialog box.

FIGURE 6.1. Formatting marks/nonprinting characters in Word.

ment in a word processor "local operations." More global discourse moves where students work with ideas, revise them, revisit them, and sometimes jettison ideas, are the real strength of word processors including those hosted on the Internet. Through collaborative composing technologies such as wikis and Google Docs, student writers can quickly see their progress using the "history" function of these tools. With the history function, writers can check previous versions, revert to those versions,

A squiggly line indicates a <u>misspellt</u> word.

FIGURE 6.2. Spelling and grammar checker.

craft a new paragraph, delete it, and retrieve it again, for example. Many examples of these tools will be explored in Part Three; however, a screenshot of a Google Doc history page (see Figure 6.3) illustrates the saved versions of a document that can be consulted, reverted to, or added to the current version. Visually, students can see their progress, the changes they have made, and the earlier versions to which they still have access.

Technology increases the means teachers might use to model written products and writing processes. Knowledge-transforming writing can be difficult, cognitive work. Scaffolding, that helping interaction between a knowledgeable person such as a teacher and student working on something new and challenging (Bruner, 1978), is a metaphor that teachers use to describe that help. When tasks are new or challenging, experienced teachers know that models are one effective way to scaffold, or help, students learn the nuances of writing. Digital tools make it relatively easy for teachers to save examples, highlight the features of the model, and share those models with students. Like Cazden (2001), we believe that tools and techniques are only scaffolds if they actually work; that is, if students don't learn from the interaction (or they didn't need that particular interaction), it's not a scaffold.

In our work with teachers, we help scaffold such difficulties as mastering the nuances of style guides by providing examples onscreen via screencasting tools. Examples include Jing and Screentoaster. With these screencasting tools, we can record examples of written work and demonstrate via a voice recording what we are doing and thinking. Students can see the page scroll, the cursor move, menus pop up and down, and they can hear our explanations of what we are doing and why we are doing it.

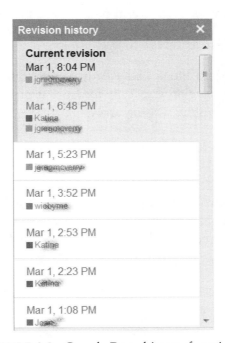

FIGURE 6.3. Google Docs history function.

We have realized, too, that students benefit from multiple models in order to broaden and deepen their thinking. One model can, at times, lock students into the approach taken in that one example. Multiple models help students understand differing approaches to a problem in writing, notice strengths from their own work, and develop strategies for working with ideas as they compose. An example of how multiple models can help will be provided in the section on using rubrics in Part Four. If you are wondering what models have to do with rubrics, feel free to skip ahead to Technique 26. Finally, it is possible to keep an archive of work available to share when it is needed with only the students who need it.

Finally, technology allows teachers to access students' work to improve feedback, and allows students to access each others' work for peer review, editing, and final publication. Technology improves the speed and efficiency of sharing work, obtaining responses, and providing feedback. Students can easily share their work in a number of ways: e-mailing a copy of their work for response, posting to an online blog (for example, Lapp, Shea, & Wolsey, 2011), or posting the work to a course management system or online storage locker, for example. Sharing work is easier with technology, but so is the feedback.

What Do I Do?

Students who can write to transform knowledge, not just retell it, need content teachers who know that they can and will be able to help them with their writing and thinking.

1 Know what software and online tools are available for writing.

2 Learn their features.

3 Subscribe to blogs and Really Simple Syndication (RSS) feeds (see Technique 13 for more on RSS-type feeds) that provide resources and updates about software and online writing tools.

Example

In this example, Dr. Wolsey and teacher Paula Dreyfuss explore how technology and writing tasks are seamlessly integrated to help students more efficiently write, use teacher feedback, and use other digital tools. The digital tools help the novice writer and the teacher interact to improve students' written work.[1]

------

[1]The following two sections are adapted from Wolsey (2008). Copyright 2008 by the California Reading Association. Adapted by permission.

Managing Student Writing Online

E-mail, at first, appears to be an obvious tool to improve rapport between the teacher and both students and parents. After all, students might e-mail teachers with questions about an assignment from the school library or over the weekend when specific guidance or clarifications are in order. It's easy to create a list or group for each class taught or another for parents to communicate homework expectations for the week, class projects, and so on. E-mail is powerful in that it is delivered right to the intended recipient, whereas information on a class website sits and waits for a reader to come to it. However, most e-mail clients like Thunderbird and Outlook are capable of sorting e-mail messages depending on the sender. What this means is that students can e-mail an assignment to a specific folder in the teacher's inbox. E-mail rules are configured differently depending on the e-mail client. Figure 6.4 shows the rules menu in Windows Live Mail (find it on the "folders" menu). If teachers set up e-mail rules, mail from specific users goes directly to subfolders in the inbox for each subject or period. Course management systems (for example, Blackboard, eCollege, and Moodle) make it similarly easy for students to upload their work to a secure account from which teachers can then download the assignments. Stacks of notebook pages with jagged edges jammed into a briefcase can be a thing of the past and returning work is as easy as clicking the "reply" button. Once the work has

FIGURE 6.4. Windows Live Mail rules. (Windows Live is a registered trademark of Microsoft Corporation in the United States and other countries.)

arrived in the class inbox, the teacher logs on and scores the assignments providing feedback that is timely and specific to the needs of the student. Another advantage of course management systems or e-mail clients set up to receive student work is that a digital archive of student work is created. From a digital archive, students can examine their work for growth and teachers can identify patterns that inform the instructional path.

There are several ways for students to turn in assignments electronically. They may post it on the teacher's webpage. Tools are available (for example, *http://www.ecollege.com/K-12_Education.learn* or digital lockers for student work) for teachers who want to set up online classes that include electronic submission of work. This is especially useful for a tech-savvy teacher, as it allows students to turn in work, participate in online discussion, and find assignments or webquests posted there. Many students today are more engaged if they find reading materials or assignments from the web. Getting students accustomed to completing assignments electronically is a good way to prepare them for future education. Besides e-mail, other ways that students can submit assignments electronically are on a flash drive (now available up to 16 gigabytes), or saved to a cloud computing account (Skydrive, Box.net, Google Docs, etc.).

Feedback for Students Using Track Changes, Insert Comment, and Highlighting

At first these tools take a bit of getting used to for both the teacher(s) and students. It requires patience from both, but it is worth the effort in time saved and improved feedback. It supports student learning by using methods that are consistent and understandable. Computers have done much to make humans more efficient in most settings, but schools have been slow to use many shortcuts available through technology. These steps should make it easier to give feedback to students on their written assignments and encourages students to use technology applications in new ways.

For the teacher, there are a few decisions to make before teaching students how to use these tools. First, which ones will be used? Second, how best to use them, and how will students be trained to learn from the teacher's feedback? Third, what are the limitations of the tool?

Of the three tools, only track changes can be used with Microsoft Works. The others do not show up if something is annotated in Word and saved as a Works document. It is also possible to save a Word file in portable document format (.pdf) and preserve the comments so that anyone with a .pdf reader can view them. Teachers may also insert comments by typing text of a different color or font directly into the student document.

Track changes and annotated comments work well alone or together (see Figure 6.5). For some students, a teacher may need to show the changes, whereas for others, just a comment in the margin may be sufficient. Picture the handwritten corrections normally made in the margins and between the lines on a handwritten or printed paper being done on the page that shows up on the student's computer screen. The

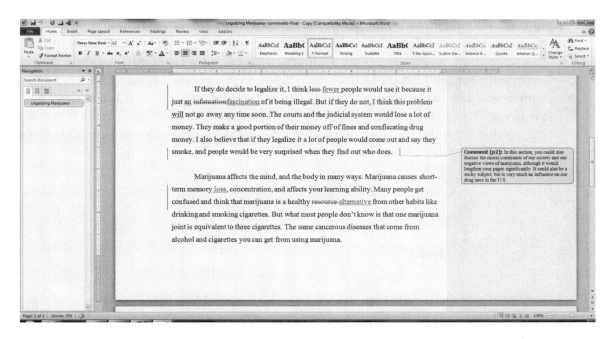

FIGURE 6.5. Track changes and comments. (Microsoft Office Word is a registered trademark of Microsoft Corporation in the United States and other countries.)

best part may be that teachers do not have to read student handwriting, and students no longer have to try to decipher the teacher's handwriting, wonder why a particular change was made, or be demoralized by the stark red ink on the page. Even red text does not seem as discouraging as red pen, although we suggest another color such as blue or green, both of which have a more positive connotation. Think green for "go ahead and make corrections" instead of red that implies "stop, this is incorrect."

The highlight tool may be used in several ways. It may be used to point out the text that is the subject of the inserted comment. Another way to help students learn to make their own corrections is to highlight different errors in different colors. For instance, yellow may be for misspelled words, pink for verb use, green for sentence structure, and so on. The important thing is to be consistent throughout the year so students will recognize the error and not have to constantly refer to a legend; although a legend should be supplied with each paper.

The key to success in using these new teaching tools, as with others, is to plan well, let students know what to expect, and practice. They will catch on quickly. If a data projector is available, it is a good way to start. The teacher may display a document with errors and demonstrate how the features will be used for class work. This may be done again when the first assignments are returned to the students electronically. Be sure not to use work belonging to one of the students in the current class without permission, or work from other students that may be recognizable. Most teachers have work from prior years that can be altered to protect the privacy of former students, or documents can be created or downloaded from the Internet.

It is important for the teacher or anyone grading the assignment to immediately save the document with a different file name so the student may compare the documents side by side after it is returned. In some cases, the student may be permitted to resubmit an assignment. This is a particularly good way to enhance the learning experience for the learner. Often students just give a cursory glance to the teacher's comments, but making corrections will encourage the student to learn from past mistakes. A system for the file names to be changed with each resubmission is critical, so that both the student and teacher know which document to open. This saves time for the teacher in marking and noting in the grade accounting system.

Why Writing Is a Process, and How Technology Can Help

Cross-reference hashtags: #flow, #knowledgetransformation, #languagearts, #writingprocess

What Is It?

Earlier, we suggested that the knowledge-telling and knowledge-transforming models of Bereiter and Scardamalia (1987) could be useful as we consider how we differentiate writing tasks. Before we continue to the next chapters, some exploration of how that model also informs academic writing tasks might prove helpful as we plan writing tasks for our students. As we planned this book, we asked ourselves some questions about writing and learning in the disciplines that are not easy to answer. As you read this book, think about your own content knowledge and the students you teach, and you will probably think of some rather difficult questions of your own, as well. We wondered how teachers would know when their students are using a knowledge-telling approach to writing and when they have truly transformed knowledge. From the writing itself, it is sometimes possible to tell, but not always. We asked ourselves, what can teachers do to promote knowledge transformation? And, we questioned how the writing process, as it is known in schools, informs knowledge-transforming composition.

The question about how writing process and knowledge transforming fit together seems to us a key consideration. Students with whom we have worked sometimes resist the process of writing as others have explained it, and we wonder why that might be. The knowledge-telling and knowledge-transforming models might hold part of the secret. Before we investigate this link, a review of what is called "the writing process" is in order here. We used a popular search engine to see how this process appears on teacher websites and writing resource sites. For the most part we found that with small variations in words and in structure, this process was founded around five phases that hark back to one the earliest articles on the process (Day, 1947) and an inquiry into the nature of composing processes in high school (Emig, 1971). Others have since elaborated on these processes, and we think that most of these will be familiar to you as you read this book.

Just to keep us on the same page, so to speak, here is a condensed version of the writing process Janet Emig described way back in the 1971 with the 12th graders with whom she worked. Dornan, Rosen, and Wilson (2003), similar to many others, summarized the writing process this way. They conceptualize prewriting stages that include thinking and talking about the writing, collecting ideas and generating material such as notes, actively planning the writing, and doing research. The writing stage, as they explain it, includes drafting the work, revising it, and obtaining feedback from teachers and peers. Significantly, writers can return to some of the prewriting or planning activities to rethink or reconceptualize as they draft, revise, and react to feedback. Finally, in postwriting, the writer cleans up by editing, sharing, reflecting on the writing, and obtaining evaluations including a grade. They note that writers develop an approach taking these tasks into account and that the activities of each stage are recursive within the stage and between the stages. That is, writers may be working on a draft, go back and revise, work on the draft some more, go back to prewriting and gather more research, and so on. A common understanding among those who describe the writing process is that the stages and activities are recursive; they do not move from one activity in sequence to the next (see Figure 7.1).

Young writers often resist the writing process and find revising difficult and unnecessary. In their mind, the draft they have written is fine and perhaps (but only perhaps) may need some punctuation or spelling checked. This is where the knowledge-telling and knowledge-transforming models become helpful. In knowledge telling, the idea is pretty much shaped as the writer retrieves the information needed from long-term memory in the brain. The writing does not need much work because it is close to being fully formed as the ink hits the page or the fingers hit the keyboard. More confounding for students might be the way they conceive of writing tasks in academic classes. Applebee (1981, 1984) and his colleagues studied writing tasks in secondary schools and found that teachers often constructed tasks as an expression of what students already know. In other words, it was often presented as a kind of assessment of knowledge wherein students tell what they know about what

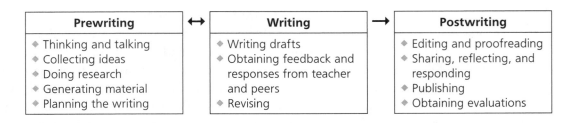

FIGURE 7.1. A model of the writing process in schools.

they have just learned. Did you catch the type of task as you read? Students are asked to engage in knowledge telling to demonstrate mastery of content.

As Applebee (1981, 1984) and his colleagues worked with teachers, they helped them formulate writing tasks in which students would construct knowledge as a result of writing, not just a demonstration of mastery. Put another way, they helped teachers construct writing tasks in which students would transform knowledge, in part, as a result of the task of writing in the disciplines. To do this, the writing needs to be engaging, and for that, we turn to what you already know how to do in your classroom.

Why Is It Important?

When students have some idea of how quality writing and thinking evolves, they become masters of the process. They come to understand that writing can be shaped through attention to a writing process when challenged with knowledge-transforming tasks, and they can become comfortable with the back and forth of writing that means that the first draft may not be the best one. They think of writing as a way to gain understanding and insight rather than as a task they must complete in order to earn a grade. This is where engagement comes in. You may have heard of the concept of "flow" (Csikszentmihalyi, 1996) where an artist, for example, is so absorbed in the art that he or she forgets to sleep or eat. This sort of engagement and focus comes from several factors that include having a complex challenge or problem, the skills necessary to work on the challenge, clear goals, and feedback that helps the person in the state of flow adjust as conditions change and develop.

In writing for academic purposes, flow helps remind us that writing that is challenging is more likely to be engaging. Writing is more engaging when the author has access to useful feedback and has the skills necessary to attempt the challenge, and knows what direction the writing should take. Understanding the processes writers use can help students with all four of these conditions as students seek to understand concepts, ideas, and big questions they have within and across disciplines. Through the cognitive work of transforming knowledge through the act of writing, students create, evaluate, and apply disciplinary knowledge that they more deeply understand.

How Will Technology Help?

With this technique, In this chapter, we asked ourselves "What can teachers do to promote knowledge transformation?" and "How does the writing process, as it is known in schools, inform knowledge-transforming composition?" We believe that technical knowledge, such as how to use software, navigate the Internet, choose media, and so forth can help students write more effectively and understand social studies, math, health, and other disciplines more deeply. Through our own prewriting activities in developing this technique, we created a mental representation of how writing to transform knowledge (Bereiter & Scardamalia, 1987) intersects with the creative conditions of "flow" (Csikszentmihalyi, 1996), and traditional writing processes (for example, Emig, 1971) through the use of composing technologies. Then, we wrote a draft of the text you are reading now and created a diagram that captured the complexity of writing tasks with technology in academic environments (see Figure 7.2).

What Do I Do?

Because the cognitive work required in transforming knowledge through writing is difficult and challenging, resist the urge to oversimplify it. Rather, consider the following ideas:

1 Make sure students have the time to write. Prewriting takes time and guidance from teachers, and complex ideas sometimes take multiple drafts and revisions. Students need time to obtain and consider feedback. Much of this is better

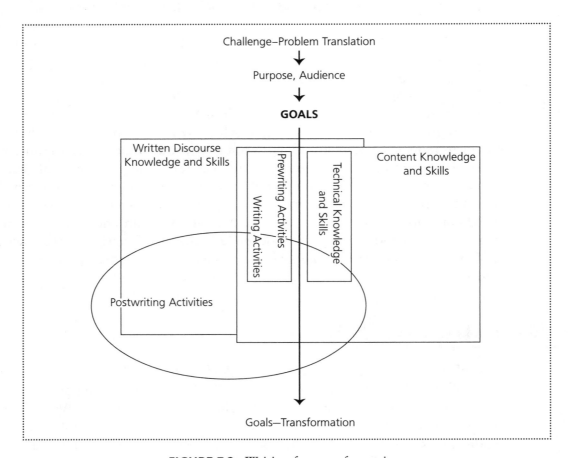

FIGURE 7.2. Writing for transformation.

done in class than at home where there is often less support and resources available.

2 Ensure that your students have technical skills and support for learning new skills from you, from expert peers, from online resources and job aids, and from others in the school community.

3 Finally, students need multiple resources and a content-rich environment form which to draw as they form their thoughts in solving problems, meeting challenges, and composing products that represent the cognitive work they have done.

4 Student proficiency develops with time, skillful instruction of content and with written discourse, and experience using the media of writing with digital tools. Taking a long view across several writing tasks can be rewarding for you as a teacher and for your students.

"Real-Time" Teaching: Example

Middle school teacher Cheryl Wozniak writes about her experience teaching students about elements of literature through writing using a process approach.

"Real-Time" Teaching by Cheryl Wozniak, San Lorenzo Unified School District, San Lorenzo, California

Commonly taught in middle school English classrooms are the literary elements of characterization, setting, theme, and plot. Many English teachers use the whole-class novel approach as a way to develop students' understanding of these literary elements and assess students' mastery of these concepts by giving an end-of-the-book test. Identifying the main characters, setting, theme, and points on a plot line often is no more than a regurgitation of ideas that were discussed at some length during whole-group conversations. On Bloom's taxonomy of learning domains (Anderson & Krathwohl, 2001), this type of assessment would be considered the lowest level: remembering. Rather than assess my sixth graders' understanding of literary elements through a multiple-choice or short-answer test, my students wrote their own short fiction stories.

Using Nancie Atwell's writing workshop resource book, *Lessons That Change Writers* (2002), I adapted several of the lessons to meet the needs of the diverse group of sixth-grade writers in my classroom. As part of the prewriting phase, my students and I used three planning sheets uploaded to my teacher webpage. First, we developed our main characters by creating a character profile. Students downloaded the profile sheet and either worked on the computer or printed it out. Before writing, students decided what their main characters liked and didn't like, the problems they faced, what they valued, cared about, and feared. Second, we used plot maps to plan out the key points in the story: opening scene, two main scenes in the rising action, climax, falling action, and resolution. Third, we wrote "somebody wanted but so" (SWBS) statements (MacOn, Bewell, & Vogt, 1991), which are brief summary statements, so we had a vision in mind for what would happen overall, and, more specifically, what would happen in the beginning, middle, and end. For example, from the following SWBS statement, you can tell the writer had an overall plan for her story: *Claire wanted* to hide her newly formed friendship with an awkward neighbor girl from her popular friends at school, *but* her school friends eventually find out *so* Claire has to make a hard decision and learns a valuable lesson about true friendship. Each statement was posted on the classroom wiki, so all students could see the ideas of the peers and build on those for their own writing. Too often developing writers have a vague idea for a story and begin writing, with no clear idea about the path their writing will take. My students learned the value of prewriting because they had a concrete plan to follow as they wrote their short fiction stories.

An important aspect of the writing process that sometimes is overlooked is peer collaboration (Yoder, 2005). During our short fiction unit, we formed writing sharing groups (Calkins, 1994). Students worked in groups of four and each student was given generous amounts of time to discuss their stories using the wiki discussion tab and face-to-face groups in class with their other writing group members. Because the expectation was that students would create an original story with a believable character about someone in their age range who encountered some teen issue that a middle school audience could relate with, the students worked in small groups and were expected to give each other specific writing advice in the following areas: the believability of the main character and the problem he or she faced, the flow of the scenes, the intensity of the climax, and the level of contentment from the resolution. Many of my students stated that being able to discuss with their sharing groups made a significant difference in the quality of their writing ideas.

As part of my own process for teaching the short fiction unit, I wrote a piece of short fiction and shared with my students modeling each step of *my* writing process. Students could view my drafts online, as well. My planning sheets served as examples for how to plan their writing. My rough drafts were filled with revisions and served as an example of how good writing is never one draft only. I gave the drafts of my writing to two colleagues and relayed their feedback to my students. By making transparent each step of my writing and thinking, I modeled for students how writers use the process of writing to construct and reconstruct meaning.

In my school district, we are fortunate to have carts of laptop computers on hand for student use. After many revisions were made to their written drafts, students saved them to their online folders, and submitted them to me by electronically dropping them into my Teacher Inbox, an online folder that only teachers can access. I was able to read the students' writing online, give students feedback, and drop the stories back in the students' online folders. All the final short fiction pieces were published as a class anthology, and each student received a copy of the book.

With any English language arts standard, there are many ways to assess students' knowledge of the concepts taught; yet, the lower the level of Bloom's taxonomy that a teacher uses to assess, the less likely a teacher is to know the depth of students' knowledge of those concepts. Conversely, at the highest level, students create original work that demonstrates their understanding of how the concepts learned apply to new contexts. After a year of reading and talking about literature together, I wanted more *from* my students than for them to prove to me that they knew the four basic literary elements. I also wanted more *for* my students, which was to provide them with a learning experience that would solidify their understanding of the reciprocality of the reading and writing processes *and* would allow them to learn firsthand, as published authors, how engaging in the steps of the writing process can transform a writer's thinking.

Working with Sources
Keeping Track of Learning, and Leaving a Path for Others to Follow

Cross-reference hashtags: #attribution, #citingsources, #moves, #socialbookmarking, #socialnetwork

What Is It?

Inspiration is an elusive quality when it comes to written work; however, the sources one hears, sees, and reads can be the beginning of inspired writing, somewhat like a fountain from which one takes a drink. The author Gary Soto once told us, "We can become skillful if coached, especially if we augment our writing with serious doses of reading" (Grisham & Wolsey with Soto, 2011, p. 37). This seems to be true whether we are writing fiction or nonfiction, narratives or an essay, poetry or prose. Or, a book, we should add! What one reads and experiences, informed by good coaching from peers and teachers, can result in inspired writing. However, a hallmark of academic writing is not just having read many books and articles, listened to many lectures, and observed life around us. A hallmark of scholarly work is also knowing how and where we came to know what we know. We call that metacognition (for example, Pintrich, 2002), and we know that students who understand the roots of their own learning more deeply understand concepts and can explain them in more robust ways. Here is a good place to address two aspects of metacognition as they relate to academic writing tasks. First, students must learn, with the help of expert teachers, to keep track of their learning. Second, they should learn how to attribute their learning in a way that communicates clearly to others so they, too, may follow the path the writer took.

Sometimes students view a requirement to cite a source as just a way for the teacher to determine whether readings were done and understandings created. Sometimes, this is so. But teaching students to document or track their learning by indexing their sources and citing them as they compose is a good way for students to deepen their conceptual knowledge as they learn where their ideas came from and write in such a way that others can follow the writer's path of knowledge transformation. In academic writing, even young scholars can learn to identify the sources of what they know and, hence, enrich their learning through this metacognitive act. Writers who identify the sources of their ideas are said to be attributing their work to the original author or creator. However, attribution does not mean the authors should not have a presence or should not assert ideas of their own. Authors who note that they are the source of the idea (often built on a foundation of sources attributed to other authors) are said to aver that they are responsible for the ideas and the notions presented in the writing. Hynd-Shanahan, Holschuh, and Hubbard (2004) suggested three attributes of writing history, for example, that demonstrate that writers often aver by evaluating the quality of sources they consult, contextualizing those sources in space, time, and place, and corroborating evidence from many sources.

Why Is It Important?

Students who know the literature of the discipline, understand the ideas derived from those sources, and can articulate what is contained therein are much more likely to engage in creative and substantive thinking of their own. Howard Gardner is best known for his work with multiple intelligences (1983) but his work encompasses creativity as a human quality, as well. He proposes (building on the work of his colleagues, as you might guess) that creativity is an interactive process derived from the synergy of individual talent, the parameters that commonly define the domain or discipline, and the field of experts who might judge, define, and evaluate works of a given contribution (1993). Theorists who write and study writing might think of this field of experts as a kind of audience, and "expert" might take on multiple forms and meanings depending on the students' purposes for writing. For middle and high school students, Gardner's explanation of a creative interaction is particularly helpful. As secondary-level students, their talents are often still developing as they create identities for themselves as writers and cognitive beings in the world (compare Erikson, 1968). In this pursuit, they must understand the nature of the domain or discipline as well as consider the field of experts who might evaluate their written work.

How Will Technology Help?

Research databases and online resources make a world of information available to students via the Internet. Many public and school librarians know about these resources and have subscriptions available, as well as help using them, for the students and other members of the public they serve. Having digital access to reliable sources makes it possible for students to read information that would not otherwise be available. Moreover, digital access makes it possible for students to gain multiple perspectives and levels of detail that would not be easily gained without the Internet. Figure 8.1 offers links to a number of subscription and free resources students might consult via the Internet; however, there are many more available than the examples provided here.

To help students organize their web resources, social bookmarking sites are invaluable. As important, perhaps more so, these sites make it possible for students to share their resources with others and retrieve them quickly. With a social bookmark site, students post the link to the sites they find, choose tags, and perhaps type a few notes. The tags make it very easy to find and list all the sites with the same tag. In preparing this book, Dr. Grisham and Dr. Wolsey used a social bookmarking site, Delicious (*http://www.delicious.com*), to gather, tag, and share the sites we found and that we believed we might use and share with you. You can access these tags and many more by viewing Dr. Wolsey's network (*http://www.delicious.com/TDWolsey*) or adding this uniform resource locator (URL) to your RSS feeds (see Technique 13). In Figure 8.2, we clicked on the tag for "social bookmarking" and several sites came up that we had previously tagged. Just like in the popular social networking site Facebook we invited each other to join our networks. In this way, we can see the links each of us has gathered. A screen capture of just some of our tags can be seen in Figure 8.3. By clicking on any of these tags, either of us can quickly retrieve the sites and click the links provided to take us to those sites.

What Do I Do?

While there are many things teachers can do to promote using sources to enrich their writing, here we highlight three that are particularly useful when writing with digital tools in the digital age.

- ◆ Proquest offers subscriptions to research databases for K–12 including tools for determining reading level: *http://www.proquestk12.com/productinfo.shtml*.

- ◆ EBSCO Publishing offers subscription K–12 versions of their databases of periodicals and other sources: *http://www.ebscohost.com/schools*.

- ◆ Some states offer access to a variety of useful resources to K–12 students such as Pioneer, Utah's Online Library: *http://pioneer.utah.gov/research/databases/kids.html*; the Texas K–12 Databases program: *http://web.esc20.net/k12databases/default.htm*; and the Badgerlink resources in Wisconsin: *http://www.badgerlink.net*.

- ◆ Many newspapers and magazines are available, along with other reliable resources from the Internet Public Library: *http://www.ipl.org*.

- ◆ International News databases and archives can be accessed for free at the Newspaper Index: *http://www.newspaperindex.com*; the World Press Review: *http://www.worldpress.org/edu.htm*; and the TFF News Navigator: *http://www.transnational.org/Resource_Index_Media-TNN.htm*.

FIGURE 8.1. Research databases.

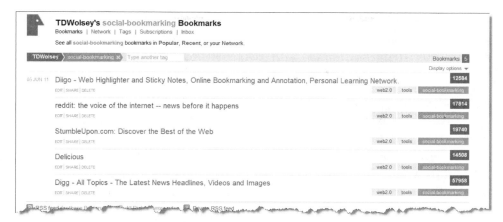

FIGURE 8.2. Dr. Wolsey's social bookmarking sites. Reprinted by permission of AVOS Systems, Inc.

1 Find out what databases for research articles and electronic books are available in your school library and from the public libraries in your community. If the subscription database collection is meager, get in touch with your curriculum and instructional technology administrators and suggest some such as those in Figure 8.1. Investigate the free resources available to your students, as well.

2 Join a social bookmarking site, invite some colleagues to join with you, and start sharing links. You will quickly see the value of the tags in organizing the many

Tags	People	Options ▼
▼ Top 10 Tags		
web2.0		26
writing		18
tools		11
collaboration		8
interactive		7
reference		7
MLA		6
presentation		6
research		6
technology		6
▼ All Tags		178
21stcenturyskills		3
6583		1
academic-language;		1
academic-vocabulary		1
access		1

FIGURE 8.3. Tags Dr. Wolsey and Dr. Grisham used in preparing this book. Reprinted by permission of AVOS Systems, Inc.

sites you find. Ask a small group of students to try a social bookmarking site as part of an upcoming writing project. Ask them to evaluate the site and report to the class how effective it is.

3 When you assign composing tasks, take some time to teach students how to structure their ideas within a framework of ideas they have gathered from others. Learning to aver when appropriate and when to attribute ideas is not just fair play to make sure that others receive credit. It is more than just a way for the teacher to determine whether students have read the sources they are assigned or that they have found. Averral and attribution are skills of critical thinkers that help them develop their own insights and conceptual understanding of big ideas in their disciplines. In the suggested reading for this section, we suggest a very useful little book that can provide a framework for thinking about academic writing. Throughout the remaining chapters, you will find examples applying the discourse moves from this book. Look for the hashtag #moves.

Example

Taking Note: Presentation Software Helps Students Take Notes

Jennifer Nation had been exploring genetics with her 12th graders at Metro High School. She knew the topic could be intriguing but difficult. Students had to understand basic genetics, but Ms. Nation also knew it was interesting to them if they could just explore the connections to their own lives. She decided a research project would help students understand how their world was impacted by what scientists knew regarding genetics. One group wanted to find out about the controversy surrounding genetically engineered foods.

To accomplish their task, the students in the group were required to summarize the sources they identified and critique those sources, then generate a plan for using genetically engineered foods. Eventually, their findings would be shared with the class, but for now they had to organize the information they encountered and work with a variety of sources that seemed to conflict at times. Ms. Nation showed them how presentation software could help.

Lisa, a student in Jennifer's class, explained what Ms. Nation had taught them. Each slide in presentation software could serve as an equivalent to one note card. Students would identify sources, type the main ideas of each source in the text field of each slide, then give each slide a title (see Figure 8.4). Since many presentation software programs allow the user to sort the slides, students didn't have to worry about the order of the slides as they worked. If they chose to, students could change the background color of the slide to correspond to the level of the outline, the type of source, and so on. In the notes field, students would type the bibliographic information they needed to correspond with the school's style guide. Metro High uses a modified version of the *Publication Manual of the American Psychological Association* (American Psychological Association, 2010), but Ms. Nation knew that many schools used the *MLA Handbook* (Modern Language Association, 2009) instead.

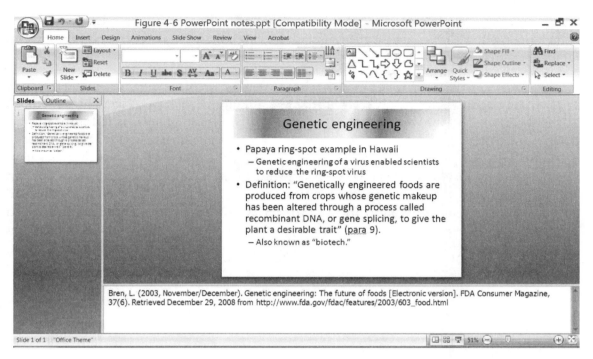

FIGURE 8.4. PowerPoint note slide.

Once most of the research was done and presentation slides created, students used the slide sorter tool to reorganize their slides according to their plan for writing. Lisa explained that they could also add slides with organizational headings and categories. Once this was done, they used the export command to send the file to a word processing document (in PowerPoint, go to file, choose "save as ... ," then choose "outline/rtf" that can be opened in Word). In Word, students can then choose the "View" menu and select the "outline" format on the "document views" group). As Lisa pointed out, this outline would then become the framework or organizational prewriting for the final report.

Best of all, hyperlinks to documents students had saved or to pages on the Internet could be linked directly on the slide. This way, students were able to double-check facts and add details they may have missed on the first reading as they synthesized their thinking and wrote their reports. With Lisa's explanation, Ms. Nation knew that presentation software could help students think about content in meaningful ways rather than simply cover the content through a series of rather meaningless bullet points. But, Ms. Nation was still thinking: How else could presentation software be used to promote thinking and effective writing?

Additional Sources

Graff, G., & Birkenstein, C. (2007). *They say, I say: The moves that matter in persuasive writing.* New York: Norton.

TECH·nique 9

Working with Sources
Using Style Guides

Cross-reference hashtags: #attribution, #citingsources

What Is It?

A style guide sets the standard for accomplishing a variety of aims by defining the manner in which some aspects of written and graphic design work is completed. The *Publication Manual of the American Psychological Association* (commonly abbreviated as APA, 2010) proposes that uniform style elements assist readers to "cull articles quickly for key points and findings." It goes on to suggest, "Rules of style in scientific writing encourage full disclosure of essential information and allow us to dispense with minor distractions" (p. xiii). Style guides and manuals also promote use of language in a way that is fair and impartial in academic writing. In short, a style guide helps writers consider the needs of the audience for the written work.

Why Is It Important?

Writers become producers of considerate texts when they use style guides with which others are already familiar. When student writers learn to use a style guide to cite their sources, they leave a path by which others can follow their thinking (see Technique 8). They also learn the metacognitive habits of noting how they have come to know what they have learned and the fair and ethical practice of attributing the work of others when those ideas are employed. As important, students learn to give themselves credit for their own ideas when they can situate or place those ideas in the company of others' work.

How Will Technology Help?

Fortunately, there are many technology tools that can assist students with style and format elements, especially those that relate to citing sources and producing reference lists or bibliographies. Figure 9.1 describes many technology tools and reference sites.

What Do I Do?

◆ First, work with colleagues at your school or department to decide on the format that makes the most sense for your students. A key attribute of a style guide is that it improves readability and communication, but only if everyone who uses the guide is familiar with its basic elements.

◆ Take a developmental approach to using a style guide. Students often cannot master all the aspects of style in any one paper. If your teaching colleagues are willing, choose a feature of the style guide to emphasize for a week or two, then move

---

ONLINE TOOLS
◆ Ottobib can format a reference entry for books with an ISBN number in APA, MLA, and other style formats (such as Turabian and Chicago style): *http://www.ottobib.com*.
◆ Bibme creates bibliography entries in APA, MLA, and other formats using either a manual entry format or an auto-fill tool: *http://www.bibme.org*.
◆ Easybib also creates bibliography entries in APA, MLA and other formats. It has premium services to which users can subscribe: *http://www.easybib.com*.
◆ The Son of Citation Machine produces citations (in text and reference entry) in APA or MLA format: *http://citationmachine.net*.
◆ The Oregon School Library Information System sponsors student-friendly citation makers for MLA, APA, and an MLA citation maker for elementary students: *http://www.oslis.org/resources/cm*.

ORGANIZING AND SHARING SOURCES
◆ Zotero is a free tool for organizing, sharing, and citing sources: *http://www.zotero.org*.

PLUG-INS FOR WORD PROCESSORS
◆ Word processors, such as WordPerfect and Microsoft Word, can make use of plug-ins or features built right into the application to format documents in APA or MLA style. Some tools that work seamlessly with word processors are available for purchase and include user interfaces that may help students navigate the complexities of style guides.
◆ Two suggested products are:
◆ Styleease: *http://www.styleease.com*.
◆ Endnote: *http://www.endnote.com*.

RESOURCES
◆ The Online Writing Lab (OWL) at Purdue University offers many examples and guides for MLA and APA citations: *http://owl.english.purdue.edu/owl/section/2*.

FIGURE 9.1. Technology resources for references.

on. Post a link to an example of that feature on the department or teacher webpages. Use direct instruction (#directinstruction) to model and explain how elements of the style guide might look. This type of direct instruction does not usually take very much time, but it improves how students understand the style guide, which means they can spend more time learning content through writing.

◆ Explain to students that citation formats, expressed in a style guide, are important, and remind them of the reasons.

◆ Style helps improve communication among readers who understand the style guide features.

◆ Style guides help writers track their own thinking, attribute sources, and treat the work of others fairly.

◆ Citing sources using a style guide provides a path others might follow who are interested in what the author has written.

◆ Using a common style guide within the school helps students because they know what to expect in science class and in English courses. There will be some specific differences for each piece students write, but by agreeing to the general principles of the style guide many problems can be averted when students write for the social studies class and the food and consumer sciences class.

◆ Remind students that they can become more proficient by taking time to review corrections from the teacher and their peers to learn why certain errors occurred or why there are sometimes differences of opinion regarding how some citations are made.

◆ Because style guides and manuals published by national and international organizations must provide resources for a broad range of writers, consider developing a style guide that highlights the important features colleagues at your school think are important and demonstrates any particular sources that are unique to your school. Creating an online template with such elements as cover pages, page numbers, headers, and heading styles can make students' work easier. Guides specific to your school are often referred to as "house style," indicating that specific modifications address the needs of your students and curriculum. Post the "house style" template on the school, department, or teacher webpages for students and faculty to download and use.

Example

The Wayzata High School in Plymouth, Minnesota, created an online style guide (WHS Style Guide Committee, 2011) that emphasized the Big 6 problem-solving approach (Wurster, 2011) that faculty at the school are encouraged to use with their students. With this guide, the teachers and students have a uniform approach to writing that all students know, and it is designed to meet the needs of the faculty and students at Wayzata High School.

Additional Resource

Read more about the intersections of content knowledge, pedagogical knowledge, and technological knowledge by visiting the TPCK (now known as TAPCK) website:

Koehler, M., & Mishra, P. (2010). TPCK—*Technological pedagogical content knowledge.* Retrieved from *http://www.tpck.org.*

PART THREE

Writing to Understand
It's All about the Discipline

> All genuine learning is active, not passive.... It is a process of discovery
> in which the student is the main agent, not the teacher.
> —MORTIMER J. ADLER (1982, p. 50)

We noted in Part I that teaching students to write is a complex construct that requires both art and skill from teachers. In Part III, we share some ideas for using the Internet and other digital technologies to help middle grades teachers provide writing instruction for their students in the disciplines

Writing in the disciplines requires knowledge of text structures and ways of writing that may be taught and practiced in short bursts. When we talk about writing "across the content areas," we are usually talking about academic language and writing practices that are common to all content areas. When we talk about writing "in the discipline," we mean writing practices common to a particular discipline area, such as writing that is found in social sciences, which differs from writing practices in mathematics. Students need to become conversant with academic language in both types of writing (Dutro & Moran, 2003).

We cannot assume that secondary students come to us knowing how to write in the disciplines. Content teachers, then, must assist their students to both read and write in their discipline. When we teach our students to write in a particular genre or discipline, we must expect to scaffold such instruction through several experiences before we can expect more than novice outcomes. Recently, Klein and Rose (2010, p. 437) reported research conducted to find out how students at the high school level learn to write explanations.

They recommend several important instructional components germane to our purposes in this chapter:

◆ Frequent writing in the content area (shorter pieces three times per week).
◆ A conception of writing as learning (interpretation of experiences).
◆ Education in analytic genres (and reading to experience the genre).
◆ Assessment designed to support self-evaluation.
◆ Building intrinsic motivation (interesting projects).
◆ Remediation of mechanics.

Montelongo, Berber-Jiminez, Hernandez, and Hosking (2006) found that a combination of writing and reading instruction is necessary for students to gain awareness of informational text structures. They suggest that students first be given instruction on writing paragraphs in expository formats; then students may use the writing they have done to help them understand the different text structures they encounter in reading.

Klein and Rose (2010) refer to "the explanation" strategy, where an event is watched, then students go through several steps—get informed, include all steps, tell why each event happened—thereby engaging in content problem solving, while the teachers provide sentence-combining strategies for the support of students' academic writing. When students reconstructed text through writing, both reading and writing were connected and understanding grew significantly deeper for the experimental group. In this respect, writing is truly used to learn.

It is also important for teachers to remember that learning should be active. Gorham (1988) identified essential elements of teaching that can promote student learning. Among these are praising student performance, encouraging students to talk (including an appropriate level of teacher humor and self-disclosure), following up on student-suggested topics, and creating a sense of community.

Good readers tend to be better writers, but good reading skills, although necessary, are not sufficient in themselves to make good writers (Lenski & Verbruggen, 2010). The quality of writing instruction has a great impact on the development of writing skills and structured writing seems to have a more beneficial influence on writing skills than does free writing. Lenski and Verbruggen (2010, p. 8) remind us that whether they have learning disabilities or just need extra help, struggling writers can improve their skills dramatically if they get the detailed, explicit instruction they need: "Writing activities offer students not only the opportunity to showcase their knowledge, understanding, and creativity but also a means through which they acquire knowledge, process and organize their thinking to find and fill in holes in their understanding, and build their creative skills."

Discussion and Writing

Cross-reference hashtags: #discussion, #languagearts, #science

What Is It?

The language students use demonstrates the development and organization of their thinking (Berry, 1985; Lee, 2006; Lyle, 1993; Lyle, 1993) and provides the means to acquire, construct, and share ideas (Lee, 2006; Lemke, 1989). The language arts are usually conceived of as reading, writing, listening, and speaking (for example, California Department of Education, 2007). Reading and listening are receptive activities, whereas speaking and writing are expressive activities.

Why Is It Important?

All the language arts (listening, speaking, reading, and writing) help us to communicate with each other, but the expressive activities require a different process than the receptive activities. A person may hear and understand many words in spoken language, but not use all of them in speech. We may read and understand many words but not use them in our written communications. When we link the receptive and expressive processes through carefully chosen activities, we strengthen learning and communication (Rupley, Nichols, & Blair, 2008). In this technique, we stress that discussion of ideas and words need to be linked with writing and composition. Students need to discuss ideas and new learning before they write about it and after they write, they also need to discuss what they have written to clarify new learning.

How Will Technology Help?

We want to stress that composition may use many modalities, including audio, video, multimedia, and hypertext. Composing, then, unites these modalities through technology (Karchmer-Klein, 2007).

Technology can assist us to teach writing in the disciplines. According to Karchmer-Klein (2007), electronic text has several useful differences from pencil-and-paper assignments that allow for (1) the seamless incorporation of audiovisual features such as graphics, audio, and video; and (2) the inclusion of these features may add depth to text make the text interactive. Students may have technological skills, but teaching them to use these academically may be needed to allow students to fully utilize the possibilities of electronic text.

What Do I Do?

Technology changes rapidly so that it is hard to keep up sometimes. However, teachers need to look upon technology as a tool, something that we use to achieve an end. The end is, of course, communication through literacy. The essence of communication is social—at the turn of the 19th century John Dewey (1900) noted that the organization of schools should help to prepare students to enter society by connecting them to a rich social life. At the turn of the 20th century Don Leu (2000) referred to changes in technology as "deictic," but his recommendations were similar to Dewey's a century before. Students must be prepared for the society they will enter, and schools must do their utmost to meet those needs.

As teachers, we don't need to know everything about technology. Our students are sometimes well ahead of us in the social uses of technology. Consider this example of how many of today's adolescents operate with technology:

> Sarah and I go home and she calls me on the phone when she's ready to log on. We keep the phone conversations going while we log on and decide where to go. We're always on the talker, but sometimes we go idle to visit other places. I keep telling dad I need a bigger monitor, because I wind up with so many windows open that I can't always follow what's going on in each one. Then we do about six different things at the same time. We'll have my talker open, our ICQ on, we'll have the role-playing MOO we just joined open, we have our homework open (which I'm pleased to report we both get done at the end of the night and its soooo much more fun doing it this way!), we have the palace open, we have our own private conversation windows open for different friends, and we have our phone conversations going on at the same time. (Thomas, 2007, p. 167)

What we can do as teachers is let students show us the way in technology, while we guide their academic uses of technology. Instead of bemoaning the social networking that students do, we need to take advantage of it and use it as a bridge to learning.

Differentiation Possibilities

Process

Discussions may occur in small groups face-to-face, in partner pairs, or with the whole class. Our experience is that small groups and partners are generally more effective than whole-class discussion; however, small groups give students the opportunity to explore a topic that they may then share in whole-class formats. Discussions may also be enhanced in online formats, and the asynchronous nature of discussion in some online environments (for example, the threaded discussion group) allows students time to think about what they wish to write while ensuring that all students have the opportunity to respond.

It's hard to get out of a pair! Johnson and Johnson (1990), who are credited with much of the organizational thought on cooperative learning, recommend that teachers begin with pairs for conversations about new ideas and information.

"Real-Time" Teaching: Example 1

Laura Kretschmar is a middle-grades teacher. She teaches science and mathematics in an inner city charter school where 85% of the students are low income. The charter school is part of the Oakland Unified School District, but it operates semi-autonomously. For example, the teachers "loop" for 2 years, following children for 2 years, when they move on to another set of teachers who loop. This year, Laura finished a group of children whom she taught in fifth and sixth grades. She partners each year with another teacher to collaborate around a common curriculum and essential questions.

"Real-Time" Teaching by Laura Kretschmar, Lighthouse Community Charter School, Oakland, California

This year we completed several projects that involved inquiry and research, integrating science and mathematics, around a central essential question, which was, "Sharks: Friend or Foe?" While we only get to the computer lab every 2 weeks or so, in my classroom I have four operating computers and we often use them to research our questions. Our investigation of sharks this year had some pretty wide-ranging repercussions after the write up of our results. One result of our study about shark-fin soup resulted in persuasive letters to restaurant owners who served that delicacy! But before we got to that point, we did a great deal of inquiry on sharks.

We began with an engaging scenario where six different sharks washed up in Arrowhead Marsh—no one had imagined that these sharks were in the bay. Photos were taken of them and students were told they needed to investigate to find out what types of sharks were there.

I downloaded pictures of six different types of sharks from the Internet, which were laminated for the students' inquiries. Then I picked the best-known shark, the Great White, and modeled the inquiry process with the LCD projector and a few relevant websites to answer my questions. The students and I did this part together, filling out a data collection sheet collaboratively. Then students completed a data collection sheet (see Figure 10.1) recording their observations on the pictures of six different sharks.

Name _____

Observations
Species # _____ of 6
Sketch
Fins and Tail—Number, Size, Shape
Coloring
Jaws and Teeth
Other Unique and Distinguishing Characteristics
Based on observations, what name would you give it and why?

FIGURE 10.1. Data collection chart.

After students completed their observation records, we "discovered" the six species of sharks and students were allowed to choose one to investigate further. This data inquiry opportunity combines mathematics and science to complete and involves partner or small-group work on the shark that the students picked.

I brought library books for the inquiry, but websites were very useful also. The students worked hard to find out about the species and to prepare an oral presentation using PowerPoint. I provided guiding questions for the investigation, a form called "Anchor Boxes of Evidence," because scientists use evidence for their inferences (see Figure 10.2) and a rubric for student self-assessment for the project.

As students researched their shark species they used other data collection forms to collect more specific information. On these sheets they also cited their sources of information. For example, one student noted that the Tope shark's scientific name was *Galeorhinus galeus* and noted also the information came from the Florida Museum of Natural History (*http://www.flmnh.ufl.edu*). For this shark report, two other websites were also used. I require at least three sources of information be consulted—Wikipedia is good, but students need to confirm the information from two other more legitimate scientific sources, whether print or online.

After the oral presentations, students were excited at the next phase of the research that involved the shark perception survey project. A survey was conducted by the students involving a large sampling of people. First, as a class we posed a number of questions, which we compiled into a list that we then examined carefully as we crafted our survey. Then we tested our survey on a few people and, as a result, refined the survey to the questions that appear in Figure 10.3. After students completed their surveys with one person, I asked them to reflect on the process. The written questions were:

1 What were your overall thoughts about giving the survey? Challenging? Easy?

2 Did you ask the questions and record the responses or did you give the person the survey to take?

3 Were there any questions that you would change the wording of? Responses? Share your revisions.

4 Any questions that you think do not address or get information on people's perceptions of sharks? What can we get rid of?

5 Can you think of any questions we should add?

Where it lives (tail shape/size, skin coloring)

Bottom Dwelling	Bottom Dwelling and Shallow Ocean	Pelagic (Open Sea)
Anatomical evidence	Anatomical evidence	Anatomical evidence

What it eats (characteristics of teeth as evidence)

Feeds on Plankton/ Zooplankton	Feeds on Fish, Crustaceans, Mollusks	Feeds on Fish, Seals
Anatomical evidence	Anatomical evidence	Anatomical evidence

The species' potential for survival (reproductive habits, rates/habitat)

Evidence for Long-Term Survival	Evidence for Endangerment/Extinction

FIGURE 10.2. Anchor boxes of evidence (because scientists use evidence for their inferences).

Demographic Information (background information on the person you interview)

1. Gender   Male   Female

2. How old are you?

   | child | preteen | teen | young adult | adult |
   | under 11 | 11–12 | 13–19 | 20–40 | over 40 |

3. Do you have any phobias or fears?

   snakes   spiders   dogs   other: _____   none

4. How do you identify yourself?

   African American   Latino   Asian   White   other: _____

5. What religion do you practice?

   Christian   Buddhist   Muslim   nothing   other: _____

6. Where do you live in Oakland?

   North   Downtown   Central   West   East   other: _____

7. What is your job or occupation? _____

   (If none, are you a student? Unemployed? Full-time caregiver or parent?)

8. What state and/or country were you born in?   _____

9. How many people live in your household? _____

10. What is your education level?

    K–12 student   high school diploma   college degree   master's   PhD

11. Do you go swimming/surfing/wading in the ocean?

    never   once a year   2–5 times/year   every month   once a week

12. Do you go swimming/surfing/wading in the bay?

    never   once a year   2–5 times/year   every month   once a week

13. Do you surf?   yes   no

14. Are you: single   dating   married

QUESTIONS ABOUT SHARKS

15. Which adjective best describes how you feel about sharks?

    terrified   scared   nervous   curious   thrilled   other: _____

16. Do you think sharks are friend or foe?   friend   foe   both

17. Have you seen any of the following movies with sharks?

    Deep Blue Sea   *Jaws* (or any sequel)   *Finding Nemo*   other: _____

    1 (all)   2 (2–3)   3 (1 of them)   4 (none)   5 (never heard of them)

18. Did you know that 100 million sharks are caught a year by humans for food and sport? On a scale of 1–5 do you think this is:

    | 1 | 2 | 3 | 4 | 5 |
    | (a good thing) | (no big deal) | (not sure) | (some concern) | (troublesome) |

FIGURE 10.3. Question about sharks.

19. Do you think sharks are dangerous?

    1 (all)   2 (most)   3 (some)   4 (very few)   5 (none)

20. Would you be willing to swim in waters where there are sharks?

    1 (jump at the opportunity)   2 (yes)   3 (might)   4 (not likely)   5 (never)

21. Have you ever been attacked by a shark?   yes   no

22. Do you know someone who has been attacked by a shark?   yes   no

23. What do you think one of your parents or guardians thinks about sharks?

    friend   foe   both

FIGURE 10.3 (*cont.*)

When we got the survey responses back, we worked with the LCD projector and made an Excel spreadsheet of the data (see example, Figure 10.4). The LCD projector allowed the students to see the data we collected in a large enough version that we could easily discuss our findings. The students were able to ask research questions, formulate hypotheses, and write several different reports based on the data set we compiled. For example, Will and Jon asked whether ethnicity affects the way people think about sharks as friend or foe. They listed their findings: Seventy-one percent of African Americans felt that it was dangerous to swim with most sharks, compared with 48% of Latinos. The boys noted: "Ethnicity does seem to affect whether people tend to believe that it is dangerous to swim with sharks." In comparison, two girls, Elena and Talia, examined the effect of age upon attitude toward swimming with sharks. Survey data found that age didn't matter, from the sample that was collected, and that the findings conflicted with their original hypothesis that age would matter.

The culminating activity for the shark unit was an informational essay. For this

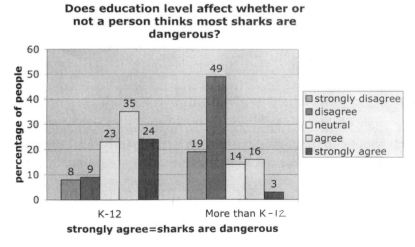

FIGURE 10.4. Excel spreadsheet.

the students used a series of graphic organizers that would assist them to marshal their evidence and information for the essay. We did separate graphic organizers on which to form our paragraphs: eating habits and prey, how a shark uses its senses, habitat, anatomy, and reproduction. Donny's example on Tope shark reproduction is shown in Figure 10.5.

The final multipage essays were published with tables of facts, a map of habitat, and a list of references (both print and online). In prior years, I had asked students to make trifold informational brochures on their sharks. As I mentioned earlier, I have also taught persuasive writing through this unit.

Example 2

Ernie Hemming decided to start small in his 10th-grade English course. He replaced a "low-tech" task (a book report) with a higher-tech task, enhancing writing tasks by incorporating technology. Later in the semester, it had been Mr. Hemming's way to have students write an essay comparing the themes of two novels. He had six computers in his classroom, so he decided that after reading novels in literature circles (Daniels, 2002), he would teach them to use presentation software to promote discussion. Students would present a poster session summarizing the book and exploring the theme. These presentations would seed discussions about the theme of the books the students had read that would, in turn, help students organize their thoughts for the longer essay they would write in a few weeks.

Mr. Hemming used one computer with an LED projector and large screen to demonstrate for students ways to use the PowerPoint program. He taught students how to construct a slide show, how to choose slide layouts, how to incorporate pictures and graphics into their slides, how to record voiceovers, and how to embed

Topic sentence:
The Tope shark is ovoviviparous.
Description/explanation of internal fertilization with details:
When the female gives the chemical perfume the male goes in and bites her pectoral fin. After that the male shark inserts one of his claspers into the female's cloaca and releases his sperm.
Type of reproduction with explanation:
Ovoviviparous is when the eggs grow and hatch inside the female.
Facts about pup size, gestation, how often they reproduce, litter size.
After they hatch, the female gives life birth to 6–52 pups. Each pup can be 12–14 inches long.
Lifespan:
Tope sharks can live more than 55 years.

FIGURE 10.5. Paragraph on reproduction. (Donny's responses are in italics.)

hyperlinks for the slides. Half the students worked in groups at the computers building the PowerPoint (which, by the way, were not new to many students) while the other half of the class worked on planning the slide show for their book. Students read their assigned books in class and at home.

Presentations could take no longer than 3 minutes or have no more than five slides. The presentations also had to include connections to other literature and ask the small-group audience to suggest other connections. The second week, students completed their PowerPoint presentations and on Friday, students viewed each other's presentations in small groups. Presentations were uploaded to presentation sites.

The students were enthusiastic about the poster session, where they were able to view every student's presentation in one class period. The presentations were available for students to view whenever they chose a new book to read. Mr. Hemming was pleased with his first effort and began to look at other ways he might enhance his instruction with technology.

Writing Short Pieces

Cross-reference hashtags: #science, #shortcues

What Is It?

Frequent and brief writing assignments are versatile and useful ways to build writers' stamina and teach multiple genres of writing (Common Core Standards Initiative, 2010; Graham & Perrin, 2007). Short writing assignments are activities that typically take place during one classroom session and do not feature all components of the writing process. These bounded sessions may be used for multiple purposes. One such purpose is building stamina for writing.

Short writing can be particularly useful in promoting reflection, as you will note in the exit slip example below. Fearn and Farnan (2001; Farnan & Fearn, 2008) refer to many short writing tasks as "short cues." When students share their short writing, they generate ideas by comparing their own with those of their peers, thus combining writing and discussion.

Although students might pass their 1-minute papers to a neighbor, another option for the millennial generation is to use electronic environments, such as the threaded discussion group. In threaded discussion, students post their short writing online, and others read and respond (English, 2007; Grisham & Wolsey, 2006; Wolsey, 2004). Hornik (1999) found that graduate students in a master's of business administration program performed well, in part, as a result of an electronic form of the 1-minute paper. Students were able to respond to the unanswered questions of their peers building ownership of the concepts and learning to rely on someone other than the teacher at the same time.

Why Is It Important?

Usually, stamina for writing is conceptualized as writing with paper and pen on a daily basis. Teachers may provide prompts to guide children or allow them to write on a topic of their choice. For example, in one class we observed, the journal writing occurred at the beginning of each day with a prompt written on the whiteboard. The teacher, Mrs. Crosby, noted that as the year progressed, her students were able to begin writing sooner and complete the task more easily (Grisham, Bicais, & Crosby, 2012). Pencil-and-paper writing stamina is essential for most of our "on demand" writing assessments today, but we would argue that the same concept applies to the creation of electronic text.

Because many elementary and middle school teachers ask students to write daily in journals on various topics and differing genre, we suggest that part of building that stamina should be electronic in nature and offer several suggestions for ways teachers can implement electronic journal writing and other short electronic writing tasks for their students.

How Will Technology Help?

Technology is motivating to students, and today's students have been described as "media crazed" (Clarke & Besnoy, 2010) but it is also essential for us as teachers to take the lead in equipping students with the academic skills needed to work with technology. Students using such social networking tools as Twitter, for example, can learn to "tweet" academically. Recently (2010), at an international research conference, researchers and conference attendees were taught to tweet in response to the sessions that they attended. Learning to make pithy comments within the character bounds of Twitter led to an interesting commentary on the conference proceedings. In grades 6–12, we know that virtually every student has a mobile phone—these are the perfect instruments for tweeting in response to learning.

Using technology can add "time" to a class. If your students are reading outside of class, they can be writing outside of class on their home or on library computers. If you are a content teacher, you can add blogs and wikis that maximize your students' interactions over text and new learning. Clarke and Besnoy (2010) found that using technology gave students control over their reading, connected to their lives outside school, and provided new ways to teach content-area literacy strategies.

What Do I Do?

The Electronic 1-Minute Paper

The 1-minute paper is well suited to the electronic environment. In general, short writing tasks ask students to write with these traits in mind:

- Concise or focused on specific curricular goals.
- Precise.

It would not be uncommon to see students jotting a few brief notes, creating a brief outline, checking notes or another text, or sitting quietly thinking before beginning to write a short task. The mental activity that leads to concise and precise writing is as important as the final written piece.

Differentiation Possibilities

Process

Given the appropriate access to technology, students might write from any location at school or home. They might seek the feedback from peers, as well.

Product

Students, working with group members, may choose to use different short cues formats, such as a VoiceThread or threaded discussion group.

"Real-Time" Teaching: Example

A perfect example of the 1-minute paper is tweeting. Many students bring their mobile wireless devices to school. Sometimes they are even allowed to use them! If the teacher establishes a site for students to tweet to from their phones, a question can be posed and students will use their mobile phones, laptops, or desktop computers, or a combination of all three to respond. For example, in an eighth-grade science class, Ms. Obi asked students to respond to the following prompt based on the activity of a previously dormant volcano in Chile:

> "We live close to Mt. Rainier, which is thought to be an active, if currently dormant volcano. What would it mean to us if Mt. Rainier suddenly became active again?"

Students had 1 minute to think and 1 minute to write. The tweets appeared as a "front channel" on the teacher's computer projected on the screen at the front of the room. All students could read each other's tweets. Ms. Obi found that she could use Twitter for several academic purposes. As a way of building background knowledge, increasing interest, focusing on a learning unit, reviewing a topic, and assessing students' learning, to name just a few.

Additional Resource

Lewis, C., & Fabos, B. (2005). Instant messaging, literacies, and social identities. *Reading Research Quarterly, 40*(4), 470–501.

Short Writing
Electronic Journals

Cross-referenced hashtags: #journals, #languagearts,
#socialstudies, #shortcues

What Is It?

Journals Then and Now

About three decades ago, Applebee (1981) and his colleagues set out to describe the writing tasks in secondary schools. The Applebee study used a framework that included four different categories that include different types of tasks. The framework included (1) writing without composing, (2) informational writing, (3) personal writing, and (4) imaginative writing.

Writing without composing includes fill-in-the-blank-type exercises, transcription (copying or dictation) tasks, and so on. Writing-without-composing tasks do not require students to write coherent and connected text. While these tasks do have a place and do involve putting words on paper or screen, we do not address these in this book given the limited cognitive engagement such tasks typically require.

Informational writing includes a range of tasks such as taking notes, reporting events, analyzing, theorizing, and writing persuasively. Personal uses of writing include journals and letters intended to "keep in touch" (Applebee, 1981, p. 29). Imaginative writing includes composing short stories, poems, and the like.

Journals and learning logs have long been one of the learning tasks in content-area classrooms. Journals and logs are similar in some ways but different in other important respects. Journals are more personal in nature. McIntosh (1991) suggests that journals in a math class might give students the opportunity to record new words and profound thoughts, connections to other content, questions, and so on. She encourages students to write as well as they can using elegant and elaborate sentence structures as well as in single words or short phrases with numbers, pictures, and diagrams. Journals are often expressive in nature and fit in the personal writing category from the Applebee (1981) framework.

Typically, short writing tasks are practice in writing and thinking for specific purposes. For the teacher, it also means less work than reading several sets of long papers. Journals and notes are important short writing tasks that many teachers use and know well. Shorter tasks increase the amount of writing that can be done, but short writing tasks also make the paper load manageable in many ways. In fact, short writing takes many forms and offers other advantages in addition to reducing the reading and scoring load for the teacher. A recent study of college students (Drabick, Weisberg, Paul, & Bubier, 2007) showed that students who were given short writing tasks were more engaged and attended class more often, and they responded more accurately on multiple-choice exams. They were able to use the conceptual development afforded by the writing task and transfer it to the selected-response exam format. In addition, short writing tasks often better reflect the types of writing that most of us do in our working lives.

Before choosing a short-cue writing task, the teacher's first consideration, as with any classroom activity, is to determine the instructional purpose and the achievement targets or objectives for the task. We identified these, relying on Pimple (2002) and our own research as potential purposes for assigning short written pieces in your classroom:

- Guides instruction (such as the entry or exit slip).
- Encourages reflection on the topic (experiential learning, such as the double-entry journal).
- Students can read each other's entries and note progression.
- Teacher responds to students' ideas rather than the mechanics and conventions of their writing.
- When done electronically, the instructor tends to reply in greater depth and so do students.

Short written pieces can provide important information about what students know and understand; teachers may then use this information to guide instruction. The exit slip (for example, Fisher & Frey, 2004; Gallagher, 2006; Tchudi, 1986) is one useful tool that can be used in this way. Students write a short response to a prompt from the teacher at the end of the class period and submit it as they leave. Writing an exit slip gives students the opportunity to reflect and synthesize ideas from that day's lesson, and the teacher can then review the exit slip responses looking for key ideas for further exploration the next day, to clear up misunderstandings, or to generate questions for inquiry and discussion. In this way, the students' responses help the teacher to fine-tune instruction. If students are assigned to the six computers on a rotating basis for the exit slips, you have added an electronic component to the short writing. Students may also use their mobile phones for this assignment.

According to Killion (1999), journal writing is fundamentally writing to learn and journals are permanent records of our thoughts and ideas. When we transform an idea into language, we process and clarify that idea. Killion was referring to journal reflections for teachers, but the benefits of journals for clarifying and expressing thoughts for our K–12 students are similar and well documented.

Why Is It Important?

The benefit of e-journaling for adults has been established. Grisham (1997) used e-mail dialogue journals for her masters-level teachers to promote reflection and learning about literacy content. King and LaRocco (2006) documented the benefits of e-journals for graduate students in education in two case studies. Little has been written about the benefits of e-journals for K–12 students; however, Campbell (2009) reported increased engagement and self-efficacy of middle-grade boys in Australia as a result of writing e-journal entries.

What Do I Do?

In electronic journal writing, teachers can teach skills to their K–12 students in short lessons. One journaling resource is Penzu Post (*http://penzu.com/content/products/pro*), which is a free online site, where individuals can sign up to post journal entries at no cost. Penzu Post will also send e-mail reminders for you to post to your journal, if you set it up that way. Students will need e-mail accounts to access Penzu. Students share their posts via e-mail or discussion board. The same is true for sites such as e-Daily Diary (*http://www.edailydiary.com*). Many course management systems (CMS), such as eCollege or Moodle, have journal functions that only the student and teacher may read.

Differentiation Possibilities

Process

Posts to electronic journals may be made via laptop computers, mobile devices, e-mail, flash drives to teacher file, or direct post to the media type.

Example

In Ms. Gabriel's seventh-grade humanities core (English and social science), the students were asked to respond to a journal entry each day. Sometimes, Ms. Gabriel provided a prompt. Other times students were allowed to write on a topic of their choice. Ms. Gabriel had a bank of six computers in her classroom and there were over 30 students in each section of her humanities core. But the teacher knew that most students disliked writing in their paper journals, so she worked out a schedule where every student was able to post in an e-journal once a week on the computers in her room. She also had access to four computers in the library. Essentially, 10 students were able to write electronically each day at the beginning of the period. Students also had paper journals they could use if they wished.

Blogs and Classroom Websites for Writing

Cross-reference hashtags: #blogs, #languagearts, #multimedia, #podcast, #TDG

What Is It?

Some definitions will be particularly helpful to get us started thinking about writing with 21st-century tools. First we define an RSS (Really Simple Syndication) feed as a family of webfeed formats used to publish frequently updated works—such as blog entries—online. There is an image that identifies it:

Readers may use RSS or other news aggregators to "subscribe" to blogs and other websites. If you read blogs, you will see the symbol quite regularly. However, you will increasingly also see "Atom Syndication Formats," which are a technologically improved webfeed that is on the rise. Google Friend Connect and Google Reader are other tools that can help readers of web content organize and manage the blogs and other webpages they follow. The webfeeds allow the continuous updating of online content, thus enabling blogs, wikis, and threaded discussions.

A weblog, called a "blog," is also an online or electronic journal. A blog is a type of website that features entries or posts in an ongoing chronological order, though tags and navigation aids make it easy to find earlier posts. Blogs are usually maintained by an individual, such as a teacher; however, student-created blogs serve useful purposes, at times. If you would like to see how a blog works, we refer you to LiteracyBeat (*http://literacybeat.wordpress.com*), a vocabulary blog maintained by four literacy researchers (Bridget Dalton, Jill Castek, Bernadette Dwyers, and Dana Grisham).

Teachers often maintain blogs and post their students' work there for review by peers or as a place to publish finished blog posts. Many academic student blogs are part of or linked to classroom websites, as well. Essentially, once a post is made to the blog site, other students (or sometimes the general public) are allowed to add comments. Thus a blog can resemble an online conversation with new elements of learning sometimes appearing.

Why Is It Important?

Blogs are a phenomenon that is changing the way information is collected, revised, disseminated, and absorbed. A blog is, according to November (2008), an enabling technology, but the strength of the blog is that it connects students to an authentic audience while making their voices potentially available anywhere in the world (p. 79). The Pew Internet and American Life Project (2010) reports that the number of teens using blogs is declining, possibly due to an uptick in use of social networks such as Facebook. Still, the blog remains a very useful classroom tool. Denise Johnson underscores the usefulness of blogging in the secondary classroom and recounts the experiences of high school students with three authors' blogs (Johnson, 2010), for example.

What Do I Do?

Student-Created Blogs

Adolescent writers can and do create and maintain blogs. When students are asked to create blogs, it is important as noted in Technique 1, that they know and are responsible for following the rules. Student-created rules are usually more persuasive to students. One website, *http://budtheteacher.com/wiki/index.php?title=Student_Created_Blog_Policies*, posts the rules the students created and the contract they sign agreeing to abide by the rules. One such set of rules is shown in Figure 13.1. Please note the "I" messages! Also, please refer to Part One for instructing students on the responsibilities and care regarding technological tools.

Classroom Blogs

What must the teacher know and be able to teach students about blogging? Classroom blogs are sites where students and/or adults contribute information or commentary on educational topics. No particular knowledge or skill is required, but before starting a classroom blog, it is important to think about what should be placed on it, how often it should be updated, who will do the uploading, and what role students, parents, teachers, and school administration (if required) shall play. There are a number of free sites that allow you to post blogs. For example, we

---

BLOG CONTRACT—6TH PERIOD

On my group's blog:

- ◆ I will only use first names (and last initial if necessary).
- ◆ I will not gang up on anyone.
- ◆ I am responsible for anything posted in my name.
- ◆ I will only post links that are relevant to the topic.
- ◆ I will not plagiarize other groups.
- ◆ I will try to use "correct" spelling.
- ◆ I will write in an "adultlike" manner.
- ◆ I will stay on topic (I won't discuss the "latest hotties" or summer plans).
- ◆ I will only link to appropriate websites.
- ◆ I won't say anything I wouldn't say in school.
- ◆ I will not use destructive criticism.
- ◆ I won't post personal information about other people or myself.
- ◆ I WILL USE COMMON SENSE.

I recognize that breaking any of these rules could lead to any of the following consequences depending on severity and repetition: warning, deletion of post, temporary loss of blogging privileges, and permanent loss of blogging privileges.

I further recognize that the blog is considered a virtual extension of our classroom, and therefore all of Mr. Lazar's, the schools, and the county's rules and regulations apply. I am aware that violation of any of these rules may be referred to the school administration.

_____(Print Name) _____(Sign Name) _____(Date)

FIGURE 13.1. Contract for student-created blog entry.

mentioned LiteracyBeat, above, and it is hosted on *WordPress.com*, a free site for establishing blogs. Readers subscribe via an RSS feed if they choose. Once you sign up, you can experiment with the format you want to use and you can decide to make it public or private. Navigate to *http://www.delicious.com/TDWolsey/blogging* to find additional sites for hosting your class blog.

Differentiation Possibilities

Content

Consider allowing English learners to blog in their native language and let them translate for you. Group students so they can serve as language brokers for each other.

Process

If your access to technology is limited, try asking the librarian or teachers whose rooms are adjacent to yours whether you can send students to do some posting at times when their computers are not in use.

"Real-Time" Teaching: Example

Mr. Coley, whom you met in Technique 5, was a teacher (now an administrator) in Murrieta, California. One of the uses of a class website is to share with parents what students are learning about. Instead of the teacher updating the website, we suggest that students can be regular contributors, by asking students to write about what they are learning on a daily basis. Mr. Coley's fifth-grade blog, linked on his website, exemplifies this (*http://www.mrcoley.com/blog/index.htm*). Mr. Coley was a fifth-grade teacher, and his website is an exceptional example of how a class website might be structured and support learning. There are many departments on the Website and many of these feature student blog posts (*http://www.mrcoley.com/blog/index.htm*). Each day, a student in Mr. Coley's classroom is assigned to be a "Roving Reporter" who writes a piece about what takes place in class on that day. The student may use a computer at home or one of the word processors in the classroom. Students word process the article and turn them in to Mr. Coley in several ways (e-mail, CD, etc.). Students thus get an opportunity to write using technology and the teacher uploads them to The Daily Blog. With Mr. Coley's permission we include examples of the blog for May 13, 2011, in Figure 13.2.

Please note when you visit Mr. Coley's website that he also posts a schedule for the students so they have advanced notice of when they will be the Roving Reporter, a rubric for how to get the maximum points for the effort they put in, a notes sheet so students can make notes during the day they are reporters, and other support documents and reminders.

There is also a Book Blog on Mr. Coley's site, a place where students review and recommend books that they are reading. Students log in to *Kidblog.org* (see Figure

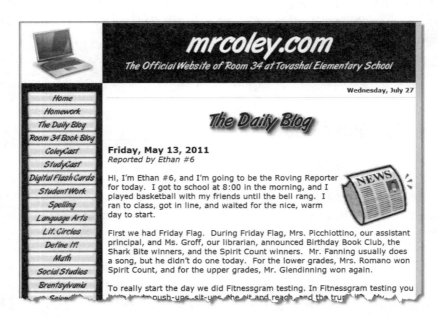

FIGURE 13.2. The Daily Blog. Copyright 1999–2012 by Brent Coley. Reprinted by permission.

FIGURE 13.3. Kidblog. Copyright 2008 by Kidblog. Reprinted by permission.

13.3) to write a short post about the book. *Kidblog.org* is a free site designed especially for students by teachers. Teachers have administrative control over student blogs and student accounts when they set up a classroom site. The site is password protected for the students and only viewable by the teacher and classmates and no student e-mail addresses are required. The site states that no personal information from either the teacher or the students is collected and that comment privacy settings block unsolicited comments from outside sources. On Deanna's (unedited) blog post on May 10, 2011, she wrote about *The Secret Garden* (Burnett, 1911):

> The book *The Secret Garden* is about a bratty little girl, Mary, who moves in with her rich sad uncle. He had a wife, but she died by falling off a broken branch on an old tree. She loved the garden very much, so she went there every day. Mary's uncle didn't want to destroy it so he lock it up and hid the key. Ten years later Mary comes. next she finds the key. If you want to know what happens next I think you might want to read it, it's a wonderfull book. I would rate the book a 10 out of 10. It has to be one of my favorite books I ever read.The auther of the book is Frances Hodgson Burnett.

At the time (May 22, 2011), there were three comments from classmates.

A productive use of multimedia that requires students to grapple with new ideas and content is to use podcasting for student presentations. A podcast is a digital recording that can be shared over the Internet, and there are many online resources for creating and sharing podcasts. Audio podcasts, usually MP3 files, are easiest to implement in your classroom, even if there is only one computer. Mr. Coley's classroom website hosts the ColeyCast section, where audio podcasts are posted.

We believe that audio podcasting is also composing, because planning and writing must be done to make the audio podcast. At the time of this writing, there are 52 ColeyCasts posted on the classroom website with topics from parts of speech to Amazing America (fascinating facts about the 50 states) included. You can listen to the podcasts on the website or subscribe to them on iTunes; just visit the website at *http://www.mrcoley.com/coleycast/index.htm*. Read more about podcasting in Technique 33.

Additional Resource

List of blog terms on Wikipedia: *http://en.wikipedia.org/wiki/Glossary_of_blogging*.

Online Literature Discussion (Threaded Discussion)

Cross-reference hashtags: #languagearts, #shortcues, #TDG

What Is It?

Online literature discussions allow students to interact without the constraint of time. We found online literature discussions (Grisham & Wolsey, 2006; Wolsey, 2004) using *Nicenet.net*, as well as a schoolwide communication suite with group discussion features, to have many benefits for our students. More recently, Lee (2008) documented the cross-cultural benefits of online literature discussion through blogs. There are other sites that support online discussion including Ning, Google Groups, and Yahoo! Groups. Locate more at *http://www.delicious.com/TDWolsey/TDG.*

Why Is It Important?

Literature provides our students with ways to learn about the human condition in all its glories and its foibles. Literature circles (Daniels, 2002) have, for the past two decades, provided teachers with a way to get students more engaged with texts. Face-to-face literature discussions are used extensively, but adding technology can assist students to respond more authentically and spontaneously to each other about what they are reading. Recently, there has been more attention to online literature discussions. Bowers-Campbell (2011) explored virtual literature circles with preservice teachers, who states, "Threaded discussions foster energetic interactions between students and teachers and promote active and collaborative learning" (p. 558).

What Do I Do?

If you do some form of literature discussion in your classes, we suggest you think about ways to move it online. We began with Nicenet, a free site where you can establish a virtual "classroom" for your students. You can put students into groups so that four to six students in one group are discussing one reading and four to six other students are discussing another text. Or if your class is reading the same book, group your students according to your own criteria. For information on different grouping strategies (heterogeneous, homogeneous, purposive) consult one of the following resources: Daniels, 2002; Grisham and Molinelli, 1995; Johnson et al., 1994. You can set up cross-class groups if you want (Period 1 students interacting with Period 6 students, for example) based on what students are reading or your purposes for interaction. If you have little access to technology, students can do asynchronous discussion from home or from the library, since Nicenet and other threaded discussion forums are accessible from anywhere.

You can also experiment with putting some students online if technology is limited. For example, if you have access to four computers on a regular basis, you can try online literature circles with a small group to see how it goes. You may wish to rotate students through the online discussion as the year progresses giving everyone the opportunity to experience it and providing you with evidence of its efficacy.

Differentiation Possibilities

Process

Threaded discussion groups (TDGs) have built into them the differentiating possibility of students choosing when to post their discussion contributions. They may do so at home, during lunch, or in class. For students whose learning strengths include working with others, the forums build on the positive aspects of peer interactions to encourage each other, add ideas, and offer useful critiques.

Online Example

Although literature circles are normally considered to be something done with literature in English classes, this doesn't have to be the case. Laura Candler maintains a website where she has "tweaked" the normal literature circle roles and responsibilities so that nonfiction texts can be read and discussed in groups. She describes these on her website (*http://www.lauracandler.com/strategies/litcirclemodels.php#NonfictionLiteratureCircles*). Although her site is designed for younger students, she provides resources and ideas that middle and high school teachers can be use to get started.

Example: Science at Community Middle School

In Ms. Gutierrez's eighth-grade science class at Community Middle School, she used text sets to assist her diverse population of students with certain key concepts. A text set is a group of nonfiction trade books on the same topic, but with different readability and complexity levels. In this case, Ms. Gutierrez wanted her students to know more about force and velocity. She knew that some of her students were struggling readers and some were English learners, and so she decided to look at books on the topic and see whether she could find books at different reading levels. In addition, Ms. Gutierrez looked for online resources that had text-to-speech features for her struggling readers.

The textbook for the class proved to be dense in text and the topic was covered in a somewhat dry and factual way, so Ms. Gutierrez decided to look for sources elsewhere. She wanted a number of books on physical science focusing on the topics at different levels of complexity. In the summer, Ms. Gutierrez visited the local public library to find books on force and velocity, but found very few at her students' reading levels and much outdated information. She looked online at the National Science Teachers Association website, which features outstanding science trade books for students K–12, and she located some books her students would like:

Gurstelle, W. (2004). *The art of the catapult.* Chicago: Chicago Review Press.
Lepora, N. (2008). *Twists and turns: Forces in motion.* New York: Stevens.
Smith, A. (2001). *Energy, forces, & motion.* Tulsa, OK: Usborne Books.

Then, on a website called "Secondary Science" (*https://www.msu.edu/course/ te/407/FS05Sec3/te802/tradebooks/phy_science.htm*), she found some excellent books, but they tended to be biographies and they were written at high levels of complexity in the text. Ms. Gutierrez found the Wieser Educational website, where there are resources for struggling learners (*http://www.wiesereducational.com/ products/i_science/39-i_physical-science/ags-physical-science.htm*).

Additional Resources

When looking for text sets, English teachers might also use Linked Text Sets (LTS; Wold, Elish-Piper, & Schultz, 2010). Wold and her colleagues provide explicit directions for conducting a unit on the heroic journey using LTS and many different genres of resources, including graphic novels. A similar Hero Journey unit with Deaf high school students is recounted in Smetana, Odelson, Burns, and Grisham (2009), using graphic novels to support struggling readers.

.... TECH·nique 15 ....

Vocabulary and Writing

Cross-reference hashtag: #vocabulary

What Is It?

Prompting Students to Use Sophisticated Vocabulary

A hallmark of the scholar is precise word choice in speech and in written work. The structure writing prompts take might promote more sophisticated vocabulary uptake in student writing products. First, some evidence suggests that if students are given challenging and complex tasks to grapple with in their writing experiences, they will work toward precision by using more sophisticated vocabulary (Wolsey, 2010). Second, specific vocabulary can be included in the prompt. Often, linguists and educators who study word choice and vocabulary classify words students might use in three categories (Beck, McKeown, & Kucan, 2002; Coxhead, 2000; Zwiers, 2008). Tier one words, according to Beck and her colleagues, are those that are common in the language and widely known, for example: "run," "happy," "work." Such words do not require much attention in secondary schools as vocabulary learning tasks go. Tier two words are the workhorses of the mature language user's vocabulary. They include words that occur relatively frequently in the language, but are more likely to occur in the language of the sophisticated language user. Zwiers calls these words the brick-and-mortar words that link concepts and increase sophisticated language use. Examples of tier two words are "quantity," "essential," and "industrious." Tier three words are generally specific to a domain or content area. In science, a tier three word is "mitosis." In social studies, "feudalism" and "emirate" are example tier three words because they are unlikely to be used frequently or in contexts outside the discipline of social sciences.

Why Is It Important?

Words represent concepts—the wider the conceptual knowledge, the deeper new learning will be (Bravo & Cervetti, 2008; Marzano, 2004). As new vocabulary is acquired, there is essentially no limit to the conceptual knowledge that individuals may develop. The prompts for writing can promote uptake of vocabulary, as well. In Technique 24, you can learn more about the relationship of prompts for writing and uptake of academic vocabulary. Digital media and Web 2.0 tools offer some unique opportunities for students to learn new vocabulary, create multimodal products, and collaborate in online communities (Castek, Dalton, & Grisham, 2012). Students are often motivated by creative and thoughtful integration of technology and media.

How Will Technology Help?

One such example offered was a response to literature using digital recording. A fourth-grade boy in a special day class responded to a piece of literature, a picture book, *Martina, the Beautiful Cockroach: A Cuban Folktale* (Deedy, 2007). When the researchers (Smetana & Grisham, 2011) examined the language he used, they discovered that he used the vocabulary from the book extensively. The researchers recorded "Greg's" (a pseudonym) voice through a digital microphone on a Macintosh computer and created an MP3 file. Greg did not use the book to recount the story, but he did see a picture from the book as a prompt. When we teach vocabulary, even struggling readers like Greg can benefit from the use of technology. Greg listened to the story as read by the teacher, talked with other students who shared the book experience, and picked a character to talk about. He was excited to recount his version of the story from his character's perspective and he used the new vocabulary of the book.

Recently, Dalton and Grisham (2011) proposed e-voc strategies—those that "evoke" strong engagement of students with technology and vocabulary learning. One such strategy is the vocabulary video. Using a Flip camera, students produce 60-second videos acting out the word's meaning and situating it in a specific context. For a glimpse of such a vocabulary video, visit *http://literacybeat.wordpress.com/2011/05/03/vocabvid-stories-developing-vocabulary-depth-and-breadth-through-live-action-video*. First, the teacher must team with someone—a student, a parent, another teacher—to create a model for students. The Flip camera or other high definition (HD) camera is inexpensive and easy to use, plugging into the universal serial bus (USB) port of a personal computer to download the video file. To record the vocabulary video, students must write a short script.

Another e-voc strategy we really like involves gaming, the Internet, and public service. An example is the FreeRice website (*http://www.freerice.com*), where students can play a multiple-choice vocabulary game that earns students a donation of free rice to the World Health Organization. We like to put our students in groups and have the groups compete for the answers. The winning team has to collaborate to create a sentence with the word in it and losing teams can also make up a sentence at the same time, so that several different uses are made of the target word. Students can also be placed in teams to use the new vocabulary in a short story.

There are several levels of FreeRice vocabulary words that allow you to target vocabulary at simpler or more complex levels to differentiate for your students. The whole class can be in on solving each word's definition. Another thing we like about FreeRice is that it can be done with only one computer station and projector. Teachers can extend the lessons by picking (or having students pick) selected words and students then illustrate them and/or find graphics and photos to create vocabulary pages in a computerized reference for the entire class.

Because most of the words that are featured on FreeRice are academic language, this engaging site assists the teacher to teach academic writing in English (Scarcella, 2003; Zwiers, 2008). Have student teams answer 10 vocabulary words, thereby donating 100 grains of rice to assuage world hunger. Then, using any of the short-cues formats, such as a threaded discussion group or online journal entry, have them write a paragraph using the 10 words in correct context. This team writing approach can also be used with PowerPoint slides to create slide shows on different topics. For example, graduate students in a writing class used Google images to write as a team preparing a presentation on a science topic. One class session saw the students in teams going on the Google site, entering a search term (for example, "trash") and downloading images that fit their needs. Then they collaboratively wrote a short text about the image to present to classmates (Figure 15.1). Using the "trash" example, students wrote about how much and what types of trash spoiled the environment and provided tips for recycling. The teacher can create themes for the PowerPoint slides so that the whole may be assembled in a presentation that can be placed on the classroom website.

VoiceThread can also be used for students' responses to new vocabulary and concepts. A VoiceThread is a collaborative, multimedia slide show that holds images, documents, and videos and allows people to navigate slides and leave comments in five ways: using voice with a microphone, voice with a telephone, text, audio file, or

FIGURE 15.1. Screen capture of VoiceThread ("trash"). Copyright 2012 VoiceThread LLC. Reprinted by permission.

video (via a webcam). With VoiceThread (*http://voicethread.com*) the teacher can place images or text on a page, then invite students to respond in one or more of the five ways. Grisham and Smetana (2011) provided examples completed by prospective teachers who had their own e-mail accounts. In that case, VoiceThread was free. However, if your middle or high school students do not have e-mail accounts, you can use a teacher account, which VoiceThread provides to educators for free. Voice-Threads can be made public or private.

What Do I Do?

No matter our reading level, we all encounter words in our reading that we are not sure about. Students may skip these words if they must go fetch a reference such as a dictionary or thesaurus. Think about how easy word choice in writing can be by using the thesaurus in MSWord. If you highlight the word "said," you get about eight synonyms. There are other resources online that may be less limited. For example, at *Thesaurus.com* (*http://thesaurus.com*), you can access over 50 synonyms for "said." On *Dictionary.com* (*http://dictionary.reference.com*), there are 17 entries for "said." Bookmark them on your computer or social bookmarking account so that your students can go directly there when composing. If you need to provide translation of words for your English learners, try Babelfish (*http://babelfish.yahoo.com*) and Google Translate (*http://translate.google.com*), where you can translate from English to other languages ("friend" to *freund* in German) or from another language to English (*ami* to "friend" from French). This, too, can be bookmarked on your classroom, library, lab, or personal computers and mobile devices or linked on your social bookmark page.

"Real-Time" Teaching: Example 1

Kristy Brown is a teacher in the St. Augustine, Florida. Here she integrates the physical classroom walls with learning in a digital environment.

"Real-Time" Teaching by Kristy Brown, St. John's County School District, St. Augustine, Florida

In my language arts classes I had students create a graffiti wall based on Chapman and King's (2009) "design signs." This was their first exposure to this unit's words. We used chalk on black construction paper. Students were fascinated by the words and kept asking what each one meant. They wanted to know what their word meant, what the most colorful word meant, and they even wanted to know what the other grade-level's words meant. I teach sixth and seventh grades, so students were exposed to both sets of words on display (see Figures 15.2 and 15.3). Each time I change the wall to be slightly different. Students see the words daily, and they use

FIGURE 15.2. Ms. Brown's graffiti wall.

the wall as a reference when they write (Chapman & King, 2009). I envision using the wall for vocabulary games throughout the unit.

Since the wall has been up, I have overheard the students using the words in conversation. Not all of them, as some are not common everyday words, but the strategy is definitely a good one for reminding students of words to use and become familiar with. I think the wall could be used for either tier two or tier three terms (Zwiers, 2008). In writing, tier two words may be more useful for encouraging students to elaborate and enhance ideas. I think if I were to use this strategy in my civics or world history course to enhance student writing, I would mix tier two and three words. Some students will need the tier two words to help with elaboration, and to keep students focused on the concept or topic, I want them to be reminded of the tier three words as well. For me, exposing them to the words daily is the important part. The words intrigue them, and since I won't tell them the meanings directly, they are encouraged to seek them out. Next school year, I will encourage the students to take photos of their graffiti wall to place on the class webpage so they can share it with their parents.

FIGURE 15.3. Ms. Brown's graffiti wall.

Example 2

Mr. Hemming and Mr. Adams were talking in the faculty lounge as Mr. Adams described the difficulty in getting students to use the vocabulary they encountered in reading, lectures, and videos when they wrote. Mr. Hemming agreed it was not an easy task in his English courses, but he had happened on an idea that seemed to help. Every time he started a new short story or novel, he chose key terms students needed to know in order to understand the fiction. He also noted that some vocabulary described the discipline itself, in his case, the elements of literature such as "plot" or "theme," whereas others were derived from the reading.

Mr. Hemming created a graphic to help students see the terms in relation to each other (see Figure 15.4). When his students read "The Scarlet Ibis" (Hurst, 1960), they needed to understand the literary term "symbolism," as well as the terms "vermillion" and "piazza" that were derived from the story. He knew that if students would use these terms in their writing, they would come to a deeper understanding of the term and how it is used. This would improve both their reading and writing capacities. For each new novel, unit, or short story, he simply put the words up on the wall with a sample sentence and sometimes a definition.

Then, whenever students were writing Mr. Hemming would challenge his students to use five of the 10 words from the story whenever they wrote about it. He also included the literary terms and asked students to be sure to use at least four of the terms that also appeared on the wall. A side benefit for the students was that because the words were right on the wall, they never needed to misspell them—all they had to do was look up and there they were. But in the digital age, he decided to take things to the next level. Whenever the wall was changed to add new words or take old words down that students would know, he had a student take a digital photo and post it on the class website. Students logged on to the class wiki and selected the vocabulary page where they added examples they found of the words used in books, on signs around the community, and in conversation. Students posted written descriptions of conversations and posted photos taken with their cell phones of places where the terms were found. For his students, it became a contest to see

Example: English-language arts

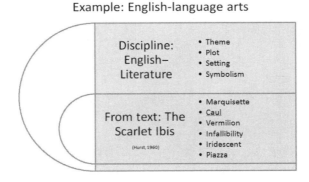

FIGURE 15.4. Vocabulary for "The Scarlet Ibis."

who could use or find the terms, and their word consciousness was improved even as they used the terms themselves. The best part of it was that the more aware students became of the terms, the more the literature made sense to them and the more likely they were to use discipline-specific terms (for example, "plot," "setting") and terms found in the literature they read (for example, "caul," "infallibility") when they wrote on discussion boards and in longer papers.

TECH·nique 16

Collaborative Writing

Cross-reference hashtags: #shareddoc, #wiki

What Is It?

When students think and compose together, they often "share the pen." Grisham (1989) wrote about the benefits and drawbacks of writing for her students. Cooperative learning structures in the classroom (compare Johnson et al., 1994) can assist teachers to provide essential components such as positive interdependence, productive interactions, and personal responsibilities to the group. Given a goal (such as a writing task), the group must come together to compose the product. During the process, they discuss the topic, approaches, knowledge required, and the writing components to complete the task. When we add technology, students no longer share a pen, but they do share a computer.

Why Is It Important?

When students work collaboratively, the outcomes can often be good, but what is equally important is the process that students go through when they work together toward a learning outcome (DuFour & Eaker, 1998; Johnson et al., 1994). In our secondary classrooms, it is important to establish a culture of learning and a sense that every individual may contribute to the learning community. Teachers and students can work together to achieve this. An important part of this is knowing your students (sometimes 150 of them in a day) and demonstrating not only your knowledge but your willingness to inquire with them on important new topics.

Shared documents and websites allow multiple users to revise and edit a single document or page. These include wikis, Google Docs, and Office Live. Most shared documents include a feature that archives earlier versions of the document. This is helpful because if an earlier idea that was edited out is later found to be useful, there is no need to retype the text. Rather, just choose the earlier version from the "history" menu and restore what had appeared before. Moreover, student writers can work from home, from the library, and from the classroom on one common written product.

As students work together they discuss and think about the topic of learning, reading resources, and writing to learn. Increasingly, students will join a workforce where they collaborate with others using collaborative writing tools. As they do, they will come to new understandings about how written work is created. When one student writes something and another joins in editing the work of the original author, the effect can be disconcerting, at first. However, the power of collaborative writing lies in the ability to build ideas together, write your own thoughts, edit someone else's ideas, and know that at any time the author can revert to an earlier version. Additional examples of a shared document, such as Google Docs, can be found in Technique 6.

How Will Technology Help?

Writing tasks are easier on the computer and when students share the keyboarding and the composing, the task becomes even easier and more motivating. It is simpler to revise and edit the group's writing—and discussion of the revisions and editing can help students build knowledge that they may apply to individual writing products. In addition, the secondary teacher may have anywhere from 70 to 150 students per day. If they are writing in groups, you can divide the number of papers you must read by four (the optimum number for a collaborative writing team). Publication and dissemination of the students' work is also simpler. It can be posted to a website or included in an electronic file that may be accessed by others. In fact, the teacher may assign groups to assess each other's writing projects, thus deepening their knowledge about a given topic. Work products may be preserved from year to year as models for the next group of students.

What Do I Do?

Google Docs can add to our repertoire of resources for teaching. A form of cloud computing, Google Docs are repositories for documents that are collaboratively written. When chair of the Technology Committee for the International Reading Association (IRA), one of the authors led a committee to revise the IRA's Position Statement on New Literacies (IRA, 2009). It was the first time that most of the participants had used Google Docs. It was set up by the chair of the committee and other members were invited by e-mail. These participants spanned the United States and there was a member from Great Britain as well. Each of the participants could make changes to the document and a record of the contributions could be seen by all. The Position Statement reflected the best efforts of the committee without the committee having to meet. Both authors of this book and a third colleague used

Google Docs to organize a special themed edition of a journal (Cernohous, Wolsey, & Grisham, 2010). It is easy to use and free. So teachers may have students work in teams to create documents for their content classes that can then be downloaded and shared with others via a link to the classroom webpage or in an e-mail to the teacher.

Another resource that we have used is a free program called TypeWithMe (*http:// typewith.me*). Two students can be sitting at separate computers typing on the same document—a real example of collaborative writing. Of course, they may also be doing this from home. We suggest you try out Google Docs and/or TypeWithMe with partner teachers or other friends and examine the possibilities for writing in your class.

Differentiation Possibilities

Product

There are several types of shared documents and collaborative work environments. In some cases, students might choose a wiki or a shared document such as a Google Doc after considering the nature of the final product, the learning outcomes, and the strengths of each type of collaborative writing media. Because these formats have different strengths and limitations, there are implications for process, as well.

"Real-Time" Teaching: Example

Gina Girlando teaches middle school language arts. She uses Wikispaces to help students find and organize their resources. At the same time, students also publish a Wikispace that others may view. Gina describes the project here.

"Real-Time" Teaching by Gina Girlando, Sparta School District, Sparta, New Jersey

To promote the writing in my language arts class, students are given the task to develop an online research paper on the Harlem Renaissance. The purpose of the assignment is for students to research a selected topic from the Harlem Renaissance and display their knowledge through writing a collaborative research paper within a group of four. The categories for research include music, art, history, and literature of the time period.

Using Wikispace makes their research paper a live document. This means that the group always has access to the page, allowing them to edit and revise as much as they choose. This gives the students the sense that the page represents them as a whole, and they must work together to be sure their spelling, punctuation, grammar, information, and so on is correct. Because they are aware that other people are viewing their work, I have found that students take much more pride in their work, and often are very careful to watch what other group members are changing on the page.

While this may seem a simple collaborative writing task, this project is far from an ordinary research paper. Students are required to embed media clips, pictures, podcasting, and slide shows on their wiki page to support their information (Figure 16.1). This has been an extremely useful feature, as it provides an opportunity to identify and organize their information through visual and written expression. Once students have completed their research paper, they must teach their information to the rest of the class. Students will be creative in designing a lesson that will have the students participate in an activity to exemplify their knowledge of the information presented. Such lessons in the past have included art auctions, dance-offs, sing-alongs, poetry night, and news broadcasting.

Wikispace has served as a useful tool as it allowed students to work collaboratively from any computer. With the issue of time during the school day, students are given the opportunity to work at any time with their group. The history tab feature (Figure 16.2; students' names are hidden) is also a tremendously helpful tool, as it allows the teacher to view who has been working on specific sections. With students always concerned about their partners' efforts, they are more comfortable knowing that I am able to see the interaction, as well as their work at any given time.

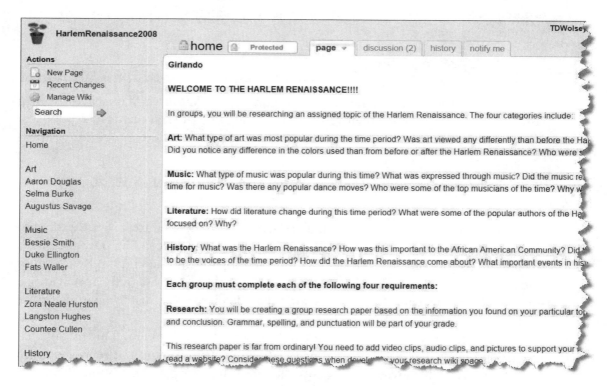

FIGURE 16.1. Gina Girlando's wiki project home page. *Wikispaces.com* is copyright 2011 by Tangient LLC. Reprinted by permission.

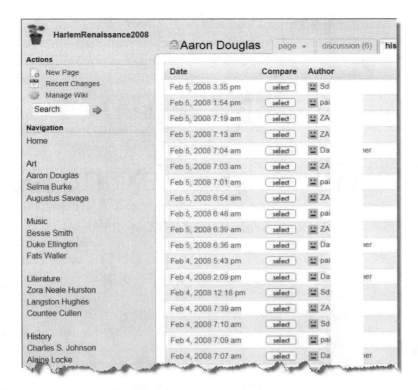

FIGURE 16.2. Ms. Girlando's wiki showing user history (names blocked out). *Wikispaces. com* is copyright 2011 by Tangient LLC. Reprinted by permission.

Are Those Kids Texting Again?

Cross-reference hashtag: #texting

What Is It?

Texting is sending short written messages via mobile phone, which is extraordinarily popular among teens (not to mention adults). Text messaging is used not only for personal communications but is also used for advertising, online ordering, and other commercial purposes. Studies show that economic status does not play a factor in ownership of cell phones (Tibbs, 2010) and that about 98% of students from fifth grade on up have their own cell phones. Although most districts and schools ban the use of cell phones during school hours, there are voices calling for a more academic use of these WMDs (wireless mobile devices, *not* weapons of mass destruction), which are far more a computer than a telephone (Rosen, 2010; Tibbs, 2010). In the world of mobile phones, there are numerous applications, better known as "apps" that allow us to communicate in more immediate ways. According to Rosen, today's students seek the newest, the fastest, and the most social of technology applications for themselves. If we wish school to be relevant to young learners, we need to learn from them. As we do so, we need to show them the educational uses of these devices.

Why Is It Important?

As we have noted before, we must find productive ways to bridge social literacies and academic literacies for our students. While mobile phones and other handheld devices can be used for disruptive purposes in school, we can also use them to students' academic benefit. In the following section we show how they can be used for polling and short forms of writing.

How Will Technology Help?

Tibbs (2010) suggests a couple of websites that can become classroom projects where students write and learn. The first, *PollEverywhere.com* (*http://www.polleverywhere.com*) lets you create instant polls for cell phones that allows up to 30 votes at no cost. *PollEverywhere.com* gives you a number to text message a vote to, and you can see the results instantly online at PollEverywhere. There are K–12 accounts that are free (if limited), and school and district accounts that are nominal in pricing. If students don't have their own cell phones or they don't have unlimited texting, they can vote using a computer in the classroom. If the teacher displays the site on the screen via LCD projector, the results would be displayed instantly and visibly. Students may then write a summary of the findings and refine their questions.

Another idea for using texting comes from Judee Shipman on *Education.com*. This webpage (*http://www.education.com/science-fair/article/texting-new-language*) provides a lesson plan for texting in social studies. The purposes of the project are for high school students to "chart the evolution of the text messaging movement, compile a glossary of standard abbreviated spellings for words commonly used in text messaging, and to discover other applications for the linguistic style of text messages" (n.d.). Students have a list of research questions to answer (such as "Is there a standardized glossary of texting abbreviations?") and a list of resources (Internet search, text on linguistics, and Wikipedia).

What Do I Do?

First, get permission to allow students to bring and use their mobile phones in your classes. Mobile phones are ubiquitous as we have mentioned. Recently, we heard a report on National Public Radio that the upcoming generation of supercomputers will be using microwave technology instead of semiconductors (chips), which have arrived at the saturation level (size and capacity). So we think that students need to use these tools as they do other tools (such as pencil and paper). We are not suggesting that mobile phone technology replace older technologies. In fact, we agree with Frey et al. (2010), that 21st-century technologies must move into the core curriculum but should be used as tools. In Table 17.1, Frey and colleagues provide us with technology functions with current tools (remember, these change considerably, in a relatively short time). Remember that this list is a guideline—as a teacher you make the decisions about what tools your students will use. But we recommend that you begin to explore (see Part One) the technological tools that are available to you.

"Real-Time" Teaching: Example

Ms. Vanessa Cristobal is a high school English teacher at the California School for the Deaf, where many of her students are achieving below grade-level standards. She

TABLE 17.1. Technology Functions with Current Tools

Searching	Listening and viewing	Storing
Google	Podcasts	MP3 players
Yahoo	iTunes	Flash drives
Lycos	Screencasts	Servers
Bing	Hulu	CDs/DVDs
Phone apps	RSS feeds	E-books
Communicating	Sharing	Collaborating
Text messaging	YouTube	Wikis
Twitter	Blogs	VoiceThread
Digg	Vlogs	Google Docs
Video conferencing	Flickr	Crowdsourcing
E-mail	Picasa	
Producing	Presenting	Networking
GarageBand	PowerPoint	MySpace
iMovie	Keynote	Facebook
ComicLife	Wimba	Ning
Voki	Smartboards	

Note. From Frey, Fisher, and Gonzalez (2010). Copyright 2010 by Solution Tree Press. Reprinted by permission.

creates a lively classroom atmosphere and loves to stimulate student interest in content with technology uses, whenever possible. Ms. Cristobal is an innovative teacher who enjoys using technology to teach her profoundly Deaf and hard-of-hearing students using Web 2.0 resources. Deaf students are avid users of technology, and indeed technologies such as closed captioning, instant messaging, and other assistive technologies are a boon to this student population.

In her classes this year, Ms. Cristobal did a unit on cyberbullying that taught her students some of the most important lessons about the uses—and possible misuses—of technology. She has created a series of lessons where her students use their cell phones to "tweet" responses to questions and topics they are discussing. Twitter is an information network made up of 140-character messages called tweets. On the Twitter website, tweets are compared to newspaper headlines that appear daily on your webpage.

> 140 characters is the space limitation for a tweet and it is quite short, like Haiku, so thought must reflect the essence of communication. (139 characters)

Ms. Cristobal provides written directions for her students through an introductory PowerPoint (see Figure 17.1). The slides show students how to sign up for their Twitter account, and Mrs. Cristobal reminds students of the rules for using tweets—that they may only use the tweets for academic purposes. In addition, students learn how they may keep the tweets private by "following" only the students in the class and Ms. Cristobal.

How do I get started?

- Go to www.twitter.com to set up your account.
- To help me memorize your name, be sure that your username has the following information:
  - First name, block number
  - vanessa3loveswarriors
- Add me to your "followers" list.
- Add only people from your class.

PROTECT YOUR TWEETS

FIGURE 17.1. Screen capture of Twitter directions.

This year, with her honors English class, Ms. Cristobal did two units with Twitter. The first was on cyberbullying—a very timely topic. Later, students participated in another project on the treatment of women. The following tweets from students are on the topic of cyberbullying:

It really hurts to be hated and makes me so angry, but I can't respond that way. Instead, I must report. I would never do this to another! (138)

A sad boy cringes from his former friends in such pain that he might suicide. It is betrayal, but don't despair. Tell someone and escape. (137)

You must not believe the lies and the hate, but trust this will pass. Report the abuse and you will then be free. Be strong. Don't despair. (139)

Cyberbullying is a crime. Don't commit it. If you are a victim, report it. It is not your fault. Sometimes so called friends make mistakes. (139)

In the end, you will survive, but it can make you angry and sad. Cyberbullying is a crime, so don't let yourself believe the bad messages. (138)

Ms. Cristobal's honor students did an excellent job with the form and the language and cyberbullying is a topic that all students, particularly middle and high school students, need to review, much like safely crossing the street for younger students.

Ms. Cristobal's website (*https://sites.google.com/site/cristobal2014*) reflects her interest in educational technology and she has done a number of other projects, such as students using Glogs for reports and for semester-end finals.

PART FOUR

Inquiry and Long Thinking Meet the Disciplines

Writing in school is just writing, right? It would seem so, at times. If students can write a persuasive essay in English, then they should be able to write one in science, too. However, though it stands to reason that writing skills are transferable, there are important differences between the work that exemplifies effective writing in science and the work that is exemplary in social studies. In this part of the book, we explore those differences. As you read, think about how science writing is different than writing about sports or about social studies.

FAQs about Writing in the Disciplines

Cross-reference hashtags: #styleguide

Is writing easy or is it hard?

William Zinsser (1980; see Technique 6), a professional writer, asserted that writing is hard work. Murray suggests that easy writing makes for easy reading (2005) and hard writing makes for labored reading. While writing *East of Eden* (1952), Steinbeck often wrote only two or three pages per day (1969), laboring over each word, organization of the novel, the characters, and the theme. Clearly, his work as a novelist was difficult at times. Ray Bradbury countered that as a young writer, he "thought you could beat, pummel, and thrash an idea into existence. Under such treatment, of course, any decent idea folds up its paws, turns on its back, fixes its eyes on eternity, and dies" (1974, p. vii). In our writing, we find that sometimes the words flow rather easily from the keyboard to the screen—often after much thought, discussion, research, and planning. At other times, the sentences have to be coaxed into coherence and the paragraphs revised until they make sense. It has not served us as writers and teachers, nor has it served the students with whom we have worked, to think of writing as either hard or easy. Rather, it has helped us to think of writing as an opportunity to learn and a rewarding use of our time.

What is a draft?

A draft is any written product that is not yet ready for general release. It may be shared with peers, the teacher, or others for the purpose of obtaining responses to the writing and feedback on its effectiveness. Drafts may not be technically flawless; however, we discourage the students with whom we work from using terms such as "sloppy copy." Strunk and White (2000) advised that drafts can be reasonably well written if they are planned well, and we discourage the notion that sloppy work is acceptable. This doesn't mean that writers do not learn, revise, adjust, and edit their work as they write. Rather, drafts are frequently filled with notes, annotations, crossed-out or deleted text, track changes, responses from colleagues, and so on. This may not look neat, but it is not sloppy work—it is purposeful and done with the intent to communicate effectively.

What is the role of responding and revising?

Responding and revising are often woven together, but the threads of each are noticeable. Writers ask for information about their writing from teachers, peers, or sometimes from others outside the school. In responding, the reader provides a reaction based on personal criteria or effect and established criteria (such as a prompt, rubric, or model) as to the piece's effectiveness. Peer responders need to know what effective writing in the discipline looks like and what the criteria for effectiveness might be. The purpose of the response is to help the writer know how others perceive the work, and benefits accrue to both reader/responder and to the writer. The reader notices perspectives that perhaps should be considered, while writers have the opportunity to compare their own purposes and intended messages with that which was actually received. Teachers often provide responses after the student writers have submitted the work, but students may benefit from teacher response during the construction of the draft.

When students have the opportunity to revise their work based on the responses they receive from peers and teachers, their written work can improve substantively. To make effective use of the response and revisions, teachers consider:

- Time for students to share their work with peers and with the teacher.
- A means of determining what effective writing might look like via models, prompts, and scoring criteria.
- The opportunity to revise with time provided to affect relevant revisions.
- Technology that improves the capacity for sharing work with peers. These include shared files (Google Docs, Office Live, *Box.net*, and so on), e-mail, and blogs dedicated to reviewing drafts of student work.
- Opportunities to confer with the teacher or peers for clarification on responses provided.

Conferring with students is a good idea. With 150 students, how do I do it?

At times, conferring with students is a time-consuming endeavor. However, if teachers make time for writing in class, conferences can be as simple as praise, prompt, and leave to confer with the next student (Jones, 2007). If the teacher has clear criteria in mind, a conference can take less than a minute. In the praise, prompt, and leave model applied to writing, the teacher quickly reads part of a student's draft (or asks the student to point out a problematic area), praises some aspect of the writing, then prompts the student with further feedback (here, a prompt is a hint serving as feedback rather than as a general direction for writing). The prompt can be to encourage the student to address a deficient area of the writing, but it can also be a suggested way forward with the writing that might improve the writing from the reader's perspective. Using the praise, prompt, and leave model, every student engaged in some aspect of writing in a classroom can receive feedback from the teacher in less than one class period (often in less than a half hour). Longer conferences can be scheduled for students who need additional help or clarifications.

Isn't editing the same thing as revising?

Editing is often associated with the job of editor. However, editors in professional arenas do far more the proofread copy for mistakes or errors in style, usage, and spelling. Professional editors supervise and approve stories, rewrite them, manage the budget for the publication, work with and supervise others in the organization, and so on. However, in school environments, the task known as editing is often restricted to matters of usage, spelling, and some style matters (#styleguide). This seems a simple matter, but these tasks are complicated and involve wide knowledge of conventions in the discipline, the school, standard English (we never use the unfortunate term "proper" English), and colloquialisms. Effective writers often edit their work themselves knowing that errors can creep in even for the most conscientious of writers. However, they often consult experts to help them. Online, the expert may reside in the grammar and spell-checking tool in the word processor, but it doesn't stop there. Writers may choose to share their work with a competent peer who can help find typographical and other errors of usage.

Revising and editing in school environments are not interchangeable concepts. Indeed, sometimes teachers and peer editors respond to matters of usage ignoring content and organization (compare, Beach & Friedrich, 2006). Thus, it is useful to think of response to content and organization as different than editing for conventions and usage.

How important are usage and spelling?

Spelling and matters of usage (commonly called grammar) are not the biggest deals in the world, but they are important. Writers who attend to spelling and usage convey a sense of competence, whereas those who ignore or cannot control these features (often called "local operations" in this book) are viewed as, well, less than competent. What can be done about this?

◆ Provide time for students to write (that is, for students to learn while they write) in the classroom. Teachers and peers can assist students as they write. If the teacher has a word wall (either virtual or actually on a wall), students can refer to it to ensure that key vocabulary is correctly spelled—after all, it's right in front of them on the wall or the screen. Even in a rough draft, students can be expected to spell words correctly that are right there for them when orthography matters.

◆ Structure the scoring criteria for spelling or usage such that it counts for something, but won't submarine the grade overall. Do all you can to make sure students know which elements of spelling or usage will be the focus of the teacher's attention during scoring.

Why are so many essays in school in the five-paragraph format or rely on those food metaphors?

We don't know. Paragraphs are not like hamburgers except in school (you know, bun, wilted lettuce, dry meat, a splash of pickle relish from a gallon jar, another bun). Essays are not like sandwiches, tacos, or any other food. No one we know (and we know a lot of people including students in many middle and high schools) writes five-paragraph essays unless they have been "forced" (we chose this word carefully) to do so. Five-paragraph essays are easy to score because, well, all the teacher has to do is count. One introduction, three body paragraphs, one conclusion. Seriously. Other than that, we can't think of any reason to use the five-paragraph essay or think of writing as fast food.

It's All the Same, or Maybe Not?

Cross-reference hashtags: #disciplines, #science

What Is It?

Writing is sometimes thought of in a sort of two-valued manner (Hayakawa & Hayakawa, 1990); that is, it is either something students can do or something they cannot do. In recent years, we have come to understand that literacy practices are much more nuanced than that. For example, academic discourse in one disciplinary community looks somewhat different in other disciplinary communities. Readers approach reading tasks in different ways depending on the discipline or content area (compare Shanahan & Shanahan, 2008). Writers, like readers, approach writing tasks in different ways from one discipline to another (for example, Fang & Schleppegrell, 2010; Fang, Schleppegrell, & Cox, 2006) and as one's sense of accomplishment within a discipline increases (for example, Hyland & Tse, 2004). Writers approaching mathematics tasks write in different ways using different structures than those writing of social science topics, for instance. The job confronting researchers and teachers is to define in what ways the language characteristics of writing in different disciplines varies. Teachers need pedagogies that promote understanding on the part of students about how best to write in science, math, and other disciplines. This book takes the view that expert content teachers are in the best position to teach students how to write in that discipline.

Why Is It Important?

Writing, as we have explored in this book, is constrained in some ways by the purposes the author has for writing and by the contexts in which the writing occurs and for which it occurs. Robert Frost (2006) was known for his mastery of form, especially rhyme. He famously claimed that writing free verse would be something like playing tennis without a net. It might be fun, but it would not be tennis, he asserted.

Like Frost's poems, disciplines taught in schools have constraints that define them and help participants in the discourse community understand what is written. These constraints are useful in that they provide context and help establish a purpose for writing (and, these serve a similar purpose for the reader of those texts). Constraints provide a set of assumptions about what the message conveyed in the text that those familiar with the discipline will recognize. Thought of in this way, constraints facilitate communication. For teachers, the constraints of any discipline also present an opportunity to learn how to write like, and think like, a scientist, a mathematician, an athlete, a writer of short stories, or a historian.

The characteristics of writing in any discipline, or academic register, might be thought of in terms of the local operations and global moves discussed earlier. Register refers to the choice of words, sentence structures, and other grammatical features that are commonly used within a discourse community, such as historians or theoretical mathematicians. Local operations, for example, might include the way disciplines use nouns and noun phrases (Fang et al., 2006), which vary somewhat. Science texts may contain more nouns and noun phrases in somewhat dense texts that place additional cognitive demands on the writer who strives to write accurately and robustly. Global moves can attend to a number of features that are also specific to school disciplines. These can include attention to an established framework (common in science), observation, problem–solution, analysis, argumentation, and so forth. Often, these are expressed in even more specific formats such as the lab report in science, or the brief constructed response in social science. However, they are also dynamic as the discourse community for any given discipline evolves, shares ideas, and defines the nature of that community. Specific academic registers are further complicated by the functions the text will serve and the audience for which the text is intended.

What Do I Do?

There are several actions that teachers in specific disciplines can take. They are not steps so much as a set of actions that can help in regard to knowing how scientists, historians, authors, mathematicians, and so forth might use them when they write that provide guidance for students in grades 5–12.

1 The first action we advocate is that content teachers read as much as they can and as widely as they can in their disciplines. Finding and reading sources that would be appropriate for the grade levels they teach can be especially helpful. Teachers who know what is current and what good writing in the discipline looks like are far more prone to notice and be able to teach their students to write similarly. More important, well-read content teachers are more likely to recognize and be able to teach those features.

2 Use an RSS feed (see Technique 13) or listserv to subscribe to news from professional organizations in literacy and in the content area. Not everything that comes to the inbox will be useful, but often, very good ideas can be found this way.

3 Conduct an inventory of the materials and student-created writing you have available to determine what some of the content-specific features are. Form 19.1 at the end of this chapter provides some guidelines for evaluating the way work students will read can inform your teaching and the way students will write in your content area. Many of these texts can serve as mentor texts (that is, texts that serve as models for student writing) for your students as they write. The content literacy analysis inventory is a place to begin considering the demands of writing tasks in your classroom and content area.

Differentiation Possibilities

Content

Identify sources that might serve as models of writing at various levels that students can read.

Process

Allow students to consult from multiple sources with some choices among them.

Example: Science Writing at Metro High

Ms. Nation teaches science, and her students explore the domain by observing demonstrations, experimenting in controlled environments, and reading about the principles of science as well as current discoveries. However, Ms. Nation knows that her students will more deeply understand science when they write about it. In the current unit, her students are exploring the evidence on how the red shift provides evidence that supports the big bang theory, which attempts to explain the development of the known universe. Though the basic principle of the big bang is not difficult for her high school students to understand, the evidence that supports the theory requires some very sophisticated thinking on the part of her students. Students need prior knowledge of the principles of the Doppler effect, wave theory applied to light, and gravitation. Students have read about these principles, observed demonstrations, and listened to Ms. Nation's presentations.

Before Ms. Nation felt comfortable assigning students to write about the big bang, she examined the texts students read including some online sources appropriate for her 10th-grade students. She reviewed five written pieces from the last year her students had written, as well as the directions she gave those students. Next, she adjusted her assignment for this year. Her plan included these steps:

Ms. Nation used one professionally written text intended for 10th-grade audiences and two exemplary writings from her students last year (she saved these with the permission of the students who wrote them). She drew on her knowledge of science writing for high schoolers and her knowledge of science writing for popular and expert audiences, as well, to highlight the features of the text that students might use when they write. She planned to use the word processing programs and the interactive whiteboard in her classroom to call out these features. Features included:

- How the professional and student authors used key terms specific to science.
- How the sentences were constructed to show relationships between key concepts.
- How tier two words indicated precision thinking on the part of the author.
- How the authors attributed their ideas, when appropriate to lectures, written texts provided by the teacher, and other sources they found on their own.

In preparing her assignment for students, Ms. Nation created three different writing scenarios from which students could choose. Over her career, she found that students often responded well to choices that helped them meet curriculum goals and standards, but also gave them freedom to choose key aspects of the assignment that would engage the students and still help them meet curricular goals. She chose to differentiate the written product by permitting students to write either a narrative or evaluative piece that was primarily informative in nature. She purposefully chose narrative or evaluative options because much of the writing about the big bang was descriptive in character. Because she was aware of this feature of science writing regarding the big bang, she wanted students to transform their knowledge that could not be simply repeated, copied, or emulated. At the same time, she provided choice by varying the mode of the written product and keeping the informative nature of the writing at the forefront. Later in Part Four, an example of Ms. Nation's prompts for writing (the directions she gives her students) can be found. Look for #prompts.

Content Literacy Analysis Inventory

Directions:

◆ Choose three or more representative texts that students in your content area might be expected to read, then reread these. They should be appropriate for the students' grade level and age, and for the background knowledge students might reasonably have at their command. Evaluate the texts as a set using the criteria below. As you evaluate the texts your students might read, note what features seem to predominate. These features can inform what you ask of your students as they write.

◆ Choose three or more prompts for writing you have assigned in your content area over the last semester. If you can, also reread student responses to those prompts, as well.

◆ Choose three or more examples of student-created writing from your content area and grade level over the last semester. If possible, select a sample from an accomplished grade-level writer in your discipline, a writer who meets grade-level and content standards, and a writer who struggles sometimes with grade-level content writing.

Teacher Name: _____

Content Area or Subject: _____ **Grade Level:** _____

1 **Purpose and Mode in Reading:** Determine the primary mode and purpose you observe most often in the materials your students read on the matrix, below. Place three X's for the most common, two X's for the next most common, and one X for the next most common. Leave other areas blank.

Primary Mode	Primary Purpose			
	Expressive	Literary	Informative	Persuasive
Narrative				
Descriptive				
Classificatory				
Evaluative				

2 **Purpose and Mode for Student Writing:** Next, consider the primary mode and purpose you observe most often in the materials you assigned your students to write about in your content area. Place three X's for the most common, two X's for the next most common, and one X for the next most common. Leave other areas blank.

(cont.)

Primary Mode	Primary Purpose			
	Expressive	Literary	Informative	Persuasive
Narrative				
Descriptive				
Classificatory				
Evaluative				

3 **Semantic features:** Estimate how often tier two and three vocabulary are used in each context and note key examples.

Academic Vocabulary Use	Based on what students read, indicate key examples:	Based on writing tasks students are asked to complete (prompts), indicate key examples:
Tier Two Vocabulary (academic terms found across several disciplines)	Reading 1:	Prompt 1:
	Reading 2:	Prompt 2:
	Reading 3:	Prompt 3:
Tier Three Vocabulary (academic terms found primarily in my discipline).	Reading 1:	Prompt 1:
	Reading 2:	Prompt 2:
	Reading 3:	Prompt 3:

4 **Syntactic Structures:** Syntactic structures often indicate a degree of complexity in associating ideas or employing background knowledge to read or write in content areas.

Syntactic Structures	Based on what students read, indicate key examples:	Based on writing tasks students actually completed (as available), indicate key examples:
Use of sentences with more than one main clause.	Reading 1:	Student work 1:
	Reading 2:	Student work 2:
	Reading 3:	Student work 3:
Use of sentences with two or more main clauses.	Reading 1:	Student work 1:
	Reading 2:	Student work 2:
	Reading 3:	Student work 3:

(*cont.*)

Syntactic Structures	Based on what students read, indicate key examples:	Based on writing tasks students actually completed (as available), indicate key examples:
Note anything that stands out about the nouns in the reading or student work samples.	Reading 1:	Student work 1:
	Reading 2:	Student work 2:
	Reading 3:	Student work 3:
Note anything that stands out about the verbs in the reading or student work samples.	Reading 1:	Student work 1:
	Reading 2:	Student work 2:
	Reading 3:	Student work 3:

5   Argumentation and Attribution

Argumentation and Attribution	Based on what students read, indicate key examples:	Based on writing tasks students are asked to complete (prompts), indicate key examples:
What format or styleguide (for example, APA, MLA, schoolhouse style) do the materials selected rely upon?	Reading 1:	Prompt 1:
	Reading 2:	Prompt 2:
	Reading 3:	Prompt 3:
In what ways are arguments (the means by which a proposition or claim is established) constructed?	Reading 1:	Prompt 1:
	Reading 2:	Prompt 2:
	Reading 3:	Prompt 3:
In what ways are sources attributed for key ideas? What assumptions are taken as received knowledge without attribution?	Reading 1:	Prompt 1:
	Reading 2:	Prompt 2:
	Reading 3:	Prompt 3:

6   What conclusions can you draw about the use of language in your content area based on the samples from the inventory, above?

7   How might you modify instruction regarding writing tasks in your content area based on these conclusions?

What Was That Essential Question Again?

Cross-reference hashtags: #essentialquestions,
#shortcues, #socialstudies

What Is It?

Essential questions are "signposts to big ideas" (Wiggins & McTighe, 2005, p. 106) and guide student inquiry. The interplay of learning spaces, access to technology and print texts, teacher expectations, and opportunities to engage in literate activities in school creates the case for the interdisciplinary essential question. At Health Sciences High and Middle College, a charter school in San Diego, California, students explored these questions during the 2010–2011 school year:

1   What is beauty and/or beautiful?

2   Does gender matter?

3   Who are your heroes and role models?

4   What's worth fighting, or even dying, for?

We know the idea of the essential question is deployed in a variety of ways in schools across the continent. In some cases, teachers develop essential questions for each lesson they lead. Sometimes, teachers work together in departments to develop essential questions for each unit or semester. However, we are intrigued with the essential questions at Health Sciences High. Teachers develop essential questions and seek student input for the questions that will guide inquiry throughout the school year. The questions are used throughout the school, and they change every year without ever repeating. Because of this, teachers and students have opportunities to make new connections between big ideas and the content they teach. Each teacher uses the question to guide inquiry and written tasks that seek answers to the essential questions while maintaining on state standards for content and Common Core Standards for Literacy and Mathematics (Common Core Standards Initiative, 2010; see Appendix A). Over the course of the year, through multiple writing assignments and other tasks, the students draw on multiple sources and integrate their understanding of content within each discipline and across them, as well.

Why Is It Important?

Essential questions help students learn, or relearn, to wonder about things. Because he chose to wonder, Einstein (1961) helped us understand the universe we inhabit and consider the immense possibilities and dangers in the incredibly small world of the atom. Because they wondered, Watson and Crick (Crick, 1988) unlocked the dynamics of the DNA molecule and changed the quality of our lives forever. Because the universe inspired him, Stephen Hawking overcame great challenges and wrote (Hawking, 1988) an elegantly simple explanation of the wonderfully complex universe we all inhabit. More important, perhaps, is that he shared his wonderment with anyone who can read his books. And because he wondered about the relationships in human families and the circles that surround those relationships, Robert Munsch (1986) wrote a book that is deceptively simple because it is a children's book and that touches the heart of every reader who picks it up regardless of age. Essential questions are the bedrock of what causes humans to wonder about the world and even the universe they inhabit, the nature of their relationships with other humans, and the interactions between that world and humans. As readers of this book know, what we wonder about and question leads to inquiry, research, and insight. Inquiry, research, and insight are the fuel of the thoughtful writer in school and everywhere else an author can find a stylus, a pencil, or a keyboard.

How Will Technology Help?

If you have ever wondered about something in the digital age, chances are good you found a search engine and looked up the details, the related variables, or the names of others who wondered what piqued your curiosity. Did you ever wonder what a map of the Internet might look like? Go to Google and type "Map of the Internet" and you'll see how some thinkers conjured an image or an explanation of the almost limitless Internet. If you ever considered the possibility that thousands of individual photographs might be joined to create a seamless virtual experience, visit *Photosynth.com* to see how two-dimensional photographs can create a three-dimensional experience you can share with your students (or that they can create and share with you). Technology brings together resources and people that can inspire wonderment. In the following paragraphs, we explore how that might happen. Oh yeah, and we wonder what you might think of to inspire your students with technology or how they might inspire others through their own uses of technology.

What Do I Do?

◆ Work with other faculty at your school to determine essential questions that inspire wonder and scholarly inquiry. Although some essential questions can be derived for each lesson, it may be helpful to develop overarching questions that span content areas and units within those content areas. Wiggins (2007) also recommends questions that get at the heart of critical concepts within a discipline. When appropriate, involve students in selecting the essential questions that will guide their inquiry for that year.

◆ Again, working with students and other faculty, note possible links to Common Core Standards (2010; see Appendix A) or state standards for the content area.

◆ Ensure that students have many resources, including digital resources, available in addition to assigned textbooks and teacher presentations.

◆ Link writing tasks to essential questions whenever appropriate. Doing so makes it possible for students to explore universal ideas and key ideas within and across disciplines. When essential questions guide student writing, they are more able to transform knowledge from one writing task to the next.

Differentiation Possibilities

Content

Essential questions rarely have a single, correct answer, and they may draw from multiple sources and multiple disciplines.

Process

Writing tasks based on essential questions permit student writers to develop a process of inquiry that corresponds to disciplinary norms or adapts processes to create a new approach. For example, students might write a typical lab report in science, or they may choose to write a short story about a lab experience that conveys the ideas derived from their inquiry.

Product

Like processes, the products that result from robust inquiry can be expressed via multiple genres or multiple media.

Example: Essential Questions at Metro High

Millie Nial, literacy coach at Metro High, checked in with Mr. Hemming to see how his unit on the Holocaust was coming. She had another idea in mind, and she wondered if Mr. Hemming was up for it. In the social studies wing of the building, Hank Adams had developed a unit on World War II and he knew his students in Mr. Hemming's class were reading *Night* (Wiesel, 1960). The 10th-grade teachers had decided to use the essential question, "Is there really a difference between a cultural generalization and a stereotype?" (Wiggins, 2007) as one signpost for their instruction during the school year. The students had voted on several and this was one of the most popular among students and faculty.

Thinking that Mr. Hemming's English class and Mr. Adam's social studies class could partner up to explore the essential question if students read *Night* (Wiesel, 1960) and *Maus I* (Spiegelman, 1986), a well-known graphic novel about the Holocaust, Ms. Nial wondered whether she could get the two teachers together. Because students would have the social studies textbook, *Night*, and *Maus I* they would have many resources in addition to the presentations and web explorations on which they could draw for their written work in both Mr. Hemming's and Mr. Adams's classes. Ms. Nial was right—both Hemming and Adams were quick to jump on this opportunity to coordinate their efforts to help students learn how cultural understanding, cultural generalizations, and stereotypes might be part of their worlds. More important, both teachers believed that students could change their views of the world and contribute their voices to help others more fully understand cultures not like their own, as well. They devised a writing task they hoped would be transformative.

The students at Mr. Hemming and Mr. Adams's school were a diverse group. They came from homes where money was not a major concern, and from homes where sometimes it was uncertain how the next trip to the grocery store would turn out. They were sometimes new immigrants spending their first year in an American school, and sometimes they could trace their family histories to the 13 American colonies of the 18th century. They were African American, Native American, white, and Hispanic. What they did share was a sense that school was a learning community. For the most part, they wanted to share what they composed, and they wanted to read what their peers had written. Their teachers chose to build on the strength of the learning community at school to help students connect to events in the present and conditions in the past through writing tasks.

TECH·nique 21

Learning Because I'm Writing
Logs and Journals

Cross-reference hashtags: #journals, #languagearts,
#science, #shortcues

What Is It?

More than 30 years ago, Applebee suggested that teachers take a stance that "encourages students to explore and discover and seldom dominates the class" (1981, p. 105). Like so many readers of this book, Applebee knew that we learn best by working with ideas rather than by having them thrown at us with the hope they will stick. Earlier, we explored how transformation is a critical aspect of writing and other composing tasks. Through composing our thoughts, the potential exists for transforming the known and the routine to insight, understanding, and improved thinking about any given concept. Short and informal writing can serve as a catalyst for thinking when teachers plan it well (yep—it's not just picking up a pencil and starting to write).

Why Is It Important?

Writing short pieces, such as logs or journals, offer multiple opportunities for engagement with a variety of texts, for interaction with other students and the world beyond the school walls, and for exploration of wide-ranging topics. Farnan and Fearn (2008) tell us that short writing is particularly effective at promoting thinking and writing in the disciplines. Writing short offers a manageable format for teachers who often see 150 or more students in a day making scoring longer works a daunting task. Moreover, short writing tasks may be tightly focused chances for students to shape and refine their understanding as they write. In Technique 2, we explored the notion that the millennial generation is interested in interaction with content and creating it. Short writing tasks fit well with technologies available in schools today.

While the transformative effect of writing longer works cannot be ignored, the role of short works such as logs and journals deserve our sustained attention. Logs ask students to engage in a range of writing tasks that are transactional in nature; that is, students must interact with other texts and sources of information. Learning logs ask students to reflect on what they have learned or are attempting to learn. A log may ask students to report, summarize, or apply knowledge, as well. They might also write extended definitions of curricular concepts and illustrate those with drawings or specific examples. In addition, logs may provide students with opportunities to engage with academic vocabulary and the formats, modes, and other conventions of specific disciplines. Price (1989) asks mathematics students to write regularly, but notes that written work that looks like an English composition is not likely to be successful in a math course. In Figure 21.1, an eighth-grade student writes a log entry exploring insights into a memoir she is reading. Although similar to a journal because it includes personal connections, this log entry is transactional in nature. The student writer engages in a reflective manner with the text she is reading. In the process, she transforms her thinking about herself, her family, and the life of the person in the memoir *A Child Called "It"* (Pelzer, 1995).

The distinctions between journals and logs are not always clearly delineated. Daniels, Zemelman, and Steineke (2007) describe double-entry journals that require students to engage with other texts. There are a variety of double-entry journal formats, but a common form has students divide a paper in half. On the left side, students record quotations, summaries, paraphrases, and so on as they engage with a text that could include a lecture or video. On the other side, students write their observations, points of agreement or disagreement, connections to other texts or personal experiences, and so on. Wolsey and Fisher with Burns (2009) describe a metacognitive double-entry journal that asks students to identify the thinking they are doing as they read novels. In the double-entry metacognitive journal, students code their responses according to the cognitive activity the text prompted. A list of codes might include those from instructional routines such as reciprocal teaching (Palincsar & Brown, 1984). Students might code predictions as a "1," clarifications

```
A Child Called "It"

6.30-7 pgs 1-14

Wow is this an intense book? I can't believe what this little boy
has had to go through. His mom torments him to the point of no end.
Sometimes she doesn't feed him and once she even stabbed him. I would
have no idea as to what he has been through because I have been lucky
enough to have been blessed w/a great family. His school nurse checks
him daily for bruises, cuts, and wounds which his mother gave him. I
have had to read pages twice 'cause I didn't believe it. He tries to
hide it, but every now & then he can't. It is traumatizing what this
boy had to go through.
```

FIGURE 21.1. Journal writing.

as a "2," and so on. Additional codes can be added for visualizations, connections to other literature, and so forth. In general, we use the terms as indicated in Table 21.1.

What Do I Do?

◆ Determine directions for writing that ask students to transform what they know and can learn.

◆ Decide what digital tools are most effective for this type of journal or log writing. Should the students share it with the world? With their classmates? With the teacher solely? See Figure 21.2 for some ideas regarding each of these audiences and associated digital tools.

TABLE 21.1. Advantages, challenges, and management: Journals and Logs

Journals	Logs
Advantages	
Mostly expressive or creative in nature.	Mainly transactive in nature.
Journals appeal to the imagination, emotions affect and permit exploration of background knowledge.	Logs ask students to engage with other texts and sources of information. They may assist students to understand concepts that are cognitively difficult or challenging.
Category: Personal	Category: Informational
Challenges	
Students often need guidelines for writing, but personal writing resists format and rules. Models of well-written journals can help students learn the attributes of such journal entries.	Learning to differentiate, attribute, and recognize other sources of information can be difficult cognitive work.

Management

Journal entries and logs can be written on individual sheets of paper or typed into an online tool. Other times, cumulative entries are more desirable. Students can return to previous entries for review and teachers might note growth over time. If students keep a notebook or formal journal, teachers might collect and score these by assigning a due date on different days for each class: Period 1 journals are due on Monday, period 2 are due on Tuesday, and so on. In this way, the task is less daunting and stacks of notebooks are physically manageable. Journals and logs kept online via a threaded discussion or journal tool can be read by the teacher wherever an Internet connection is available, and such writing introduces the possibility of students sharing their writing with one another.

Grading

Journals and logs resist grading because the writing task is often formative. Minimum expectations may be established that identify specific features for the journal or log entry. Those entries that meet the expectation might be counted or scored as complete.

◆ Use models of journal entries written by other students of approximately the same grade level and on related topics.

◆ Set a purpose for writing the journal or log entry that coincides with the curricular objective, promotes transformative thinking, and draws on students' experiences as appropriate.

Differentiation Possibilities

Content

Depending on the learning objective for the log or journal, students might be given choices to choose the sources of their own experience, or the perspective from which the journal entry will be written.

Process

Students might be permitted to submit a journal entry from home or from their cell phones or to write the journal entry in class on a computer or on paper. They may also choose the nature of the written journal according to possibilities in Figure 21.2 by determining whether to post for the whole world, classmates, just the teacher, or perhaps just for themselves.

Example: Writing in the Science Classroom at Metro High

Millie Nial needed ideas as she sought to differentiate support for other teachers at her school (for example, Blamey, Meyer, & Walpole, 2009). She arranged to stop

---

For the world
◆ Blogs.
◆ Wikis also include some discussion features that may be set to share with the public or just with those authorized to use the wiki.

For classmates
◆ Blogs associated with course management systems (CMS).
◆ Threaded discussion groups (TDG).

Only for the teacher
◆ Journal functions of course management systems.
◆ Journal tools such as *http://penzu.com*.

Private
◆ Save work to a flash drive or on a private network.
◆ Use an online tool such as *http://current.im/login*.

FIGURE 21.2. Digital tools for journal writing. Course management systems often include blogs, threaded discussion groups, and journal tools.

by a ninth-grade science class to observe the nuances of how short writing might work in a content-area classroom. Ms. Ondas's ninth-grade students were making waves—just as she wanted them to do. After a demonstration with an aquarium full of water, her students logged onto the computers and navigated to the wave generator on the National Geographic website *http://www.nationalgeographic.com/volvo-oceanrace/interactives/waves/index.html*, where they could manipulate the length, height, and period of waves on the ocean. In preparation for this activity, she posted the link on the class webpage for easy navigation. After a few minutes, she asked students to go to the next link on the class webpage from the PBS online website (*http://www.pbs.org/wnet/savageseas/neptune-article.html*). Here, they read articles about different types of waves on the ocean, viewed a video clip, and tried out a tsunami wave generator.

With about 10 minutes left in the class period, students logged onto the eCollege course management system. They found the module for the unit on waves, then the discussion board for the wave topic. Ms. Ondas had already posted directions for a short writing task that day. Following the construction writing format (Farnan & Fearn, 2008), students were to write everything they understood about waves on the ocean. They needed to type for 5 minutes before logging off the computers and replacing them on the laptop cart. She uses a virtual timer using the data projector for all students to see (*http://www.timeme.com/timer.htm*). During her preparation period, she logged on and read through the students' responses noting for herself any misconceptions or big ideas students had about waves. She posted a brief note to the entire class, but she did not respond to any specific students.

The next day, students once again navigated to the class webpage where a new link waited for them. This one was a link to the science textbook's support site, and it addressed waves. But this time, light and not the ocean was the subject. Students read about the wavelike behavior of light. Students were then directed to the lab stations where they conducted experiments to note interference, refraction, and diffraction. When they finished, students read Chapter 13 of their textbooks that discussed the properties of light that behave like waves. And once more, as the class period came near to the end, students logged onto the computer where Ms. Ondas had posted a new task for them on the discussion boards. This short writing task asked students to read a peer's post from yesterday, and then type a response summarizing what the peer had written, and then add as much new information about waves and how they are propagated from their reading and experiments with light.

By building on the posts of others, students also had to connect their observations from their work on the first day with the new observations on the second day. By interacting with peers, they also develop a sense of inquiry and community, as well. As the unit progresses, students will eventually write a much longer description with illustrations of an experiment of their own design to test questions they have about the behavior of waves depending on the medium. But the longer paper is a topic for another technique in this book.

Writing Is (Hard) Cognitive Work
Bloom's Taxonomy Matters

Cross-reference hashtags: #blooms, #prompts, #science

What Is It?

In addition to the considerations of discourse type, data and sources, audience, and topic, we encourage teachers to plan writing tasks by approaching them as an integral part of the learning activities. On one hand, teachers must think of writing as a seamless part of learning in the classroom; on the other hand, writing tasks must be carefully planned to match the learning objectives while providing students with opportunities to learn through writing and eventually demonstrate command of course concepts through their writing.

Why Is It Important?

In Part Two, we cited William Zinsser (1980), a professional writer who claimed that writing was hard work. For students who are trying to grasp or explain a difficult concept by writing about it, this principle applies. Writing can be, and often is, hard work. This is a worthwhile consideration because if the thinking crystallized as writing is difficult and challenging, then there are implications for instruction, as well.

Teachers are familiar with Bloom's taxonomy of cognitive tasks, though it is less widely known that in 2001 the taxonomy was revised with a new framework and descriptors. The taxonomy provides teachers a useful framework for thinking about how to structure learning tasks and experiences. In Table 22.1, we summarize the elements of the old taxonomy and the new revision (Krathwohl, 2002). One thing readers may notice about the revision is that the cognitive process categories are now

TABLE 22.1. Comparison of Bloom's Original taxonomy of cognitive tasks with the revised taxonomy

Revised taxonomy	Original taxonomy
1.0 Remember	**1.0 Knowledge**
1.1 Recognizing	1.1 Knowledge of specifics
1.2 Recalling	1.2 Knowledge of ways and means of dealing with specifics
	1.3 Knowledge of universals and abstractions in a field
2.0 Understand	**2.0 Comprehension**
2.1 Interpreting	2.1 Translation
2.2 Exemplifying	2.2 Interpretation
2.3 Classifying	2.3 Extrapolation
2.4 Summarizing	
2.5 Inferring	
2.6 Comparing	
2.7 Explaining	
3.0 Apply	**3.0 Application**
3.1 Executing	
3.2 Implementing	
4.0 Analyze	**4.0 Analysis**
4.1 Differentiating	4.1 Analysis of elements
4.2 Organizing	4.2 Analysis of relationships
4.3 Attributing	4.3 Analysis of organizational principles
5.0 Evaluate	**5.0 Synthesis**
5.1 Checking	5.1 Production of a unique communication
5.2 Critiquing	5.2 Production of a plan or proposed set of operations
6.0 Create	**6.0 Evaluation**
6.1 Generating	6.1 Evaluation in terms of internal evidence
6.2 Planning	6.2 Judgments in terms of external criteria
6.3 Producing	

Note. Based on Anderson and Krathwohl (2001).

verbs instead of nouns (for example, *understanding* instead of *comprehension*). The verbs help teachers to talk about their work and plan student tasks by focusing on the cognitive action that learning entails.

The authors of the new taxonomy also added a second dimension that asks teachers to consider factual knowledge, conceptual knowledge, procedural knowledge, and metacognitive knowledge. Conceptual knowledge deals with interrelationships within larger conceptual frameworks. Procedural knowledge has to do with how something is done and the conditions under which different procedures might be best employed. Metacognitive knowledge is awareness of cognitive processes that might result in control and refinement of those processes. Together, the two dimensions create a matrix for designing learning experiences. We suggest creating a chart with the cognitive processes listed in the right-hand column and a checklist for several recent writing tasks you have assigned. How many of your tasks call for higher-order thinking? An example you can use appears in Form 22.1 at the end of this chapter.

This is all very interesting, you might be thinking. But what does this have to do with planning writing assignments for students? It stands to reason that if students struggle with simple writing tasks that more complex tasks will elude them. Our experience as teachers and in working with thousands of teachers over the years suggests a counterintuitive stance, however. If students are to succeed with complex thinking tasks that involve writing, more opportunities for writing such tasks are needed. This is where the taxonomy can be helpful. We know that the most common question type students are asked in oral discussion are at the lowest levels of the taxonomy (Daines, 1986) unless teachers take positive steps to plan higher-level questions in advance. The same idea applies here: If we take time to plan the cognitive activities we intend to promote that help students do the cognitive work negotiating complex ideas, student writing and learning about content will improve.

What Do I Do?

◆ An important step in planning a writing task is to consider the instructional objectives and the standards the task will help students address. Is the composing task one that demands a great deal of thinking on the part of the students? If not, why not?

◆ Plan the task using key types of cognitive tasks found on Bloom's taxonomy (Anderson & Krathwohl, 2001). Don't discount the utility of tasks such as summarization, which is in the second category (that is, understanding) of the new taxonomy but still requires significant thinking to accomplish. At the same time, plan tasks that specify creation, evaluation, and analysis, as well.

◆ Because writing can be and often is hard work, students will need your support and the assistance of their peers in the classroom. Writing can be and should be a learning activity, and one for which time should be set aside in the classroom as part of effective instruction.

◆ Model your own writing processes and help students think about their own composing processes and thinking approaches as they write.

Differentiation Possibilities

Content

Where the object of writing is not content dependent, students might compose using topics of their choice. For example, if students are learning the nuances of scientific inquiry, it may not matter if they choose to write about the human genome or about the process of erosion as manifested in the Grand Canyon.

Process

Bloom's taxonomy has built into it options for differentiation. Students might write a summary of a particular text or they may apply the knowledge gained from that text in a novel situation. An important consideration for teachers is to ensure students know the nature of the task they are choosing to complete and the cognitive work involved in accomplishing it. Thus, this approach has implications for differentiating by product, as well.

Example: Writing about Energy at Metro High

The science objective asked students to understand that waves carry energy. Neal Boer realized that if writing is a means by which students might learn about this principle, obviously the topic for writing should not be about cellular mitosis. However, it's really more complex than just matching up topics between the learning objectives and the writing task, he reasoned. He needed to determine the type of cognitive work students would do to help them learn. If students need only be familiar with the principle of waves, a summarization task based on a specific source might be appropriate. He knew that summarization tasks can help students think about content (for example, Marzano, Pickering, & Pollock, 2001).

Mr. Boer handed out an article from *High School Science Monthly* (a fictional journal) about the motion of waves. He gave this direction: "Please read and summarize this article in five to ten sentences." Brown, Campione, and Day (1981) suggest the following rules for summarizing:

1 Delete trivial or redundant information.

2 Label categories for listed information—cats and dogs can be recategorized as "pets."

3 Identify and relabel subordinate actions to a superordinate—"Napoleon crossed the Alps through the Great Saint Bernard Pass to reinforce French troops at Genoa. He intended to surprise his Austrian adversaries. Eventually, his army crushed the Austrians at Montebello" can be relabeled as "Napoleon surprised the Austrians and defeated them at Montebello."

4 Find and select the author's topic sentence in each paragraph where one exists. Create or invent a topic sentence if the author has not written one into the text.

If students know how to summarize, a learned skill, completing this task will help them become familiar with the content. Often, however, teachers want their students to understand a concept at a deeper level. For this, a summarization task may not be enough. To effectively plan a writing task for students, planning the cognitive work students do in completing the task is important. In Technique 31 on prompts (#prompts), further examples of assignments are provided that illustrate other types of thinking using Bloom's taxonomy.

Writing Task Analysis Form

	Teacher's name: _____ Week of: _____		
	Writing Task: _____ _____ (example: exit slip, Tuesday)	**Writing Task:** _____ _____ (example: essay, Thursday)	**Writing Task:** _____ _____ (example: log entry, Friday)
1.0 Remember			
1.1 Recognizing			
1.2 Recalling			
2.0 Understand			
2.1 Interpreting			
2.2 Exemplifying			
2.3 Classifying			
2.4 Summarizing			
2.5 Inferring			
2.6 Comparing			
2.7 Explaining			
3.0 Apply			
3.1 Executing			
3.2 Implementing			
4.0 Analyze			
4.1 Differentiating			
4.2 Organizing			
4.3 Attributing			
5.0 Evaluate			
5.1 Checking			
5.2 Critiquing			
6.0 Create			
6.1 Generating			
6.2 Planning			
6.3 Producing			

Internet Inquiry

Cross-reference hashtags: #directinstruction, #essentialquestions, #inquiry, #RAFT, #science, #socialbookmarking

What Is It?

Internet inquiry permits students to explore topics of special meaning for them (Leu, Leu, & Coiro, 2004). The possibility of exploring a topic in depth engages students in content learning and knowledge transformation that results in lasting understanding. In Internet inquiry, students learn to develop a question and use the Internet to search for the answers in such a way that they make over that knowledge and retain it. The potential for students is that they can, with appropriate guidance, help themselves to become self-directed learners.

There are two major models of Internet inquiry. In the original five phases (Leu et al., 2004), Internet inquiry consists of:

1 Developing a question.

2 Searching for the information on the Internet and other sources.

3 Evaluating the quality of the information relevant to the question identified in Step 1.

4 Composing a response or answer to the question.

5 Sharing the final composition with others.

Another iteration of Internet inquiry proposed by Eagleton and Dobler (2007) develops the notion of transformation that we explored earlier. This model, called QUEST, also consists of five phases but with an emphasis on synthesis and transformation (see Figure 23.1).

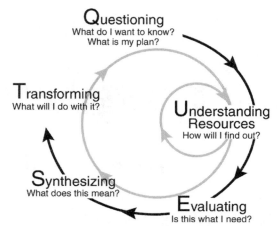

FIGURE 23.1. QUEST inquiry model. From Eagleton and Dobler (2007). Copyright 2007 by The Guilford Press. Reprinted by permission.

1 Asking a question.

2 Understanding and choosing resources.

3 Evaluating resources and information.

4 Synthesizing the relevant ideas and concepts from the resources.

5 Transforming ideas in a new and insightful way.

Why Is It Important?

For students writing about the concepts they encounter in content-area classrooms, inquiry is the heartbeat of learning. Although it is important for students to either know some facts as big ideas or important details, the act of inquiry transforms knowledge through encounters with essential questions (#essentialquestions), multiple sources of information sometimes representing many perspectives, and the students' own experiences that are relevant to the questions they develop and their teachers pose. The process of asking questions, determining appropriate resources, evaluating those resources, and synthesizing ideas from them leads to the opportunity to transform that knowledge. As important, young writers continue to learn as they compose, and they can share their insights as a result of the inquiry process.

What Do I Do?

   ◆ Provide opportunities for inquiry using the Internet and other digital resources that align with curriculum, Common Core Standards (2010) and state content standards, and students' interests.

◆ Ensure that students have the resources available (such as access to the Internet on a regular basis in or near the classroom).

◆ Include time in the lesson or unit plan for students to develop their inquiry. Determine how much time students need at school and whether students have the time and resources to complete portions of the task at home.

◆ Develop potential scaffolds for inquiry to assist students with the learning tasks. Inquiry is a process that can be learned, and teachers can and should be available to assist students virtually and in face-to-face environments with planned and unplanned direct instruction (#directinstruction) in content and inquiry processes. Each phase of inquiry is a potential stumbling block for students unless the teacher and capable peers are able to help and have the resources to do so.

◆ Determine the compositions, which can often be presented as choices, for student transformation and sharing. As with other aspects of inquiry, students will need some guidance to select an appropriate type of media and an appropriate genre for their work. Not every inquiry will lend itself to the essay genre, for example. Not every inquiry will lend itself to a podcast. Some curricular standards will demand that students write with pen and paper or at the keyboard, whereas others will permit and encourage creation of an online video. Some inquiries may be expressed as narrative or as exposition. Student writers need guidance in choosing the best fit for the message their inquiry generates and the audience for whom the message is intended.

Differentiation Possibilities

Content

The topics of inquiry that may result in written products may be varied keeping in mind essential questions and content-area standards. Sources for the inquiry may be left to the student to choose, but teachers might select a few sources as jumping-off points for students who struggle to identify a topic or approach to the inquiry.

Product

Teachers might design composition tasks that result in different types of written products, again aligning them with content standards and Common Core Standards for Language Arts (2010; Appendix A).

Example: Internet Inquiry and Writing at Metro High

Neal Boer had lectured with nifty PowerPoint shows on the scientific thinking that led to modern understanding of the atom for years. He was animated when he spoke, and his presentations included colorful graphics. The students seemed to respond well to his lectures. However, when the students took the multiple-choice test at the end of the unit, they almost invariably did not do very well. This year, he resolved to engage his students in a new way that would result in solid learning. All summer long, he thought about how a new approach might look. Ms. Nial had been gently nudging all faculty to incorporate writing as a way to learn, not just a means of assessing what students already understood. In addition, she had been gently promoting the idea of the Internet inquiry as a way to get students wondering about things, not just replicating someone else's ideas in their written work. Mr. Boer listened and decided a composing task was worth a try.

On the day Mr. Boer introduced his unit, he was worried. He knew that his students were effective note takers when he presented content as a PowerPoint lecture. Today, they would be taking notes for a different purpose. Instead of giving students information, he challenged them to find their own information and transform it in order to make it their own. This had always been his goal, but having students listen to a lecture and read from the textbook was not enough. The bell rang, and the class session began. Mr. Boer told his students to take out their netbooks and prepare to make notes, something they had done many times before. Instead, this time, students were not going to just transcribe his presentation into note form. He did briefly outline the history of the atom as scientists conceptualized it. Next, he described the limitations of some of the historical models of the atom and how that led scientists to consider new models of the atom that describe its behaviors and the implications for the models depending on the purpose the model might serve in research. Students began to wonder—they had always believed that there was just one model of the atom; now Mr. Boer was telling them that there were several models and each of those models was useful. Rachel, a ninth-grade student in Mr. Boer's integrated science class thought she knew what was coming: after the lecture, the students would be sent to the textbook to find an answer that was buried in chapter 7 of the book somewhere. She was quite surprised because nothing like that happened.

Instead, Mr. Boer left the students with a cliffhanger. Here were all these models for an atom that had developed over time and many were used by scientists today. Mr. Boer did not tell Rachel which one was the right one that scientists use. Instead, he challenged them. "Get a netbook from the charging station," he told them. "Work with two of your classmates. You will use a search engine of your choice and the school's database of online journals and find at least one model of the atom that is no longer considered useful. Find at least two more models or representations, and preferably three, scientists use in the 21st century to explain certain aspects of the atom and how it behaves under certain conditions." Next, he further challenged the students to find a graphic representation and a written explanation of it. He knew that scientists often wrote about the results of their research and they also used graphic representations. Together, these could be quite powerful, but he wasn't quite done challenging his students. He wanted students to find an animated or video representation of at least one of the models, as well. His goal: encourage students to explore the world of the atom via the Internet without telling them exactly where to look. He knew that after they poked around, they would have many questions. Sure enough, they did.

"Why is the quantum model of the atom different from the Bohr model?" Armando asked. "What makes the electron cloud model useful from the Rutherford model?" Rachel chimed in. "The Thomson representation has a cool name called the plum pudding model," Raoul added. "Perfect," Mr. Boer thought, "this is working out better than I planned. The students were developing questions because of the way I challenged them to use the Internet." Instead of telling them to find something specific, he asked them to explore. Their explorations led to inquiry, and from inquiry he hoped they would develop a deep understanding of how modern science conceives of the atom. Just then, Ceci noticed that the symbols on some of the models were just like the symbols on the battery she just installed in her digital camera. Yep, the students were engaged and they had begun to make connections that led to wonder.

Now that students had questions to answer, they needed some focus. Because some students took to the idea of developing questions about content more readily than others, Mr. Boer asked Wanda to log onto the class wiki and list all the questions from the discussion. Those who were a bit stuck for a question could log on and build a question based on those their classmates had asked. In doing so, they would also have to explore who Bohr and Thomson were and what the term "quantum" means. "Phase I was complete, or was it?" Mr. Boer wondered. The students had questions, but perhaps they would think of new questions as they explored their initial questions.

Next, students needed to refine their searches for information and decide how valid the sources were for the inquiry that was beginning to take shape. Some initial resources turned out to be a bit more unreliable than others. Mr. Boer posted a link on the class wiki to an evaluation tool they could use to help them evaluate the utility and reliability of a website (Form 23.1 at the end of this chapter). Students were encouraged to use websites such as Wikipedia to help guide their search; however, they needed to consult more authoritative sites as well as textbooks and books from the Metro High School library to guide their search.

Mr. Boer's students worked together in groups of three to choose websites that they might use to help them respond to the questions they had developed and to share resources. As they worked, they posted their links on a social bookmarking site (#socialbookmarking), adding notes about the site and tags so the sites would be easier to locate again. They rated each site and added a tag as "reliable," "maybe," and "background." Those sites that were not useful were not linked on the social bookmarking site. Those that would not be effective primary or otherwise reliable sources were marked as "background" and would not be included as a reference for the final product.

As students searched the Internet and other resources, they started to synthesize their ideas. Mr. Boer had not told students they must use a particular approach or genre, but as the students worked, he visited with them about their findings. Sometimes, as the students talked, he suggested that they use a compare-and-contrast approach to guide their thinking. Other times, a chronological or cause–effect approach seemed to make sense. The students did not always agree with him, and

Mr. Boer encouraged them to choose an approach that fit their ideas as those ideas developed. As important, he worked with students by asking questions about the sources.

"What did your first website suggest? What about the second source? Did they agree? Or were there different perspectives? Did the sites contain the same information or was it different in some important way? Why do you suppose that was so? What do you think?" As Mr. Boer moved from group to group to talk with the students, his repertoire of questions to prod synthesis of sources improved, as well. He was careful not to tell students what he thought; rather, he guided the students to question the sources they found online and to question their own thinking. Students used a word processor to keep notes and embedded websites in their notes.

Rachel was the first to ask, "What are we supposed to do now? I have all these ideas in my head, and I need to get them out somehow." Though Mr. Boer had some ideas in mind, Rachel was ahead of him on this. Both he and Rachel knew that though they were at the last phase of the QUEST model (Eagleton & Dobler, 2007), there was still learning to do. Both realized that though there would be a final product, such as an essay or blog entry, the synthesis would continue through the transformation phase of the project.

Because Mr. Boer wanted students to understand the atom as well as conceptualize how scientists built their ideas over time, he asked students to write about their inquiries. Borrowing from the RAFT format (Santa, 1988), he gave students some choices regarding role and audience (#RAFT) For this project, he asked students to choose media type, as well, between a blog post and a standard essay composed in a word processor. They were encouraged to add open-source images or created their own to supplement their final product that would then be shared via a link on the class website.

Additional Resources

Big Six: Information and Technology Skills for Student Achievement (*http://www.big6.com*).

Eagleton, M. B., & Dobler, E. (2007). *Reading the web: Strategies for internet inquiry*. New York: Guilford Press.

Form for Evaluating Websites

Respond yes, maybe, or no, and include narrative where appropriate.

Part I—Looking at and Using the Site

1 What search engine did you use? _____

2 What is the URL of the webpage you are evaluating? _____

3 What is the name of the website? _____

About how many words on the screen did you feel you did not know at all? _____

4 Are there any words you learned while browsing the site? _____ Which ones? _____

_____

5 What concepts seem to be easy to understand? _____

6 What concepts will require more research? _____

	Yes	Maybe	No
Are the images on the page helpful?			
Is each section of the page labeled with a heading?			
Can you tell who the author of the site is?			
If so, who is it? _____			
Is there a date on the page that tells you when it was last updated?			
If you go to another page on the site, can you easily get back to the main page?			
Summary: Is this a good site for you to find information about atomic models?			

(cont.)

Form for Evaluating Websites *(cont.)*

Part II—What's on the Webpage?

	Yes	Maybe	No
Does the title of the page tell you what it is about?			
Is there a paragraph on the page explaining what it is about?			
Is the information on the site useful for finding out about the models of the atom? If not, what can you do next?			
Does the site lead you to some other good information or links?			
Is there information on the site you think is incorrect?			
Does some information contradict information you found somewhere else?			
Do you feel the author is knowledgeable about the topic?			
Are there videos, images, or sound files that add to what can be read on the page?			

Summary:

◆ Who created the page or site?

◆ Are there limitations to the credibility of the site's authors?

◆ Is the author affiliated with a reputable organization?

◆ Are you sure the information is accurate? How do you know?

◆ What are the main ideas you found on this site?

Prompts

Cross-reference hashtags: #languagearts, #math, #prompts, #RAFT, #socialstudies

What Are They?

A writing prompt is simply a direction for writing. Emig (1971) decried what she called school-sponsored prompts; however, Hillocks (1986) countered that there is little evidence to support the idea that school-sponsored writing is a hindrance. A great deal of writing, in our experience, is at least partially sponsored or directed by another party. For example, while it may seem this book is entirely the ideas initiated by the authors, in reality it is the result of discussion with the series editors and the publisher, all of whom helped shape the work through their directions to the authors and the needs they believe will drive ultimate sales of the work. The same is true for student writers. Audiences necessarily impose restrictions on the written product. What might the author assume the audience knows? What format will be most accessible to that audience? For students, what curriculum needs does the writing fulfill? The list of questions is somewhat unlimited, but the prompt or direction for writing determines the amount of freedom within which the author might work as well as the constraints for a specific or perceived (or hypothetical) audience. In reality, the audience is rarely authentic.

To illustrate the practical nature of the prompt and how it can help or hinder the written work students attempt, consider the work of Beck and Jeffrey (2007). They found that terms in a prompt for writing assessment, such as "explain," might be understood in several ways by novice writers who had purposes of their own for writing their responses to the prompt. "Explain" could mean describe how something works or it might mean to take a position and argue for it. Because the prompt was vague in the minds of student writers, the work they produced did not always match the somewhat invisible expectations of those who scored their written products. For this reason, we believe it is useful for students to examine and analyze prompts in terms of expectations, audience, language used, and organization required.

Why Are They Important?

Because prompts are intended to help shape student writing to meet curricular goals, the best prompts tend to be aligned with literacy standards such as the Common Core Standards (2010; see the Appendix on pp. 209 for the writing standards for grades 6–12), and with objectives and goals for the lesson. The prompt sets the expectations and parameters of the assignment that align with the curricular goals. A prompt for writing or other composing tasks may be thought of as an achievement target (Stiggins, 2005), and clear targets make it possible for students to succeed at what they and their teachers intend for them to achieve.

What Do I Do?

Planning the prompt for writing is not as easy as it sounds. If a teacher says, "Write all you understand about linear equations," the students might write many pages or a single sentence. The prompt shapes the way students think about writing, about the topic, and the specificity of the writing in many ways. There are many ways to write a prompt. In Example 1, below, a traditional prompt with possibilities for differentiation is presented. In Example 2, we introduce the RAFT model based on Santa's (1988) writing prompt she called RAFT. RAFT stands for role, audience, format, and topic. We add "dm," which stands for digital media.

- ◆ **R—role:** Writers assume different roles such as news reporter, novelist, and so on.
- ◆ **A—audience:** Writers attend to the possible needs of the audience who might read the piece.
- ◆ **F—format:** Written work takes the form of letters, short stories, scholarly essays, memoirs, and so on.
  - ◆ **dm—digital media:** What types of digital media might the writer use?
- ◆ **T—topic:** Written work contains content; that is, it is about something.

We include dm for digital media because formats such as letters to the editor can be written on paper or sent in an e-mail. An essay might be typed and printed, e-mailed to the teacher, or posted on a blog. Each type of digital or traditional media changes the dynamics of the message to varying degrees. An essay on a blog might take advantage of the features of blogging that allow linking to other pages within the blog or linking to outside sources, for example. RAFTdm prompts can be differentiated by placing them on a matrix, as well (see Table 24.1). Students who have

TABLE 24.1. RAFT

Role	Audience	Format/dm	Topic
Business owner	Congressman	Letter (format) sent via e-mail (dm)	Impact of global warming legislation on business.
Environmental activist	The public	Letter to the editor posted to a major newspaper's opinion webpage (dm)	Reasons why global warming legislation might be good for business, too.
U.S. ambassador to a country that contributes excessively to air pollutants	Head of state in a country that contributes excessively to air pollutants	Report to the head of state with recommendations using a word processor (dm)	Persuade the head of state to adopt policies to curtail emissions.

just read several articles on global warming might explore the topic through RAFT prompts with several possibilities.

1 Decide what the purpose of the composing task will be and how it will align with standards, unit goals, and lesson objectives.

2 Determine the format for the prompt keeping in mind the idea that student writers should not have to guess what the intent of the assignment is or how it will be scored.

3 Determine the elements of the prompt. Each element can be fixed to meet curricular goals or flexible to provide choices that might fit the demands of the writing task. Prompts for writing can be analyzed in terms of what they do or do not contain. Hillocks (2002) examined prompts for assessment of student writing and suggested that prompts might consist of directions regarding the type or structure of the discourse, the topic or subject matter for the composition, the data sources students might consult, and the audience for which the piece is intended. Each element might be included or not included, and if included, it might be specific or general.

4 Create the prompt.

5 Ask a student to read it and summarize it as a check to ensure that the teachers' intent is clear to the student.

6 Post the prompt in a place where students can easily access it. It might be a handout or on the whiteboard, but posting the prompt on the class webpage or blog could make the prompt accessible from the classroom library, on a smartphone, or at home as well as in the classroom.

Differentiation Possibilities

Process

Prompts might include options for various discourse types, audience, data sources on which students might draw, and so on. Students who need assistance might be given a prompt with clearly specified audience, discourse type, and source of data. Students who are ready to explore the content in depth might be given a prompt with additional options regarding the most appropriate discourse type, audience to be addressed, or -topics.

Example 1: Prompts, Technology, and Prewriting Work Together at Metro High

The memoir is a difficult genre for 10th-grade students; the genre requires an accumulation of experiences and time for reflection about those experiences. From reflection, the writer organizes themes, selecting some experiences for intense scrutiny and downplaying others. Millie Nial, the literacy coach at Metro High School, knew 10th-grade students have relatively few experiences from which to draw and state standards often require sophisticated vocabulary and sentence structures that they are working to master. Ms. Nial discussed the memoir with Mr. Hemming, a 10th-grade English teacher. During a professional development conference, Ms. Nial and Mr. Hemming discussed an upcoming memoir students would read and planned a response to literature as a writing task.

In Elie Wiesel's powerful memoir of the Holocaust, *Night* (1960), high school students are confronted with one of the darkest periods of earth's history, a time long before their own time on the planet began. Wiesel's powerful memoir asks readers to understand events that are incomprehensible and to identify with a narrator whose experiences are unlike any they have known. Mr. Hemming knows his students will face a loss of innocence as they read this piece of literature. They may mistake the real events of the novel with the desensitized world of some video games and other media. If that happens, he knows, the power of the memoir will be lost on his 10th-grade readers.

To assist students to make the events of the Holocaust more immediate and real, Ms. Nial and Mr. Hemming planned a number of activities that build historical knowledge of the time period, and more important, an emotional response. First, Mr. Hemming identified the state standards and achievement targets that would be the focus for this unit. Then, he and Ms. Nial wrote two prompts for a composition students would write near the end of their reading of *Night* (Wiesel, 1960). Each was based on an essential question (Wiggins & McTighe, 2005) the 10th-grade English teachers identified as they planned their curriculum. To guide instruction, the essential question they ask students to consider is "How does the memoir help us understand the Holocaust as it affects us in the 21st century?" Ms. Nial typed the prompts as she and Mr. Hemming discussed the essential question.

Prompt #1

Wiesel's memoir is a powerful description of a dark time in human history. Though the Holocaust occurred more than 60 years ago, it affects us in the 21st century. Having read *Night* (1960), you have unique insights that fit your experiences and those Wiesel reported in the book. Using Wiesel's book, your own experiences, and the sources you identified with your classmates on VoiceThread, write a blog entry that describes why you feel *Night* helps us understand genocide in today's world. Cite sources of information and include appropriate links to other websites.

This prompt included the main elements of discourse type (blog entry, expository response to literature), audience (blog readers on the Internet), data sources (*Night* [1960], Internet sources), and topic (the Holocaust and *Night*). Length is implied in the discourse type; blog entries are fairly concise with several paragraphs requiring readers to scroll the screen a minimal amount. Next, Mr. Hemming and Ms. Nial discussed the cognitive tasks the writing might require. The task seemed to ask students to compare Wiesel's experience in *Night* with genocides students read about on the Internet, and students would have to attribute causes and effects. But, Mr. Hemming wanted more. Deep thinking would require students to transform what they know rather than just report it. Using verbs from Bloom's taxonomy (Krathwohl, 2002), he wanted students to try out and become increasingly sophisticated with their use of vocabulary. Here is the second prompt Ms. Nial typed:

Prompt #2

Wiesel's memoir is a powerful description of a dark time in human history. Though the Holocaust occurred more than 60 years ago, it affects us in the 21st century. Having read *Night* (1960), you have unique insights that fit your experiences and those Wiesel reported in the book. Using Wiesel's book, your own experiences, and the sources you identified with your classmates on VoiceThread, write a blog entry that **evaluates and plans for the responsibilities of global citizens in preventing** genocide in today's world. Cite sources of information and include appropriate links to other websites.

Challenge: critique the effects of poverty or war as factors leading to genocide

Word bank: economy, evident, fascism, Holocaust, Nazi, policy.

In this prompt, students were asked to evaluate and plan, and they were given a challenge (Benjamin, 1999). The challenge promotes higher-order thinking and gives students a choice as to whether they want to take on the challenge. To encourage uptake of tier two and tier three words, a word bank is included from which students select words they might not otherwise use.

Next, the two teachers planned prewriting activities. Images can evoke complex emotions, but the written word might assist students to connect those emotions with the events of the memoir. Understanding begins with questions, and Mr. Hemming set up an online tool called VoiceThread (*http://www.VoiceThread.com*) to combine images he located on the Internet and the questions his students generate in an online discussion group. This short writing activity scaffolds what students understand about the novel and their subsequent response to this piece of literature. As important, students may actually engage in an online discussion using their voices, typed comments, images found on the Internet, and other sources.

A VoiceThread permits the user to upload an image or set of images. Students may then respond either by recording their voices or typing text. As each student contributes to the discussion, making observations and asking questions, others respond adding to what others have said as well as commenting on or asking questions about the image (see Figure 15.1 for an example slide). In responding to literature, students must empathize with the characters, express questions about their understanding of the narrator's situation, and respond eloquently. Eloquence, Mr. Hemming has found, is partly sensory description and rich experience born of discussion and inquiry. The VoiceThread evokes responses by combining images with a shared community in which students engage with each other asking difficult questions and responding by adding their own background knowledge, additional sources on the topic, and the image itself.

Reading the memoir, identifying other sources, and responding to images in VoiceThread helped students think about the work of literature they read. However, more structure would help students write a concise blog entry. Ms. Nial stopped by Mr. Hemming's class to learn how he would help students use prewriting to organize and make sense of all they had read and experienced. After roll call, Mr. Hemming reminded students of the prompt they were given before they started reading the book. He provided copies to them via their student e-mail accounts and posted a copy on the class webpage. Then, he asked them to think about their plans for writing. Instead of passing out a graphic organizer for students to fill in, he asked them to choose the type of organizer they felt would best fit the writing they would do.

John suggested that a cluster map would work for his blog entry. He sketched out his cluster map with genocide in the center and elements of the prompt in the outer circles: a bubble for his own experiences, another for attributes of the book, and a bubble for Internet resources he read online with his classmates. Tamika thought a timeline might help her understand the memoir, but she would also need to create a cause–effect map with elements of the book across the top row and her experiences and other Internet sources detailed across the bottom row. At the end of the arrow point, she would add a box for her ideas about civic responsibility and social justice as they relate to genocide. In small groups, students worked on their prewriting and thinking, then shared the results with each other. As they did so, they added details to their own plans for writing their blog entries.

Ms. Nial knew Mr. Hemming's students were well on their way to writing effective blog entries, and more important, they had learned something about themselves as global citizens and a particularly dark period of human history. She snuck out the side door and headed down the hall, straight to Mrs. Jennifer Nation's science class.

Example 2: RAFTdm at Community Middle School

Mr. Arthur Matica, teacher at Community Middle School, knew his colleagues at the high school were using writing enhanced with technology more and more often with some remarkable results in learning and engagement. His seventh-grade advanced math students studied algebra but they often struggled to see how algebra was useful in any place other than in the mathematics classroom. Drawing on the RAFTdm model, Mr. Matica devised a prompt for his students where they might use writing to learn and explore the utility of algebra and demonstrate their knowledge of it in the process. He wanted to differentiate for students who were up for it by including a challenge under the digital media component. Students who chose to take on the challenge would have to use the symbol tools in a word processor as well as apply their knowledge of algebra beyond the walls of the math classroom.

Here is how Mr. Matica's RAFTdm prompt looked:

- **R—role:** Write as a seventh-grade student who is completing the first year of study in algebra.
- **A—audience:** Write to Muḥammad ibn Mūsā al-Khwārizmī, the author who introduced linear and quadratic equations to a large part of the world. You will also assume the role of al-Khwārizmī for some of your work.
- **F—format:** Write a series of four to five letters between yourself and al-Khwārizmī.

    - **dm—digital media:** Choose to write using a simulated Facebook page, or a blog post with comments from al-Khwārizmī and yourself. **Challenge:** Use algebraic notation in your explanation using the symbol tools in your word processor.

- **T—topic:** Explore and explain how algebra is used in everyday activities such as cooking and in specialized activities such as engineering.

Prewriting
Composing before Writing with Pen or Keyboard

Cross-reference hashtags: #journal, #PE, #prewriting, #socialbookmarking

What Is It?

Just as teachers should plan the stimulus or prompts for writing tasks, student writers need time and guidance in planning their writing. In their excellent little book *The Elements of Style*, Strunk and White (2000) remind writers that choosing a design for the writing is the first principle of composition. Writers may deviate and adjust their plan as they write, but these wizards of the written word tell us effective writers "foresee or determine the shape of what is to come and pursue that shape" (p. 15). Prewriting is the part of the writing task where planning occurs. Often, prewriting activities are prescribed by the teacher. Students writing about the buildup to the Gulf War might be given a graphic organizer with a clear cause–effect design. Students choose the facts and determine how to fit these into the cause–effect graphic organizer. Then, they begin writing their compositions based on this design.

Why Is It Important?

Prewriting can be thought of as a more complex cognitive activity. It can and often should be more than just one activity in complex writing tasks. As we found in our discussion of creating prompts for writing, prewriting encompasses a variety of considerations. These mirror many of the elements in the prompt.

What Do I Do?

The first principle of planning writing is establishing a purpose through prewriting. Some purposes include:

- Determining the best fit of tools for prewriting for content or topic, genre, mode, format, audience, and data sources available.
- Exploring what the writer already knows about a topic.
- Exposing areas that the writer needs to explore or research in further detail before and during drafting.
- Organizing and ordering concepts.
- Identifying ideas, concepts, and data that should not be included in the final composition.
- Narrowing ideas from the general to the specific.
- Reminding the writer of the plan (see also Strunk & White, 2000) while the written draft takes shape.
- Informal prewriting.

Planning a piece starts from the moment writers are aware that they will be composing text. This suggests that students might be better writers if we can direct their attention to sources of information, organizational approaches, and so forth early in any learning cycle. Their written notes and their mental notes are often inspiration for writing, as well as a ready reference to sources when facts and concepts must be accurately conveyed. Rather than wait for the completion of a unit before a writing task is announced, students might be alerted to the task before most other learning activities (for example, reading, viewing a video, listening to a lecture, conducting an experiment, working in small groups to discuss the topic) begin. Planning for writing thus becomes integral to the other learning tasks related to the lesson or unit. During these instructional activities, the teacher might indicate to students how that content might contribute to the written piece they will complete later. Composing happens in students' minds during all the learning activities, as a result.

Specific suggestions to students during these activities can help. For example, a teacher might say:

"Did you notice the National Archives website explained the events leading to the signing of the Declaration of Independence in chronological order, but the chapter we read in the textbook described the purposes the Declaration served? Notice that you will be able to choose from among these approaches and others when we write about independence later this week. You may want to include this in your notes."

In Technique 26, we explore the specific uses of graphic organizers as tools for writing; therefore, the discussion of these useful tools will be saved for later. Specific prewriting tasks can include the discussions students have as they grapple with complex topics and concepts. Journal entries (#journal) and exit slips might be good ways to begin thinking about longer and more complex writing tasks, for example. Of course, this means that students will need the teacher to return these short pieces in a timely manner and they will need a way to save their work for future reference. Technology makes this relatively easy to accomplish via e-mail or online journals. Students sometimes treat note-taking assignments as a perfunctory task required by their teachers. If students view their notes as a way of composing and organizing their understanding, these notes become valuable prewriting tools.

Discussion is a robust activity that can help students organize their thinking and become conversant with the content. Small groups are typically more effective than large groups because discussion requires active participation, both listening and speaking. Participation in larger groups is difficult to achieve because most students must listen while few speak. Time limits the amount of oral composing students might do as a result of the interaction in large groups. As we shall see, many electronic environments are useful in promoting interaction and discussion of ideas, as well.

Different prewriting tools serve different purposes. Discussion activities and other instructional activities such as note taking, participating in a lab, reading a text, and so on are powerful tools as students begin planning their writing. Other tools are more familiar; however, fine-tuning how we use them might help students think critically about their writing and the shape it will take. For example, freewriting and quickwriting are good ways to explore topics when the organizational pattern or important attributes are not immediately apparent. In freewriting, students write without concern for normal conventions, such as paragraphs, punctuation, and so on. Fiction writers sometimes use freewriting to develop portraits of the characters about whom they will write in their short stories or novels (Goldberg, 2000). From the freewriting piece, students may order ideas they have uncovered, strike out concepts that don't seem to fit, add details by writing in the margins, and plan further by using a graphic organizer. Quickwrites are similar but are typically structured by the teacher with a specific topic about which students write for a specified period of time. Such activities may promote writing fluency and reduce the fright some students experience when they approach a blank piece of paper.

Differentiation Possibilities

Process

Often, student writers are told what type of prewriting activity is the one they should use. However, students who have a command of many approaches to prewriting and organizing their thinking may be given the option to choose from a range of prewriting approaches. Students who are stuck for a place to begin can be given a recommended prewriting activity to get started.

Example: Writing for Physical Education at Metro High

Coach Kardio had been thinking about the students in his physical education (PE) classes. They did everything he asked, often with great skill; however, he realized that very often they were only doing what he asked. The football team did the same. They never complained about training, but they did it mainly because Coach asked them to. Training regimens, Coach Kardio knew, led to better performance on the football field and in any sport. In many ways, it was a reflective activity, and that's where Coach Kardio's lightbulb lit right up. Ms. Nial had been going on and on about writing and how writing led to reflective thinking. She claimed that reflective thinking led to better performance in almost any endeavor. He was skeptical, but he thought it was worth a try. The football team needed to understand why training was important rather than just do it because they were told to. Students in his PE classes were in the same boat—they did the training exercises, but they did not seem to know why or how it would improve their ability on the field or court.

This would be an experiment. Ms. Nial was so convincing with her arguments for writing and insistence that writing could help students learn more about any content, even PE, that Coach Kardio decided to give it a try. Drawing on his experience as a football coach for more than 20 years, he started thinking about what students might write that would help them learn PE principles. Football training had similarities to basketball training, he knew, but they were not identical. Training was often goal oriented; that is, it might focus on strength, endurance, flexibility and speed, anaerobic and aerobic training, and so on. Training should respond to the needs of the athlete, their long-term health goals, and the demands of the sport in which they are engaged. It turned out, on reflection, that the perfect topic for his PE students to consider might be the complexity of training regimens while developing the ability to apply the principles of training in high school and after graduation. Maybe there is something to this writing idea of Millie Nial's, the coach thought. Putting students' minds in service of their physical training could work.

Ms. Nial had passed out a content-literacy analysis inventory at a staff meeting a couple of weeks before with a link to another copy on her webpage. As he looked it over, Coach Kardio noticed that many of the articles about training were descriptive in nature according to his analysis from the inventory. Hmmm, he thought. What if students were to use a different mode and write an analysis of three training regimens for football, or a classificatory paper about appropriate training programs for three different sports? What if, he thought, they also wrote for an audience of skills coaches? If skills coaches were the audience, the young athletes turned writers would strive for accuracy and detail. Next step: What are the resources on which they might draw?

Fortunately, Metro High School had several netbooks and laptops. These would be very useful and fit right in to the modified circuit training activity he planned for next week. He checked out 15 netbooks, made sure the wifi network was available near the locker rooms, and designed the lesson. Students would complete the circuit-training activities with one of the stations being devoted to writing. At the writing station, students would have a chance to rest their muscles while continuing to exercise their brains. Coach Kardio created a *Delicious.com* social bookmarking page with 10 articles he had chosen, and he let students know they could locate additional sources if they wanted to. He referred them to the evaluating websites handout Ms. Nial had linked on her page to help them decide whether a site was useful or not for their purposes. Reading and thinking about reading was a way of getting started with an inquiry about training that he hoped would lead to greater engagement with training exercises and purposeful selection of training regimens that would benefit them throughout their lives. In short, the reading they would do at the netbook station would be the first of several prewriting exercises. While there, they would take a few notes and post them on a threaded discussion board with citations. By posting their notes, and citing the sources, there would be no need for students to keep track of paper and pencils while in the PE environment.

Once students had several sources, they needed to start organizing their thinking. He talked with Mr. Hemming and Dr. Samantha Johnson about what types of prewriting they did in class. While he was starting to see that writing could be very helpful in PE, he did not think it would be a good use of time for him to reteach prewriting approaches if the students already knew some that might work. After all, students in PE were supposed to be engaged in physical activity most of the time, too. Fortunately, Mr. Hemming and Dr. Johnson had a couple of ideas ready to go. They listened to Coach Kardio and suggested that he might have students do a quickwrite. In it, they would start to synthesize their thoughts about the training regimens they had explored by writing as many of their thoughts about training in just 6 minutes. At the computer station in the circuit-training routine the next day, they would stop, read the directions, reread their notes, then complete the quickwrite in a word processor. Though there were many options for sending the work, Coach Kardio asked students to copy and paste their work to a page in a wiki he set up. The wiki allowed all the students to access their classmates' thoughts, but the word processor helped them to think through what they knew before they read what others in the class had written. Finally, students would need to start organizing their papers, and that's where graphic organizers would prove useful.

Prewriting
with Graphic Organizers

Cross-reference hashtags: #graphicorganizer, #PE, #prewriting

What Is It?

Graphic organizers are familiar tools to most educators. The cause–effect graphic organizer in Figure 26.1 is one such tool. These tools present information visually and linguistically so that students can see connections between concepts, organize ideas, activate background knowledge, and add details. When students use graphic organizers, they can be simultaneously taught to think about the sources on which they have drawn their information. Transactional writing (Britton, 1992) is one form of academic writing, and it calls for students to work with ideas found in other texts beyond their own experiences. By calling attention to sources, students have a framework for thinking about what they know and how they know it. When students consciously attend to what they know they can learn to control the processes they bring to bear on the task at hand (compare Hacker, 2004). Engagement with a topic or task is often a function of the level of competence and control one feels in approaching the task. Teaching students how to work with ideas and sources during prewriting can help them assert control and gain confidence.

Several graphic organizers are displayed in Figure 26.2. Different organizers are useful for different types of cognitive tasks and written products. One potential danger with graphic organizers is that students will confine their thinking to the format enforced by the organizer. A number of software and web tools are available to assist teachers with planning and using graphic organizers.

There are at least two ways to combat the tendency of a graphic organizer to limit students' approaches to writing. First, to encourage complexity and promote sophisticated writing students might be challenged to develop a graphic organizer for their

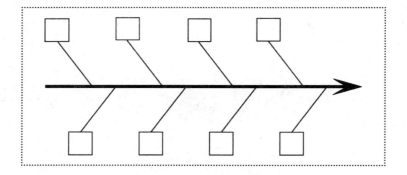

FIGURE 26.1. Cause–effect graphic organizer.

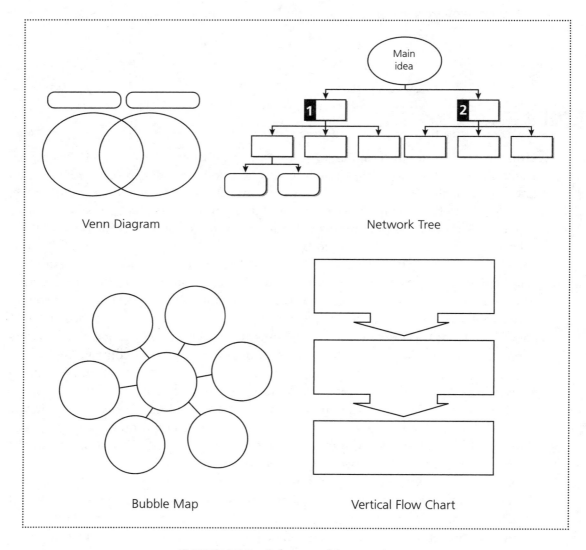

FIGURE 26.2. Other graphic organizers.

planned writing that combines both cause–effect organizers with bubble elements to add descriptive elements to the story. Since written products often include features of many different thinking and composing processes, allowing students to construct their own organizers is helpful. A piece may begin with a cause–effect structure but also include descriptive and compare–contrast elements, for instance. Second, once students are familiar with graphic organizers for different purposes, teachers can encourage students to construct their own graphic organizers and choose the types that best fit with their purposes for writing.

Earlier, we noted that familiarity with many resources on topics about which students might write is an important feature of many writing tasks in middle and high schools. For this reason, the inquiry (or I-chart; Hoffman, 1992) may be particularly useful. A recent study (Viscovich, Eschenauer, Sinatra, & Beasley, 2008) found that I-charts were effective for fifth-grade students confronted with writing a research report. The I-chart procedure, based on the well-known KWL graphic organizer (Ogle, 1986), centers around three phases: the planning phase, the interacting phase, and the integrating and evaluating phase. A strength of the I-chart is that it asks students to go back to the sources for their inspiration, sources they can use to support their ideas, and sources they can use as counterarguments, as well. In the planning phase, the topic is identified by students or teacher, questions posed, resources and materials gathered, and the I-chart constructed. During the interacting phase, students explore what they already know about the topic, identify new questions, and read while recording the information on the chart. In the final phase, students synthesize (Hoffman used the term "summary" but we prefer "synthesis") their responses to the questions posed from among the resources consulted, compare these syntheses with the information in the prior knowledge recorded on the chart, identify any remaining questions and research to be done, and report their findings. Form 26.1 at the end of this chapter is a reproducible I-chart for classroom use.

Why Is It Important?

Graphic organizers can help students see, quite literally, the relationships of the ideas and concepts they explore in their content-area classes, connect. Through constructing a graphic organizer, young writers not only demonstrate the connections they see but also build connections and depth. Herein lies the great opportunity of the graphic organizer. Students who are familiar with the formats and genre most commonly found in the content areas are able to start thinking about organization as part of a process of transforming knowledge. That which they can transform, they own; that process often starts with the ability to move beyond the bounds of a graphic organizer or formulaic writing approach. When writing in secondary school settings, the value of the graphic organizer lies not in "filling out" a graphic organizer or other formulaic approach. Rather, the value lies in the ability to combine, adapt, adjust, and create whole new organizers that help student writers plan their work.

How Will Technology Help?

Uploading a teacher-created template to the class webpage is one possible means of making graphic organizers available and editable for student use. A number of online tools are helpful, as well. Some provide graphic organizers that are predetermined, whereas others permit student writers to develop their own graphic organizers that reflect their thinking and that thinking of the sources they consult in planning their writing. In Figure 26.3, you will find several digital tools for creating graphic organizers.

What Do I Do?

As you choose graphic organizers and digital tools to create graphic organizers, consider the following:

- ◆ Use the content-literacy analysis inventory to determine which organizers are most appropriate and most used in your content area.

- ◆ Inspiration software: *http://www.inspiration.com*
- ◆ Products include Inspiration, which helps students and teachers create graphic organizers and framed outlines and InspireData helps students work visually with data. WebSpiration is a collaborative tool that users access via the web rather than download to their computers.
- ◆ SmartDraw: *http://www.smartdraw.com*
- ◆ Creates graphic organizers that can be exported in a variety of electronic formats.
- ◆ Offers a variety of tactile tools for organizing thinking and building knowledge.
- ◆ bCisive software: *http://bcisive.austhink.com*
- ◆ Developed with the business market in mind. The bCisive tool is more sophisticated in appearance and may appeal to older learners. Also note: *http://austhink.com*
- ◆ TeAchnology: *http://www.teach-nology.com/web_tools/graphic_org*
- ◆ A subscription website that provides a number of tools including graphic organizers.
- ◆ ReadWriteThink, a partnership of the International Reading Association, the National Council of Teachers of English, and the Verizon Foundation: *http://www. readwritethink.org/student_mat/index.asp*
- ◆ Provides a number of interactive tools including graphic organizers.
- ◆ Provides a number of model graphic organizers on its website.
- ◆ Thinking Maps: *http://www.thinkingmaps.com*
- ◆ Offers training and tools for using graphic organizers in the classroom.

FIGURE 26.3. Graphic organizer resources on the web.

◆ Then, consider the particular problem or inquiry your students will use to respond to the writing task you assign.

◆ What are the features of that task to which students should attend? How might they transform their thinking?

◆ What graphic organizers might they use?

◆ How might students reconstruct graphic organizers to fit the demands of the content and their own conceptualization of that content?

Differentiation Possibilities

Product

Students are often told what graphic organizer to use; however, when students understand why a particular graphic organizer is useful, they may choose from among a range of graphic organizers to transform their ideas through prewriting with graphic organizers. Graphic organizers students employ using digital tools increase the possibility that students can expand on those that might appear on paper. A bubble-type organizer on paper with one central topic and four supporting bubbles is limiting; however, a digital graphic organizer can expand in infinite directions. At times, students may combine graphic organizer types to demonstrate complex and creative thinking.

Example: Coach Kardio Uses a Graphic Organizer at Metro High

Coach Kardio knew from his own experiences in college and high school that after the students had some sources on which they could draw for ideas and written some initial pieces in the quickwrite fashion, they would still need to organize their thoughts. Based on his discussions with Dr. Johnson and Mr. Hemming, he knew that students were familiar with a variety of graphic organizers. Although he did not wish to dictate the organizational pattern the students might use, he wanted to suggest one that he thought would work in case students needed something to fall back on as they started to organize their PE writing task. He chose the I-chart format (Form 26.1) because it allowed students to organize their thoughts according to the questions they had and the sources they consulted.

I-Chart

Topic	Question	Question	Question	Question	Other interesting facts and figures	New questions
What we know						
Sources						
Synthesis						

From *Transforming Writing Instruction in the Digital Age: Techniques for Grades 5–12* by Thomas DeVere Wolsey and Dana L. Grisham. Copyright 2012 by The Guilford Press. Permission to photocopy this form is granted to purchasers of this book for personal use only (see copyright page for details).

TECH·nique 27

Feedback, Assessment, and Technology

Cross-reference hashtags: #assessment, #feedback, #model, #rubric

What Is It?

Assessment and feedback are inextricably bound together, and this is as it should be. We agree with Tomlinson (2008) when she asserts that informative assessment is not just about scores in the grade book. Informative assessment provides guidance to students and to teachers about how they may use the information available to them to improve on the task at hand and move forward on future tasks. Assessment coupled with feedback is a regular and meaningful feature in the lives of young writers in classrooms where composing tasks are a meaningful way of learning. Rubrics, accompanied by models, of the writing processes and written products expected of students improve student writing if great care is taken in aligning key elements. In Figure 27.1, notice how the standards, content expectations, and essential understandings inform the design of the prompt and rubric. In turn, all these elements become means for providing effective feedback.

Why Is It Important?

Assessment

Assessment is sometimes about grades, but it is also about information the teacher and students can collect about how students are progressing. Tomlinson (2008) calls this informative assessment. Once teachers have some idea of how students are progressing, they can share that information with students, provide feedback about how the information might be used, and use it to improve instruction.

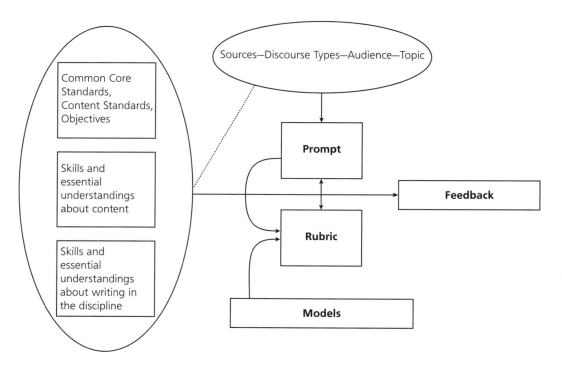

FIGURE 27.1. Planning an academic writing task to provide effective feedback.

Feedback

Feedback, based on assessment of student progress, helps students improve the work they are doing and the future work in which they will engage. Effective feedback may take three forms, according to Hattie and Timperley (2007), which they express as questions:

1   Feed up helps students answer the question "Where am I going in relation to the goal for this task?"

2   Feed back (the space between is intentional) helps students answer the question "How am I going?"

3   Feed forward helps students answer the question "What next?"

Assessment tells the teacher what the students needs might be as they relate to the task at hand and long-term curriculum goals and standards. Feedback is the information the student receives that helps the student to do well on the task as well as achieve long-term goals and standards. Not all assessment, as Tomlinson (2008) asserts, results in a grade.

Rubrics and Scoring Criteria

Rubrics are powerful tools, and they may serve as more than just a scoring device. When student writers are given rubrics in advance, they reinforce the important attributes of the writing task and may show degrees of achievement that make clear what the task may entail. The most powerful rubrics are those that are specific to the elements of the prompt and do not introduce new attributes that might confuse students. For example, it does not help students to read a prompt that asks for the writer to list or identify something only to find that the prompt asks the writer to describe or compare. Bloom's revised taxonomy (Anderson & Krathwohl, 2001) can help choose verbs that indicate the teacher's expectations and that match the directions found in the prompt and in the rubric.

On some occasions and for some instructional purposes, rubrics include elements that cut across multiple assignments. For example, students may generally be expected to use the school's styleguide (#styleguide) and to use scholarly approaches to spelling that are appropriate for the grade level and discipline. Teachers may have provided direct instruction in attending to the needs and expectations of the audience, that imaginary or real person who might read the piece, or to the organizational patterns that are appropriate for the written work or for the content area in which it is written. Rubrics are deceptively simple in design but conceptually difficult to create. They should highlight skills (Popham, 1997) and essential understandings without being overly specific to the task or being so general as to be useless.

While rubrics are generally thought of as a matrix, they need not always be presented in this way. Montgomery (2000) defines a rubric simply as "scoring guidelines." One form that is sometimes efficient is the checklist. Checklists are useful instructional tools when sequential order of tasks or lists of requirements are important (Rowlands, 2007). A checklist might be used to remind students of the process to be used as a responder to a peer's work promoting more effective peer responses that help provide feedback.

Did you remember to:

Listen hard as the author read?

Make notes about things you liked and things that confused you?

Tell the author a summary of the piece?

Give the author a narrative of your responses to the reading?

Identify things you liked and things that confused you?

Ask the author to reread passages you didn't hear well?

Answer the author's questions about the writing?

Give the author your response notes? (Rowlands, 2007, p. 63)

Checklists are useful as scoring tools if the students are mainly following a process or the individual points of the task are critically important. As with prompts, what is not on the checklist or rubric is as important as what is there. Rubrics, checklists, or other scoring schemes are useful for the teacher, as well, if they are prepared in advance of the writing task. By preparing the rubric in advance, the teacher establishes what the important attributes of the task are and does not change them after students are engaged in the task or have completed it. Building on Stiggins's (2005) work, we assert that students can hit any achievement target that they can see and stays still for them. Further, they can explore the content effectively and remain engaged when the rubrics coupled with prompts provide options for differentiation through meaningful choices and challenges.

Finally, models can help students understand the complexity of the task and what the teacher expects. Models of the written task can be inhibiting or defining in character. Because scoring criteria must of necessity generalize somewhat about what students might eventually write including the complexity of the students' ideas, the approach they may take toward the task, and variability of what may be deemed important, models can make the task comprehensible to novice writers. Because novice writers are unfamiliar with the types of writing and the expectations within the discipline for academic writing, they may find models useful or inhibiting. Sometimes the value of a model is what it does not show (for example, Macbeth, 2010) rather than what it does show students. Models, used correctly, may show students what an excellent performance looks like and what an adequate performance looks like. Several models, taken together, may show students how perspective changes the nature of the composing task and thus expand their notions of how they may employ creative approaches to resolve the problem the writing task represents.

Once the prompt is prepared, the rubric or other scoring scheme established, and models identified, the teacher is prepared to provide feedback. Because the parameters of the task are clearly articulated in the mind of the teacher and subsequently in the minds of students, the teacher is better prepared to provide meaningful feedback that takes into consideration the purposes, types, and qualities identified in Figure 27.2.

What Do I Do?

Digital technology provides tools for developing rubrics, making prompts accessible to students after school, and storing models that may be used to enhance instruction. Careful planning of the writing task can improve the opportunities for novice writers to improve their capacities to write about and within the disciplines while encouraging creativity and transformative thinking.

1 Consider the Common Core Standards (2010; Appendix A, p. 209) for writing as well as the content standards from your state or region as well as lesson or unit objectives. Link prompts and rubrics to these standards and objectives.

Purposes	Types	Qualities
◆ Feed up ("Where am I going?") ◆ Feed back ("How am I going?") ◆ Feed forward ("What next?")	◆ Affirmations ◆ Clarifications about confusing points ◆ Observations about the work ◆ Corrections ◆ Content ◆ Mechanics, usage, spelling, style, etc. ◆ Questions ◆ Exploratory ◆ Personal	◆ Identify positive aspects of the work. ◆ Explain rather than label. ◆ Perceptive. ◆ Corrective. ◆ Compassionate, ◆ Useful. ◆ Timely. ◆ Linked to specific criteria. ◆ Expand or elaborate on key ideas.

FIGURE 27.2. Feedback.

2 Develop the prompt considering how it might be differentiated based on students' instructional needs and interests.

3 Choose the scoring method: for example, a rubric, checklist, or other approach. Figure 27.3 describes several assessment tools.

4 Create rubrics or scoring criteria that highlight the essential understanding for the writing task. Align the rubric and prompt with the standards and objectives.

a Think about the essential understandings about content and the literacy skills needed to write well about that content.

b Based on models provided, students may be able to help the teacher construct a rigorous rubric that guides their own writing and helps them plan what attributes are important. Doing so reinforces for students their own knowledge of the content and how to write about that content.

5 Identify models that illustrate important criteria and attributes from the rubric and prompt. Point out to students how the models either demonstrate or fail to demonstrate the criteria and attributes. Consider using multiple models to increase the possibility that students will explore the complexity of the issue or topic about which they will write. A single model may, at times, be mistaken by students as the "right" answer (Macbeth, 2010) and lead them to replicate the model given rather than explore and transform their notions of the content and perspectives derived from the sources in the classroom and their own inquiry into the topic.

6 Introduce the prompt in tandem with models and rubrics. Consider using the rubric as a source of information about how the writing might evolve, as a means of helping students assess their own writing, as a way for peers and teacher to provide feedback, and as an evaluation instrument.

Analytical Rubric	Analytical rubrics call attention and assign points and sometimes weight to specific categories (see Figure 27.5) with points assigned for each category and achievement level.
Holistic Rubric	Scores on holistic rubrics give an overall impression of the work based on a series of expectations. Individual categories are not necessarily broken out for scoring; however, feedback can be specific to the expectations. A holistic rubric may be presented as a matrix, a checklist, or description of expectations.
Primary-Trait Assessment	Scores or grades that rely on the primary-trait assessment focus on the purpose for the writing. Purpose, for school writing tasks, may be related to the genre (for example, biography), the purpose for the assignment (for example, use of academic vocabulary), aspect of writer's craft (for example, composing powerful sentences), and so on.
Checklists	Scores based on checklists are effective when specific elements should be included or steps in a process followed.
Self-Assessment	All of the rubrics or assessment approaches described above can easily be converted for use as a self-assessment the writer uses as a tool to plan writing, execute revisions, and prepare final products for presentation. Rubrics used for scoring may also be used for self-assessment by the student in composing and preparing the final product.
Hybrid	In some cases, it is informative for students and useful for instructional purposes to combine approaches. For example, a checklist describing a process can be appended to the top of an analytical rubric. A primary trait from the discipline might be combined with an analytic rubric that helps students develop their writing skills and content knowledge.

FIGURE 27.3. Types of assessment. Based on Duke (2001); Fearn and Farnan (2001); Merritt (2003); Rowlands (2007); Spandel and Stiggins (1997).

7 Provide feedback as students write as well as with the written work once it has been submitted for a grade or score. A word processor tool may help with efficient feedback with certain types of information. (See the box on Autotext.)

Differentiation Possibilities

Process

Prompts, rubrics, and models work in tandem based on student readiness, learning strengths, and interests. Using RAFTdm, students can choose topics, roles, audiences, formats, and digital media that permit them to select based on their interests and learning strengths. Rubrics might also be written to accommodate different writing tasks based on levels of readiness or interest that focus on the content objective and Common Core Standards (2010; Appendix A). Students who are presented with several models of written products that demonstrate varying approaches and conceptualizations may choose the model most representative of their chosen areas of focus.

Autotext

Popular word processors have a feature that allows the user to reuse blocks of text and other elements (such as a URL) by storing them in a kind of library for later use. In Microsoft Word, these are part of the Building Blocks feature that includes Quick Parts and Autotext. In WordPerfect, these tools are known as QuickWords and ClipBook. Open Office also has an autotext feature. At first, this may seem interesting, but not particularly useful. However, as any teacher or editor who provides feedback on written work can attest, some types of feedback come up time and time again. An example may help: Students sometimes unintentionally transfer colloquial language to the writing for academic purposes. A common problem relates to pronoun–antecedent agreement. That is, Standard English calls for the number of the pronoun (singular or plural) to agree with the noun to which it refers. This problem occurs so frequently that the ability to insert a standard block of text may be helpful to highlight where this problem occurred. Using the "comment" feature (see the example in Technique 6) or the "track changes" feature in Word, a block of text can be inserted quickly that identifies the problem and its location. Find useful online tutorials for Microsoft Word, WordPerfect, and OpenOffice at *http://www.delicious.com/TDWolsey/autotext.*

Example 1: Using a Cumulative Feedback Table to Manage Individual and Group Writing Feedback[1]

What is more durable than a sticky note, has more clarity than handwriting, and is better organized than annotations in the margin? All these can come into play when providing writing feedback and all involve a certain labor intensity that the *copy and paste* function of electronic text can overcome. Consider creating a cumulative feedback table (CFT) instead. (See Figure 27.4; a blank version you can use is presented in Form 27.1 at the end of this chapter.) A CFT can individualize feedback, encourage students' questions, track successes, and identify misunderstandings. It affords teachers and students flexibility to add new goals and eliminate mastered ones. It can provide assessment data that is accessible to learners, their teachers, and other stakeholders in students' learning, such as parents and administrators.

When receiving the paper as electronic text, the teacher first reads the student's comments about the last paper (let's call that "Assignment 1"). The teacher then clears that space, reads the current paper (which we will call "Assignment 2"), and comment about it is shown below. The teacher places comments and highlighting within the paper that match the feedback within the checklist section of the CFT for the next assignment. The student would review the teacher's comments about

---

[1]This section was contributed by Arlene R. H. Pincus, PhD, Walden University.

Title of the paper/genre:	Date of assignment

Teacher's comments and questions about Paper 2

Student X, you can be proud of this paper for the following reasons:

— We talked about how the beginning of a paper can draw you reader right in. When I read— (first sentence is copied here) — I really wanted to know more about it.

— I also noticed that your word choices were sophisticated and really helped me see what you were talking about. I highlighted some of these terrific choices (yellow).

— You can see that you have made progress in almost every area we have discussed.

— When we have our private conference, we can add in other ideas and maybe take out some that we both think you have learned to make part of your writing.

If you look at the places where I wrote an X for this week, you might have a go at revising these run-ons (highlighted in green) by following the directions in the box about these below each. If you need assistance, we can talk about these.

Look at the other places where you see an X for this week. Let's talk about these during Writing Workshop. I will invite a group of you to meet with me about this idea.

Student's comments and questions

[These would be the student's response to the teacher's comments about the last paper, Paper 1. These comments are not shown here as this CFT shows what the teacher would return to the student with Paper 1.]

Grade or rubric subgrades can go here ...

Assignments (each number is a new assignment):	1	2	3	4	5	6	7	8	9
Purpose and audience:									
Is my lead compelling?	X	X	X						
Did I tell the reader what the reader needs to know?	X								
Does my ending work?	X	X							
Strong writing: (examples below)									
Descriptions: specific adjectives (examples: a *sizzling* meal, a *compelling* question)	X	X							
Strong verbs: powerful verbs (examples: _____ and _____)	X								
Other:									
Revising:									
Order of ideas: (example: Student considers whether the information is given in a user-friendly order.)	X								
Consider whether all of the ideas belong in this paper.		X		X					
Other:									
Editing:									
Please use the spelling and grammar checker.	X	X							
Check for run-on sentences.	X	X	X	X					

FIGURE 27.4. Sample cumulative feedback table. Reprinted by permission of Dr. Arlene Pincus.

Assignment 1, and respond to the request to edit run-on sentences within the CFT (eliminating the need to return Assignment 1). The student would then ask and answer questions in the space for the purpose of responding to Assignment 2 and paste the resulting CFT on top of Assignment 2.

Notice that this teacher has decided to offer a mini-lesson to several students about one writing idea but has asked this particular student to consider editing the run-ons in the paper before offering individual instruction about this type of error. Class members would need to learn how to select the table when a paper is returned and copy it to the top of the subsequent paper. The following could be a student's personal CFT for one marking period or for a series of assignments.

Example 2: A Rubric in an English Language Arts Classroom

Tara Minnerly teaches seventh-grade students and describes how she and her students use an analytic rubric.

"Real-Time" Teaching by Tara Minnerly, Torrington Public Schools, Torrington, Connecticut

While reading the novel *Ties That Bind, Ties That Break*, by Lensey Namioka (1999), seventh-grade students write a persuasive resume as the main character, Ailin. In order to obtain a nanny position, students include information such as educational background, personality traits, and interests.

For this assignment, students and teacher use an analytical rubric (Duke, 2001) on two areas of content: persuasive information and textual evidence. Besides content criteria, students are also assessed on two areas of writing: resume format and spelling. The content and writing tasks are separated into achievement categories. The analytical rubric for this assignment includes four categories of achievement: Exemplary, Proficient, Progressing, and Beginning.

After reading the prompt and reviewing the sample resume, students preview the rubric (see Figure 27.5), comparing content and format criteria. While previewing the rubric, the class discussed specific content, such as the experiences Ailin had that qualify her as a nanny (Namioka, 1999). Examples that would not appeal to the audience were also discussed and model essays examined. Since achievement levels for this category reflect how well students appeal to the audience, this part of the rubric review will strengthen content learning by honing the skill of selecting the most persuasive details.

Another content category, related to the persuasive information, will be textual evidence. While reviewing the rubric, the class will discuss specific details that would support, or not support, the resume categories. Teachers should explain a rubric to students (for example, Shellard & Protheroe, 2004), including the particular competencies they will need to demonstrate. Discussing examples of convincing details will help students see how choosing an inappropriate detail, or not including one at all, would result in a lower score for the category of textual evidence.

Assessment Categories	Levels of Achievement			
	Exemplary—4	Proficient—3	Progressing—2	Beginning—1
Content: Persuasive Information Common Core Standards (2010, p. 42): 1. Write arguments to support claims with clear reasons and relevant evidence. 1d. Establish and maintain a formal style.	Resume includes persuasive information such as educational background, qualities, experiences, and interests that highly appeal to the audience; includes resume objective.	Resume includes persuasive information that mostly appeals to the audience; includes resume objective.	Resume includes some persuasive information that appeals to the audience; includes resume objective.	Resume includes limited persuasive information that inadequately appeals to the audience; Information, including the resume objective, may be missing or inaccurate.
Textual Evidence Common Core Standards: 1a. Support claim(s) with logical reasoning and relevant evidence, using accurate, credible sources and demonstrating an understanding of the topic or text.	All persuasive information is supported and elaborated with accurate textual evidence.	Most of the persuasive information is supported and elaborated with accurate textual evidence.	Some of the persuasive information is supported and elaborated with accurate textual evidence.	Persuasive information is not adequately supported with textual evidence; details may be missing or inaccurate.
Resume Format/ Organization	Uses proper resume format: spacing, indentation, bold headings, and categories.	One to two errors in resume format compared to model resume.	Three to five errors in resume format that detract from presentation of information compared to model resume.	More than five errors in resume format that significantly detract from presentation of information.
Spelling	No errors in spelling.	Resume includes some minor spelling errors.	Resume include several errors in spelling that detract from the author's credibility.	Resume contains multiple spelling errors that significantly detract from the author's credibility.

FIGURE 27.5. Ailin's resume rubric: *Ties That Bind, Ties That Break* (1999) persuasive piece.

Cumulative Feedback Table

Title of the paper/genre:	Date of assignment
Teacher's comments and questions about Paper 2	Student's comments and questions

Grade or rubric subgrades can go here ...

Assignments (each number is a new assignment):	1	2	3	4	5	6	7	8	9
Purpose and audience:									
Is my lead compelling?									
Did I tell the reader what the reader needs to know?									
Does my ending work?									
Strong writing: (examples below)									
Descriptions: specific adjectives (examples: a *sizzling* meal, a *compelling* question)									
Strong verbs: powerful verbs (examples: _____ and _____)									
Other:									
Revising:									
Order of ideas: (example: Student considers whether the information is given in a user-friendly order.)									
Consider whether all of the ideas belong in this paper.									
Other:									
Editing:									
Please use the spelling and grammar checker.									
Check for run-on sentences.									

Note. Reprinted by permission of Dr. Arlene Pincus.

PART FIVE

What about Literature and English Language Arts?

English teachers in middle and high schools bear enormous teaching and grading burdens, but the bright spot for us is that we really tend to love what we teach. Reading, that is. We love to provide the opportunity for our students to *read* literature. But, when it comes time for writing instruction, we teachers may feel less positive. We may ask ourselves some questions. Why don't students already write competently? What were those elementary (middle school) teachers doing? What about having to grade everything that students write? It's too much!

Fortunately, technology can help. The American Association of Colleges for Teacher Education (AACTE) and the Partnership for 21st Century Skills (P21) collaborated and published a white paper on teaching in September 2010 (AACTE & P21, 2010). The authors make the following three important recommendations (p. 11) for teachers to know and embrace:

1 Align technologies with content and pedagogy and develop the ability to creatively use technologies to meet specific learning needs.

2 Align instruction with standards, particularly those standards that embody 21st-century knowledge and skills.

3 Balance direct instruction strategically with project-oriented teaching methods.

For many teachers, the thought of trying to accomplish these goals in addition to everything else on our plates may seem overwhelming. However, as noted in Technique 11, short writings can assist. The following strategies assume that you have at least one computer with Internet and a data projector so that students can easily view what is on the screen. It is also helpful if you have three or four student computers with Internet access and that you can send some students out—to the library to computer terminals, to another teacher's classroom to use terminals, or to a couple of the computers in the lab, if you have one that has computers set up for drop-ins. If you have portable laptops that you can obtain or if students are allowed to bring their own, they might be used in class. At any rate, if you have limited access to computers you'll need to think of some alternatives about how to get access for your students. You may also put students into pairs or triads (Grisham & Molinelli, 1995) and have them write as a team on the computer.

Short Writing
Summaries in Response to Reading

Cross-reference hashtags: #languagearts, #shortcues, #summarization

What Is It?

In Part Three, we discussed some short writing strategies using computers, mobile phones, and other handheld devices. If you are fond of literature circles (Daniels, 2002) and conduct some in your English classroom, then you may want to compile a list of summary topics for your middle or high school students to use in response to their reading. These can be used for literature circles, but you can also post them on a wiki.

Suggested Summary Topics

1 Give an overview of the plot that unfolded in the chapter you just read. Your paragraph(s) should relate back to what has already happened in the book and make a brief prediction of what you think will happen next.

2 In the chapter(s) you just read, how has the main character developed? Relate back to what has happened to the character in the previous chapters you have read and make a prediction about what will happen next to this character.

Why Is It Important?

We learn with and from each other. Literature brings us together in ways that help us to share our humanity, to understand others, and "the other." Great works of literature bring us a shared understanding of our world and our place in it. They provide a glimpse of worlds that are past, worlds that are to come, and worlds of imagination. So ... how do we get adolescents to delve meaningfully into these worlds? We believe that discussion of literature brings students to understand more than they would understand on their own.

Judith Langer (1995) theorizes that we create envisionments of what we read and that these envisionments evolve over time, becoming more sophisticated. For example, one reads *Romeo and Juliet* as an adolescent and sees the love story. Later, one may read *Romeo and Juliet* and see the heartbreak of the young. Finally, one may read *Romeo and Juliet* as a parent and find a different heartbreak.

How Will Technology Help?

We have noted that wherever we go, schools are recognizable institutions that haven't changed much over time, despite the many technological advances of the 20th century and of the first decade of the 21st century. In 2004, we journeyed to a literacy conference in the Philippines and made a side trip to Bali, where we had the delight of visiting a school. Interestingly, the school in Bali, a school in Baja California, Mexico, and the schools down the street from our homes are amazingly similar. In the wealthiest nation on earth, students still go to a square room with chalk or whiteboards, desks or tables, books, pencils, and so on. There is surprisingly little technology apparent in most schools we visit. When we do see computers, for example, they may or may not be used by the teacher.

Technology is a tool for getting the job of communication done. Moreover, today's technologies provide unprecedented opportunities for learning about literature without even reading the text, finding out what others think/know about the works of literature that our society deems essential to the education of our children. We can't afford to keep using old technologies in school without running the risk of becoming irrelevant.

What Do I Do?

Teachers can make use of Web 2.0 technologies to write about their study of literature, even when technological tools are not right at hand. One way to do this is to create wikis where students can post responses to literature. You can join a wiki site like Wikispaces or PBWorks to create a forum for students to post their responses.

Differentiation Possibilities

Content

Students select works of literature for response in literature circles or read individually selected works of literature.

Process

Posting work on wikis, blogs, or threaded discussion groups, students choose the frequency of their responses or the audience for their responses.

Product

Students post work via wikis in small groups, on blogs for the class or public, or in threaded discussions or VoiceThreads.

Example: "Real-Time" Students Write with a Wiki

Choose a prompt that suits the books that your literature groups are studying. Students will need to do their composing on the computer rather than with pencils. They should be allotted about 10 minutes to compose the summary and make the post to a website called Wikispaces (*http://www.wikispaces.com*) where you can create a wiki for students in your literature circles. In our example, we set up a wiki (*http://lrcsummaries.wikispaces.com/message/view/home/40475689*) called LRCSummaries where you can view samples of student summaries in response to selected literature.

On the LRCSummaries wiki, Team 1 is a group of students reading *Of Mice and Men* (Steinbeck, 1937/1965). These students were assigned as a team to post chapter summaries on the wiki where the entries may be accessed. Students do not have to have e-mail accounts to contribute to wikis that the teacher creates.

Team 1, consisting of Laila, Nathan, and Lindsey, all 10th-grade students at a high school in Northern California, read *Of Mice and Men* (Steinbeck, 1937) and collaborated to write summaries of the chapters. Each summary had one student as the lead in keyboarding, though the entries were all team written. The teacher then posted them to the wiki where they could be read by others. Below is Laila's (keyboarder) entry for chapter 5 of the novel (*http://lrcsummaries.wikispaces.com/Team+1*).

Act 5 by Laila, Nathan, and Lindsey

Lennie sits alone on the floor of the barn. In his lap was his now-dead puppy. He talked to the puppy, debating whether or not to tell George that he killed the animal. He worries that if George knew that Lennie had not even been able to keep a little puppy alive, George would not let Lennie tend to the rabbits. Lennie quickly buries the puppy under the hay and decides to tell George that he found the puppy dead. He then realizes that George would see right through that lie, so he unburies the puppy and angrily throws it across the room.

Just then, Curly's wife quietly creeps into the barn, right past the last stall. She asks Lennie what he is doing. Lennie tells Curly's wife that he is not allowed to speak to her. As Curly's wife attempts to convince Lennie to speak to her, she notices the dead puppy on the ground. She inquires him about it, and Lennie tells her how he played too roughly with the puppy, and it ended up dead. As Curly's wife consoles Lennie, she also tells him that the rest of the workers are out playing and will not return soon, so Lennie should not be afraid to speak to her.

Curly's wife begins to tell Lennie about her past. She tells him how a man once told her that she could make it big in Hollywood, and how she waited for him to contact her, but the man never did. She then married Curly directly after. She confided in Lennie, telling him how she truly hated Curly and wished she had gone to Hollywood and made a life there.

Lennie continues the conversation, telling Curly's wife all about his dreams for the future. He tells her how George and he want to own their own property, and how Lennie will tend to all the rabbits. When Curly's wife asks him what he likes so much about rabbits, Lennie tells her that he loves how soft they are. He says that he loves to pet soft things. Curly's wife tells him how soft her hair is, and she places Lennie's hand on a strand of her hair. Lennie strokes it and strokes it. Curly's wife tells him to stop, and Lennie reacts by grasping tighter.

As Curly's wife begins to scream, he asks her to stop, and covers her mouth with his large hand. As her screams get louder, his grasp gets tighter. Eventually, he accidentally snaps her neck. Lennie realizes what he has done and runs away, to the hiding place that George provided in the beginning of the book.

Old Candy comes into the barn, looking for Lennie. He sees Curly's wife's body and calls George in. As George looks over the body, he decides that they have to tell the rest of the guys. He goes back to the bunkhouse and Candy comes in and tells everyone what had happened. The men examine Curly's wife's body and pronounce her dead. They decide that Lennie must be found and killed immediately. The men grab their guns and run after Lennie.

Additional Resources

We suggest two good places that are free for teachers to set up wikis. One is from our example at Wikispaces (*http://www.wikispaces.com*) and the other is PBWorks (*http://pbworks. com*). You can also set up a space in Google Docs that has similar features to a wiki. A useful resource online (*http://educationalwikis.wikispaces.com*) provides you with a list of articles and resources that help you to learn how to use wikis in education, a comprehensive list of educational wikis you can refer to, and a general discussion of wikis in education. For one published example of an educational wiki set up for literature responses, go to *http:// literature.wikispaces.com/The+Hotseat*.

The Zen of Writing about Literature

Cross-reference hashtags: #internetprojects, #languagearts, #literature, #podcasts

What Is It?

Bliss is reading a great novel! So why do students resist this process? One student in one of our classes actually computed how long it would take him to read a page of a novel and then multiplied the minutes it took by the number of pages and announced that 10 hours was much too long to spend reading a book! So, how do we engage students like this?

Why Is It Important?

Students often can't relate to the things they read in the "canon." We ask students to read books from historical eras of which they are barely aware. How can we bring students to understand historical eras and moral dilemmas that are alien to them? One way is to provide the intellectual and emotional bridges from present to past, so that students can relate to great works of literature and, more importantly, so that they gain the combination of confidence and curiosity that spurs them to inquire further.

How Will Technology Help?

Technology provides a number of useful tools that we believe enable students to think more deeply about literature. English teachers can help their students accomplish this and we think you will like the example that we provide below. One way to respond to literature is through critique. Critiques of literature require inquiry and it is through interested inquiry that bridges between times and cultures can be built.

What Do I Do?

- ◆ Students need time to read and time to write online and on paper.
- ◆ Ensure students have access to the online forums you choose.

Differentiation Possibilities

Process

Students might read online critiques written by other students outside their own school, or read the critiques of their peers within the school.

Product

Critiques require wide knowledge of the literary genre as well as the genre of the critique. Students might choose audiences for their critiques that require different approaches to writing. A critique written for peers might take a very different perspective than one written with a public audience in mind.

Online Example 1

For your serious students (and even some of the not-so-serious ones) check out a site called Teen Ink (Figure 29.1). This is a website, but is also a print magazine and a publisher of student-written books, in existence since 1989. Such a stable site is accomplished by donations, partnerships, celebrity support, and, of course by the submission of quality student work. Teen Ink is online and student identity is protected by the use of a first name and a last initial (*Kate F., Long Beach, California,* is an example). Teen Ink publishes poetry, fiction, nonfiction, and reviews (of books, films, music, TV). Teen Ink also provides a forum called Writer's Workshop, where students can "meet" and share their works in progress. There are videos of poetry and other readings and of musical performances. There are links for summer programs and colleges (both searchable). In short, Teen Ink is a writer's dream come true. Getting your students to write for a real audience is engaging, and writing reviews of novels (even if not published by Teen Ink) supports both critical thinking and honing composing skills.

The book review may be written in class using the computer using the writing process. In fact, as a motivator, students could submit their best book reviews as

FIGURE 29.1. Home page for Teen Ink. Copyright 2012 by the Young Authors Foundation, Inc. Reprinted by permission.

part of a classroom competition for the top five best book reviews to be submitted to Teen Ink.

As a way to scaffold the project, have your students go online and read some of the book reviews and look over the comments other students have made in response. For example, a girl from San Jose, California, wrote a review of *Twilight* (Meyer, 2005), which was voted the number one review by other teens and had over 500 comments posted about it. As preparation, your students can read some of these posts and make some of their own. As mentioned in Part One, you need to make sure that your students have earned their chit, which shows they know how to conduct themselves online. Joining is easy, so long as you are between 13 and 19 years of age. Writing submitted to Teen Ink is copyrighted by the Young Authors Foundation, but your students also have permission to publish elsewhere, so long as that publication is not "exclusive" in nature. Oh, yes, and you may subscribe to the print version of Teen Ink for your classroom as well.

Online Example 2

Another example features podcasts. Podcasts are MP3 audio files that are posted to the Internet and are used for various purposes. For example, Frey et al. (2010) relate an example where high school students subscribed to Classic Tales (*http://classictales.libsyn.com*), where such classics as *A Room with a View* (Forster, 1908) can be downloaded in segments to iTunes and enjoyed by students who can plug in their earbuds and pretend they are listening to music. Just kidding.... You might be thinking, "Hey, wait, isn't this a book about writing?" And, you're right. In creating podcasts, students compose their responses, often in writing. They may compose their script entirely in advance, or create a draft with the final podcast derived from their initial drafts and precomposition planning.

In addition there are some wonderful sites where teachers can get ideas. Kidcast for Teachers (*http://www.intelligenic.com/kidcast/rss.xml*) is a site where blogger Dan Schmidt posted tips for kids on podcasting—they are useful and still there, although the last one was posted in 2009. *Scientific American* (*http://www.scientificamerican.com/podcast/podcasts.cfm?type=60-second-science*) has a feature called 60-second Science, where new information is posted weekly. This can be a stimulator of discussion in classrooms and it can also serve as a model for doing a 60-second podcast on literature! The podcasts are posted on the site and the exact transcript with them so it is easy to see how long a script needs to be for a 1-minute audio podcast.

Because we don't have to just listen to podcasts, we can have our students create them—and we can use these as an opportunity for students to compose a script instead of just speaking off the cuff. For some examples of podcasts that were done by secondary-teacher candidates from various disciplines on how to use literacy strategies in the content area, go to *https://sites.google.com/site/audiopodcasts* and listen to the brief (4- to 5-minute) podcasts posted there. They constitute an example of how content can be created by students. For our students in grades 6–12, we provide an example of an audio podcast from our wiki LRCSummaries that is posted on Podbean (*http://danagrisham.podbean.com*).

We should note that it is relatively easy to make a podcast on a Macintosh through the program GarageBand; however, you must convert the file to an MP3 format to post it to most websites (such as Podbean) that accept audio files. It took a little doing to understand the process. What we did:

> In GarageBand, select "new project" and then "podcast." You will then title the podcast, saving it in GarageBand. Next you select "create" and when you first try to record your podcast, a message will come up to "select an instrument." To select an instrument, you press the plus sign at the bottom left of the GarageBand screen and three choices come up. Select "real instrument." Then you may press the red record button and record your voice (or the child's voice). When done, press the red button to stop recording. Save in GarageBand, then go to the pull-down "Share" menu and select "export to iTunes." It will ask you the format—save in the MP3 format and the file is exported to iTunes. From there you can drag and drop onto your desktop, if you wish, for uploading to your website.

Once you "get the hang" of it (be sure to write down your process as you go) you can repeat for any number of podcasts. Remember that this is the bare-bones version of the podcast. You and your students may wish to experiment with GarageBand and use music, graphics, photos, and other multimedia to make the podcasts more interesting.

Persuasion
In This Essay, I'm Going to Convince You . . .

Cross-reference hashtags: #languagearts, #persuasion

What Is It?

Writing to persuade is generally regarded as the most demanding genre of all. The Common Core Standards (2010; see the Appendix on pp. 209) on writing call for making arguments at the sixth-grade level.

Thus, teaching middle and high school students to write persuasively is critical to their success. Persuasive writing may be defined as "The art and science of getting someone to believe as you want them to believe and/or act in a way that you want them to act" (Grisham, Wozniak, & Wolsey, 2010, p. 98). Easier said than done! For teachers, the hard part is teaching students the art of persuasion that goes beyond pro and con arguments or common prompts such as those that ask students to persuade the principal to reduce the amount of homework. Barone (2011) describes the problems with common persuasion prompts: "They are often polarized so that students can only take a single position. For instance, while students might argue for more homework, most students would not and they would find it difficult to craft an argument for why more homework would be laudable" (p. 15). Rather, Dejoy (1999) suggests that teachers invite writers to move from persuasion to participation through an active voice in the discourses that are the fabric of our lives.

The rhetorical bases for persuasion are well founded. Baird (2006) recommended the following: personal appeal, tone (word choices), precision of language (referring to audience), concessions (acknowledging opposing points), rebuttal, logic (syllogism), authority, and rhetorical questions. Other means of making arguments go back to Aristotle in the fourth century B.C.E. (logos, ethos, pathos, and kairos).

♦ Logos is the logic of reason or thought. The syllogism is an example: "All men are mortal. Aristotle is a man. Therefore, Aristotle is mortal." There are 256 types of syllogisms; for an explanation and examples, go to Wikipedia (*http://en.wikipedia. org/wiki/Syllogism#Examples*). Any time you add numbers or research, you are adding a rational (logos) argument.

◆ Ethos is an appeal to what is right, usually couched in terms of morality (it is the right thing to do). Appeals to righteousness depend, naturally, on our value systems. If we believe in kindness, for example, we might further an argument for what we want based on how that is the kind thing to do.

◆ Pathos is an emotional appeal—this will make us happy, sad, and so on. Often, a sympathetic portrait may be drawn. Think of children who have not had the experience of kindness in their lives!

◆ Finally, kairos is an appeal to the timeliness and importance of action. This must be done now before more children suffer!

On the ReadWriteThink website (*http://www.readwritethink.org/classroom-resources/lesson-plans/convince-developing-persuasive-writing-56.html*) you can find a lesson in persuasive writing with a graphic organizer (persuasion map) that can either be downloaded and reproduced or may be filled out by students online. There is also a PowerPoint presentation for students on the various methods of persuasion. The presentation also includes the powerful argument of "experts agree" or the power of celebrity ("Magic Johnson recommends this!"). The ReadWriteThink site links you to standards by state, provides information on resources and preparation needed, a sample instructional plan, and related resources.

Why Is It Important?

Students need to learn both how to critically read persuasive text and to note the arguments made to them and also how to marshal the arguments in their writing. As teachers, we need to scaffold this complex process for our students. When students understand argument, they can also analyze appeals made to them more critically. When we are bombarded in the media to buy products and services, this analytical stance is essential. It is even more essential to the political process in a democratic society.

How Will Technology Help?

As with other genres of writing, technology can assist you in making persuasive writing more transparent. We have already provided you with one valuable online resource: ReadWriteThink (*http://www.readwritethink.org*) and this site links to another called Thinkfinity (*http://www.thinkfinity.org*). The Thinkfinity site offers resources in a variety of disciplines at the click of a button. Once you know your way around these two sites, you are ready to involve your students with persuasion and technology. These sites include graphic organizer templates and lesson plans that can be adjusted to fit your students' needs.

What Do I Do?

A useful technique for involving students in short writing is an adaptation of Zwiers's (2008) "pro/con" discussion technique. For some content topics, such as stem-cell research or election year issues, the pro/con discussion can promote effective thinking about sources and positions, though caution is warranted that student writers don't identify themselves so closely with their arguments that they cannot look through and beyond those arguments. Zwiers places students in pairs. One person argues the pro position on a topic/issue for 1 minute, followed by the other student taking the "con" position for 1 minute. Then they switch places, arguing for 1 minute each again, taking the opposite stance. Our adaptation of pro/con involves writing. Students write for 2 minutes (one con, one pro). They share their writings for 2 minutes. Then they write again, taking the opposite stance for 2 more minutes of writing. The whole class then participates in 5 to 10 minutes of discussion about how students may have changed their ideas about the topic/issue. We believe such writing has the potential to widen the discussion beyond simple opinion and can prepare students to consider the audience and viewpoint of others when they persuade. However, we recommend cautious use of two-valued arguments with only a pro or con.

Differentiation Possibilities

Content

Topics for persuasion vary widely with human experience, even within a specific discipline.

Product

Composing processes can result in products that are appropriate for different audiences and their expectations for persuasive writing. A letter to the editor of a newspaper will result in vary concise writing with a minimum of support from additional sources, whereas an essay intended to persuade a city councilperson to support bike trails in the community might require elaboration regarding costs, possible routes, safety concerns, and so on.

Example: Prompts, the Six-Trait Model, and Technology

Prompts can be developed so that students acquire writing skills, and the six-trait model (Spandel, 2009) can assist teachers to be cognizant of how the skills are acquired by students. The six traits are ideas, organization, voice, word choice, sentence fluency, and conventions/presentation.

Our example comes from the trait of "organization." Organization encompasses the design and flow of ideas. Spandel includes the following (2009, p. 65): "[An] enticing lead pulls readers in; clear design guides readers, enhances understanding; strong transitions tie ideas together; good pacing—time spent where it counts; ending wraps up discussion." Before you write your own prompts for students, have them look at some sample papers (show these on the projector in your classroom).

First, students need to examine this piece of persuasive writing for the qualities of persuasion (appeals to reason, appeals to ethics, appeals to emotions). Then students need to examine the paper for the sense of organization. How well does it do what it attempts to do? Looking at the aspects of organization above, how well does it meet the criteria?

Finally, work with students to go online to find out more about reality TV in order to strengthen and rewrite this persuasive piece. Once they rewrite the arguments and discuss them, they are ready to respond to another persuasive prompt.

Example

Cheryl Wozniak, whom you met in Technique 7, submits the following example from her work as a literacy coach.

"Real-Time" Teaching by Cheryl Wozniak

Students in Anneka Harper's seventh-grade classroom learn how to write persuasively not just because it is a California state standard, but also because Ms. Harper believes that persuasive writing is a genre where middle school students have an opportunity to take a stand and share their opinions with their class members and community. "For some of my students, [writing their persuasive letters and essays] was the first time they really got into writing, and it was because they chose the topics and they really cared about what they were writing."

Ms. Harper teaches two sections of seventh-grade English, one consisting of students who are considered intensive learners enrolled in the Scholastic Read 180 program, which are students who are reading at least 2 years below grade level, and a second combined group of students who either are on grade level (benchmark learners) or reading 1 to 1½ years below grade level (strategic learners). Both classes received explicit writing instruction over a 6-week period as part of their two-period language arts core class. Many of the lessons were taught in similar ways to both groups of learners; however, the intensive learners required more scaffolding. At the end of the unit, all students produced one or more pieces of persuasive writing and most had progressed in their skills of writing persuasively; however, the intensive learners still were writing below grade level.

In Ms. Harper's classroom, students begin the process of learning to write in a new genre by first reading many texts in that genre. Although the texts used in her classroom may or may not be texts written by well-known authors, she refers to the samples of writing as mentor texts and students quickly learn the characteristics of the genre after being immersed in many writing examples. Students in Ms. Harper's regular English core class read an editorial titled "Should the Driving Age Be Raised to 18?" After students predicted the reasons one might give both for and against raising the driving age, students read the article and "talked to the text." After their initial read and annotation of the text, students reread the article with highlighters in hand and half of the reread to find the pro side while the other half reread to find the con side. A class discussion followed and students were prepared to provide reasons the author had given for and against raising the driving age to 18.

Using a similar approach, students in Ms. Harper's intensive intervention class read their first mentor text titled "Should Cell Phones Be Banned in Schools?" Ms. Harper chose this text for two reasons: first, she knew that cell phones was a topic of high interest for her students because her school site has a policy that limits students' use of cell phones on the school campus, and second, the article was an appropriate follow-up to the previous day's lesson where students watched a video showing two sides of a debate on the benefits and harms of technology. As part of the intensive intervention program, Read 180, Ms. Harper teaches students in both whole- and small-group sessions. During her whole-group lesson, she guided students through a discussion of what ideas were presented for each side of the cell phone argument. Then in small-group instruction, she helped students complete a three-column graphic organizer identifying sentences from the text in column 1, stating whether the sentence was a fact or opinion in column 2, and explaining why the sentence was fact or opinion in column 3. In the days that followed, students read two more texts on cyberbullies and repeated the process of identifying facts and opinions in the new mentor texts.

Throughout the persuasive writing unit, Ms. Harper's students observed many teacher demonstrations and participated in both shared demonstrations and guided practice before being asked to write a persuasive essay or letter independently. Anneka began by modeling how to write just a persuasive paragraph using one of the ideas from the pro list students generated in their discussion about raising the driving age. Students observed her write the beginning on the whiteboard and then added their ideas as she continued to write the paragraph with them. Next, students chose another idea from the pro list, wrote paragraphs, and then discussed their writing with a partner. The lesson ended with students sharing any convincing ideas that they or their partner had written.

Ms. Harper views technology as a valuable tool for literacy instruction, and she and her students access a variety of technological resources on a regular basis, including websites for mentor texts for the unit. The Internet has become a rich source for finding information during the research process; however, students must be taught how to conduct effective searches and how to evaluate the credibility of a website. Lessons to address these require further use of technology as teachers use a laptop hooked to an data projector and a wireless access point to model for students how to use Google's advanced search feature to create a "hotlist" of websites for students to use. Organizing ideas for persuasive writing can be a challenge for some students, even at the seventh-grade level. A graphic organizer that Ms. Harper has found helpful for these students is called a persuasion map and is available at *http:// www.readwritethink.org/materials/persuasion_map.*

Lastly, Ms. Harper's students used laptop computer word processors while studying persuasive writing. Students typed their persuasive essays in school and shared them with each other in the course management system. Students worked with peer-revising partners to improve their ideas and were able to make further changes in class. Ms. Harper monitored the peer-revising conferences and offered support as needed. Many students decided to name their audience by turning their persuasive essays into persuasive letters. Students requested that they be able to send their letters via the postal service so that their writing would be viewed more authentically. Ms. Harper agreed and was pleased with her students' enthusiasm for getting their writing into the hands of real readers. "I was so impressed when some of my students asked if they could really mail their letters. I could tell that they were proud of what they had written and that they were beginning to understand that writing really is a tool for thinking."

Prompts for Writing
Language Arts

Cross-reference hashtags: #languagearts, #poetry, #prompts, #RAFT

What Is It?

In Technique 24, we discussed general purpose and disciplinary prompts. In this technique, we look at writing prompts for the English classroom. A large part of writing in the English classroom involves the teaching of "genres" of writing.

Let's write a haiku. You know the English version of this Japanese poetic form: three lines with five, then seven, and finally five syllables, respectively. The constraints in the poetic form help us think creatively. When we think of creativity, we often think of free expression with no limitations. But, a closer examination suggests that constraints bring out the creative impulse and promote intellectual curiosity. In haiku, the syllable count constrains the number and types of words that can be used in composing. Further, haiku poets often focus on the seasons or nature and juxtapose ideas through comparison and contrast. Haiku remains a vibrant poetic form that inspires poets and readers alike, in part, because the rules of the form communicate information and set expectations for readers about to read a haiku. Creativity is not stunted as a result of the rules; rather, exploration and creativity are enhanced. Our attempt appears below (and we're sure you and your students can do much better).

> A yellow pencil
> Left beneath a schoolhouse tree
> Autumn leaves gather
> —T. D. Wolsey

Try it yourself. Writing a haiku takes a bit more than just counting syllables and eliminating words. As you compose, you will find that the rules of haiku help you choose words with precision and juxtapose ideas in order to highlight the idea you want to convey. As teachers, we want to choose writing tasks that promote thinking about content and about how language is used to increase student understanding. It seems a contradiction in many ways.

Why Is It Important?

How do we promote creative thinking and intellectual exploration and simultaneously help students work within the constraints entailed in learning about content and language as part of particular genres of writing? Part of the answer to that question lies in how we structure composing tasks for students. Tasks may be self-sponsored (Emig, 1971), that is, writing planned by students who choose topics, discourse modes, and so on. On the other hand, many tasks are teacher sponsored; that is, the teacher designs elements of the task but may leave some choices up to students.

Students, appropriately, take many of their learning cues from teachers. When teachers give directions for a writing task to students, they hint or highlight the attributes of the learning that are important. Consider the time-honored writing task for the first day of school: "Write an essay about your summer vacation." Student writers may have had many fascinating experiences over the summer break and perhaps learned many things. However, the prompt tells them nothing about what type of learning is valued, what purpose the writing task serves, and so on. Open-ended prompts may serve a purpose, at times, but to students trying to learn through writing, confusion may be the result. And for the teacher, scoring the results of such assignments can be frustrating as well. In this technique, we explore the aspects of student writing that teachers can plan and how teachers can promote planning among their students.

Writing Tasks and Prompts

Like the rules for writing a haiku, the constraints of the writing task can promote deep and critical thinking. Similarly, poorly constructed prompts that do not communicate important information about the writing task may limit what students are able to learn as they write.

How Will Technology Help?

With technology, we can easily publish an anthology of poetry, by printing the pages (takes less room, too) or using a digital format. Throughout the year, the student may keep a portfolio of literary writing (journals, poetry, essays, responses) that can then be published as a book to take home. While we have seen books made of students' pencil-and-paper books, for an adolescent, the notion of having a printed book is more attractive. Teachers can print out and bind the books themselves, but a more professional-looking book may also be professionally printed. For example, we recently used an online printing service to self-publish a book of poetry. The book was 60 pages long and cost $2.30 to publish (of course, shipping was $3.00) but by combining the shipment of several books, the price would be less per item. The Print to Press site was easy to navigate, membership on the site is free, and books are printed within 48 to 72 hours of the receipt of the order. You may edit any part of the book before final submission on this site and see the results. You may upload photographs or other images (for example, when doing the haiku, original student photos or photographed artwork in jpeg format can be uploaded and added to pages and/or cover. For roughly $5.00 per copy, students can have a published book of their writings as a keepsake.

With technology, formats other than books can also be used. If you are writing in response to literature, for example, students can create responses that include various media. Audio and/or video recordings of readings are easily included in electronic response journals (see the Wikispaces example in Technique 28). Podcasting, historical pictures, artwork, photographs taken by the student, and so on may be included, which teaches students how to make academic products more relevant and helps teachers feel more comfortable with the use of technology in their classes.

What Do I Do?

Elements of a Prompt

Teachers typically know what the content or topic of the writing task will be. Discourse type or structure varies in many ways from word choice to sentence structure to genre and purpose. Data and sources present difficulties for a number of reasons. First, students who rely on just one source, for example, a textbook, may not notice the critical attributes of the genre (for example, poetry, essay, short story, critical analysis of literature) as well as they might if they have had multiple exposures to the target concept from multiple sources (Rose & Meyer, 2002). Students who are provided with multiple sources of information and opportunities to read, discuss, and write about those sources are more likely to come to a greater understanding through analysis and evaluation of the sources, one with another. In preparing a prompt for a writing task, teachers should determine whether to name the data sources students will use or whether students will choose the sources for themselves. Both approaches have a place in instruction that includes thinking through writing. When students have access, time, and expert guidance in choosing multiple sources of information, what they learn deepens. Students who read a textbook, compare that information with well-chosen articles (either the student or the teacher might choose the articles), evaluate information from reliable Internet websites, and contrast that with classroom lectures, their learning becomes increasingly sophisticated and rich. As we noted earlier, using both receptive (listening, reading) and expressive (speaking, writing) modalities deepens the learning.

Audience is an assumption about the role of the writer as a competent and knowledgeable communicator, the purposes for writing, and an assumption about the knowledge, dispositions, and competence of the persons who will read the written product. Assumptions about audience change the approach the writer will take in composing a written product. For example, students in math classes learning about measures of central tendency (mean, median, mode) might survey their teen peers about their use of cell phones and text messages, then write a report that is fairly descriptive in nature. However, a daughter writing an argument for increased cell phone privileges will select some data and present it in terms that will demonstrate the advantages to the parent. The purpose for writing changes as the assumptions about the audience changes and what that audience might want or need to know. Therefore, it is helpful for students to develop some sense of who the reader might be and what the writer wants the reading audience to know. In Technique 24, you read about RAFT (Santa, 1988), which stands for role, audience, format, and topic, and RAFTdm. By now, you have seen that the elements of RAFT are the same as those outlined above where format corresponds with discourse type or structure, and role is related to audience in that the role assumed by the writer corresponds to and informs the relationship to the reader.

Example

"Writing good prompts is a challenge," according to author Vicki Spandel (2009, p. 27). She goes on to provide a few useful guidelines. Consider the interests of your students. Have them confer in groups and write lists of things that interest them. They will write more easily about these than about topics of little interest to them. Make sure it is also something that you would write about. Try to make the prompts open ended so that students can express differing viewpoints. When possible, let students select their own topics, but if that isn't possible, try to provide them with a couple of choices.

Spend time reading and deconstructing prompts that appear on writing assessments (you can get the retired prompts from many sources).

Teach students to look for and consider what their main point will be. In a persuasive piece, students need to be very blunt about their main idea! Just that will improve students' thinking about writing to prompts.

Finally, give a prompt and have students write to it. Use a rubric (see Spandel, 2009, pp. 44–46, or write your own) and have students evaluate their own writing to see whether they addressed all the parts of the prompt. Choose some good examples (and save these year to year) to share with students for analysis and debriefing. A brilliant teacher we know always gives back the actual writing assessments with scores from readers and students analyze *why* they got the scores, what they agree or disagree with, and what they would change for the next time. Her students' scores are always above the mean.

PART SIX

Composing
with Multimedia

We need a working definition of composing. How about this: The selection and ordering of ideas or concepts, often in an innovative or transformative way, with attention to the most effective means of communicating to others what has been created. While we have focused on using written language throughout this book, there are other ways of composing a product that meets the working definition above. In Part Six, images, video, and audio media meet written language. Text in many cultures started out as pictures on the wall of a desert canyon or cave wall; with technology, we can improve how we communicate through written language, images, and audio files.

Visualize It!

Cross-reference hashtags: #images, #video, #visualization

What Is It?

Images can complement written language, and they can tell a story or illustrate a point all on their own. With presentation software (for example, PowerPoint, Prezi), Web 2.0 tools (for example, blogs, glogs, and wikis), animation software, and video hosting, the authority of the image or the video is within the grasp of any student and no longer the domain of the Hollywood studio or the museum curator.

Why Is It Important, and How Will Technology Help?

The 21st century offers information visually in so many ways from image search tools to the software that allows students to compose images by mashup or derivative works from other sources. Throughout this book, we have explored together how human brains use ideas and information from other sources to transform that knowledge, own it, and share it creatively and purposefully. Images and video are equally important sources, just as articles and books are, on which young writers can draw.

What Do I Do?

◆ For student-learning tasks, create choices of media based on the strengths of each medium, the needs of the audience, and the purpose for composing with the selected media.

◆ Create a plan students can use to guide them in using media for the purpose of transforming knowledge and communicating that knowledge to others. Ask, "How will I know whether the students have learned from the multimedia product? How will students know whether they have learned and how will they articulate this learning?" An electronic poster (for example, a glog) may have a variety of images in a collage, but a variety of images on their own may not represent transformative thinking. Ask, "How might images and language be combined to enhance the communicative power of both?"

◆ Design assessment tools that underscore the type of thinking you are trying to promote.

Example: The Power of One

"Real-Time" Teaching by Stacy Miller, Patch American High School, Stuttgart, Germany

Thomas Cahill wrote, "The historian's principle task should be to raise the dead to life" (2003, p. 8). It's one thing to write a research paper on the life of someone who changed the world; it's another to make that person *real*. My tenth-grade integrated honors students have the opportunity to complete a year-long culminating project called the Power of One that would make Cahill proud. My writers bring their subjects to life. I require students to use a minimum of eight sources and a total of 25 cards, but the cards may be PowerPoint slides converted for use as a research tool. Students read and write about their subjects in short projects all year. During Quarter 4, we get to meet the subjects. They come to life through multimedia presentations. Students use the background information they obtained during Quarter 1, the research they compiled during Quarter 2, and the outline of the paper they wrote in Quarter 3 to create short presentations (no fewer than 3 minutes and 30 seconds and no longer than 4 minutes) that are mini-movies of the lives of their subjects.

I do not require that students use a specific program for creating their projects. While most are comfortable with the PowerPoint presentation that provides easy-to-follow templates, other students are comfortable with a range of programs and wouldn't want to be limited or constrained by the programs we have on our computers at school. I've had two students—future DreamWorks CEOs—hand illustrate and narrate their projects, including voiceovers that would excite even Professor Henry Higgins. As far as I'm concerned, as long as the final product meets the requirements for the assignment, the sky is the limit when it comes to production. Some students create their projects on the computers we have here at school and many use their newer, faster computers at home. One of the biggest challenges regarding the project is related to the technology involved. No matter how they create the program, it must be playable on my school computer. This may mean saving the project as an older version of a program or downloading plug-ins. The projects inspire.

In place of a second-semester final exam, we invite the parents to join us in the classroom for the world premier of the students' projects. As the students are told from the beginning that their subjects must have had a positive, significant impact on society, we're basically watching 3 hours' worth of inspirational, motivational films. I've learned more about Stephen Hawking and Johann Gutenberg (see Figure

32.1) than I ever could through a textbook, and the project allows us not only to learn about the subject of the presentation, but to learn about that person through the eyes of the student who created the project. We get to see what Stephen Hawking meant to Zach, what Johann Gutenberg meant to Will, and what Rachel Carson meant to Tess. The students' personalities and creativity are paramount to the projects and instead of getting the encyclopedia version of the story, we get emotion. We get drama. We know these people who changed our world.

In addition to what we see and read on the screen, we are also moved by what we hear. This is the fourth year doing the project, and I use student projects from the previous years as exemplars. We get to see why using a swirly, cursive font over a busy, colored picture is unreadable. We get to see why using a red font on a pink background is unreadable. We get to see why *scrolling text* is code for *migraine*. We get to see that a picture really is worth a thousand words and sometimes it's the simplicity that makes the project work. We get to see why the transitions and details are important and how a picture of Kofi Annan accepting the Nobel Prize followed by a (random) picture of a tree Annan planted takes away from the previous picture.

We use music. I play movie soundtracks in class while the kids write in their journals and this gives a feel for the evocative power of music. Students know that Hans Zimmer's scores can excite and incite, and that "Bagger and Hardy Measure the Course at Night" from Rachel Portman's *The Legend of Bagger Vance* (2000) is ethereal and mysterious. Through the exemplars, students get a feel for what music works best, and that one simple, moving piece is better than four or five that might match the pictures or text on the screen but take away from the overall effect.

Putting the projects together takes a bit of organization but the thing to do is start with the script of what text should be included in the project and go from there. For storyboards, I have students bring in printed screenshots or PowerPoint slides so I can make notes and proofread and edit where possible. This allows me to see the organizational pattern of the project, as well as what fonts, pictures, and

FIGURE 32.1. Power of One by Will Viana. Available at *http://vimeo.com/13422854.* Reprinted by permission.

graphics are being used. I can point out erroneous information and ask questions about information I'd like to see added to the project before it is completed. I also get to see how invested the students become in the research. We're lucky to live in Europe. Will went to the Gutenberg Museum in Mainz to see one of the surviving Gutenberg bibles. Paige went to Normandy to walk in the footsteps of Winters and his men. Will's initial video posted to YouTube was entirely an animation showing an animated Gutenberg talking about his invention. Subsequent revisions showed a real-life Will talking to an animated Gutenberg in a 21st-century living room. Each revision reflected greater and greater transformation of Will's thinking about his subject's contribution over the centuries and into the digital age.

Audio Podcasting
It's "Ear-resistible!"

Cross-reference hashtag: #podcasting

What Is It?

Audio podcasting can take many forms when students are asked to create the media. When complex ideas are explored in disciplinary contexts, students and teachers often draw on many sources of information as they transform ideas from their static form to dynamic understanding. Podcasts are defined as "pre-recorded audio programs that are posted to a website and made available for download so people can listen to them on personal computers or mobile devices" (Entrepreneur, 2010, n.p.). Creating an MP3 or other audio file is similar to the older technology of radio broadcasting or tape recording spoken language; however, it has advantages that these 20th-century technologies did not. An MP3 file is recorded digitally and the resulting file may be posted to a website and/or downloaded to an MP3 player, such as an iPod.

We have used podcasts in our own teaching with secondary-teacher candidates with marked success. We found that academic uses of podcasting could be teacher or student centered. This depends on the purpose for the podcast.

Why Is It Important?

Adolescents often have acquired useful levels of literacy skills, but they are faced with learning the *practices* of the various content areas they learn about in secondary and postsecondary schooling. At the heart of this is the application of literacy processes in more complex and authentic ways (for example, Marzano, 2004; Moje,

---

We thank Denise Johnson for ideas in this chapter.

Young, Readence, & Moore, 2000). Literacy is essential for effective and meaningful learning in all disciplinary areas (Moje, 2008). In order for students to engage with content, they must have foundational skills and attitudes that allow them to understand the relevance (importance) of active efforts to understand new concepts and ideas. Part of this is dispositional—they must possess or develop openness to learning. Part of it is experiential in that students must be involved in and with gradually more complex texts and analyses of texts.

How Will Technology Help?

As students grapple with discipline-specific learning, they must also learn the skills and dispositions necessary to navigate 21st-century information sources. Because the technologies change rapidly, these skills and dispositions must also evolve very quickly (Leu, Kinzer, Coiro, & Cammack, 2004). As a result, the proficiencies one has today may not be as effective next year when the tool has evolved or changed in some substantive way.

Technology recenters the dynamic of education from lecturer centered to learner centered. Podcasting is a recent technology innovation that combines the Internet with MP3 files downloadable to an iPod or personal computer.

We believe that the type of technology we employ isn't the main consideration. We argue that the difference lies along a continuum where a teacher (or a teacher educator) may believe or decide that some tasks require students to be involved in decisions and activities that affect their own learning. This, in turn, rests upon teacher dispositions toward student-centered learning and the skill with which the teacher applies his or her knowledge of content, selecting teaching strategies that are appropriate to students and context, and then considering the proper tools for learning.

In the case of "writing," we suggest that composing is not wholly a writing task; that is, composing is not always about pencil on paper or fingers on a keyboard. With today's evolving technologies, there are widely varying considerations in composing, such as collaborative online composition, shared tools such as Google Docs and VoiceThread, inclusion of multimedia texts such as audio and video, and the prevalence of graphics and color in composition. For examples of audio podcasts by our secondary-teacher candidates in different content areas, see *google.com/site/ audiopodcasts.*

What Do I Do?

Podcasts, similar to other effective composing tasks, may call for middle and high school students to transform knowledge and turn it toward more complex and specific purposes that meet their academic learning needs. The composing activities of planning, reflecting, and revising are evident in many podcasts, both those composed for the popular audiences via tools such as iTunes and those composed for the academic purposes of teacher preparation programs.

For teachers, podcasts are a way to scaffold student learning. When using lectures, record yourself and make your lectures available on your school and/or classroom website. Students may download your podcasts and listen to them again. For students with learning difficulties and/or reading difficulties, these may provide access to the content.

For your students, experiment with podcasts as ways of composing and transforming content learning. An important theoretical perspective comes from technology and "new literacies," which are frequently performance-oriented, multivoiced, and complex (for example, International Reading Association, 2009; Lewis & Fabos, 2005; New London Group, 1996). Embracing new or multiliteracies requires an expanded definition of literacy that includes practices in virtually all content areas and across a variety of media.

Example

Mr. Coley's fifth-grade students have created audio podcasts on many topics that he posts to his classroom website (*http://www.mrcoley.com/coleycast/index.htm*). On the website, he states, "ColeyCast is Room 34's very own podcast! Recorded by the students, each broadcast highlights some of the exciting things we're learning in our classroom." At the site, he provides a link for teachers who wish to try podcasting with their students.

Once on the site, you "mouse over" the podcast of your choice and sit back to listen to the students of Room 34 broadcast their knowledge about different topics. There are 53 (as of July 14, 2011) podcasts on Mr. Coley's website. Number 52 is amazing facts about America, three facts provided by each of the 33 students in Mr. Coley's class (this is a long podcast!). Podcast 53 is the students of Mr. Coley's classroom broadcasting their literature "book trailers" or summaries and responses to the literature they are reading. The first one is on *Fever, 1793* (Anderson, 2000), and the student who recorded this segment is very enthusiastic about the book. Take some time to listen to Mr. Coley's students' podcasts. They are using digital technology for academic purposes. Next year, Mr. Coley will assume a new job as principal of another school in the district, but he plans to leave his website up for teachers and students to enjoy.

PART SEVEN

Wrapping It Up

We come to the end of our work—almost. There are a few topics that we need to address before we close. We run into teachers who tell us, "We are not allowed to use anything from YouTube!" Or, they will say, "The district won't let our students go on the Internet, because students might find something objectionable." Well, we say, they might. Those very students are out on the Internet and surfing YouTube when not in school. We counter that teachers have a responsibility to make sure their students learn how to be responsible Internet citizens. In addition, we need to ensure that they are critical users of digital technologies. Teachers can be the most effective advocates for responsible digital policies. We start with advocacy.

Advocacy for Technology and New Literacies

Cross-reference hashtags: #advocacy, #art, #languagearts, #newliteracies

What Is It, and Why Is It Important?

In the early years of the 21st century, the Internet became ubiquitous. In the introduction to Chip Bruce's groundbreaking book *Literacy in the Information Age: Inquiries into Meaning Making with New Technologies* (2003), Allan Luke talks about how schools and educational institutions must grapple, not just with rapidly evolving technologies, but also with new forms of human *techne* in all walks of life, the complex effects of cultural and economic globalization, and the plight of print-trained teachers (pp. viii–ix). Since the publication of Bruce's book, we have seen incredible changes in the technologies that are now common to communication and we have seen changes in the students who are immersed in such technologies (Rosen, 2010). But Bruce's organizing questions (p. 1) remain the same: "How do young people make meaning as they both respond to and create texts with the new media?" and "How are cultural meanings reinforced or reformulated through new modes of expression?" We believe those questions are even more germane today. And it is even more incumbent upon the educational establishment to respond in appropriate ways. Denying the existence of these new modes of communication is really not an option if schools are to be at all relevant to students' lives. Bruce provides us with historical literacy transformations (p. 15):

Primitive symbol systems
Complex oral language
Early writing
Manuscript literacy

> Print literacy
> Video literacy
> Digital/multimediat/hypertext literacy
> Virtual reality

What Do I Do, and How Will Technology Help?

So, where does that leave us when we are discouraged from using the new tools of communication in our schools? Bruce (2003) would recommend a "utilitarian" stance—we need to evaluate and use these new tools. We need to teach our students to "learn how to learn" in this rapidly evolving world we inhabit.

Thus we suggest thinking out of the box and finding ways to change the stances of those schools, districts, and administrators who are fearful of underage students being exposed to the uncensored content of the Internet. For example, art on the web has created a wonderfully enriched body of work that is readily available to our students.

Example: Using Web Resources in Art at Metro High

Can we get specific permissions to use particular pieces in the classroom? What do we need to do to get this limited permission? What evidence and arguments must we provide and to whom do we provide them? What regulations exist and what exceptions are possible?

Vince Vango is an art teacher who sought approval for a unit on modern art he was planning for his junior art students. He decided to assign student groups to websites that featured modern art. He decided that students would visit the websites, collect information and images, and provide a PowerPoint report in class. He found the following sites:

Heidelberg Project: *http://heidelberg.org*
Metropolitan Museum of Art: *http://www.metmuseum.org/toah/intro/atr/02sm.htm* (includes the Heilbrunn Timeline of Art History)
Google Images: *http://google.com*
Web Gallery of Art: *http://www.wga.hu*
San Francisco Museum of Modern Art: *http://www.sfmoma.org/projects/artscope/index.html*

After Mr. Vango found the sites, he contacted his principal about getting approval for students to visit the websites. There was a process he needed to go through to get a specific exception to the general rule. He filled out the paperwork, made a presentation at a school board meeting, and eventually got specific approval for this project only. The rules didn't change, but one more successful project was conducted.

Advocacy for students' access to Web 2.0 technologies is essential if we are to make our schools responsive to student needs and enable students to operate successfully in their own futures. Reasonable policies need to be in play for the cyber-safety of students (Frey et al., 2010), but we need to be careful not to overstate the dangers. The academic benefits that Web 2.0 technologies provide to students far outweigh the potential risks. We teach students to be safe when crossing the street, when learning to drive, when beginning to date. We teach them to be careful. We do our best to teach our students to be critical of what they read—there is as much misinformation in printed materials as there is in online materials. We teach our students to be critical of what they read.

High-Stakes Writing Assessments

Cross-reference hashtag: #assessment

What Are They?

High-stakes writing assessments are those that students must complete with long-term ramifications for students that may impact graduation, entrance into college, obtaining a job, and so on. They are also assessments with long-term and significant impacts on the schools and the curriculum enacted there.

Why Are They Important?

Performance on college entrance assessments and high school exit exams with a writing component carries with it high stakes for students, teachers, and schools. For example, a graduation requirement in California is attaining a successful score on the California High School Exit Exam (known as CAHSEE; California Department of Education, 2010) that includes an on-demand response to a writing task. Some colleges and universities either require or recommend that students who want to enter their programs must complete the writing test on a college entrance exam. Most school districts or states also administer an on-demand writing assessment to students in selected grade levels.

What Do I Do, and How Will Technology Help?

◆ Consider and discuss the parameters of the writing for a given type of assessment and in relation to the models.

◆ Consider and discuss what the purpose of the writing task (as represented by the model) might be.

◆ To this, we add that teachers consider the effect, called "washback," of such tests on teaching and instruction (Alderson & Wall, 1993).

Additional Resource

Gere, A., Christenbury, L., & Sassi, K. (2005). *Writing on demand: Best practices and strategies for success*. Portsmouth, NH: Heinemann.

Automated Tools

Cross-reference hashtag: #tools

What Are They?

A number of tools are increasingly available to teachers and students that may automate some tasks associated with writing. Plagiarism detection and automated essay scoring are two of these. Plagiarism detection services compare student writing with databases of Internet and other electronic resources and sometimes with other students' work. Automated essay scoring makes it possible for students and teachers to derive a score for some aspects of written work automatically when a written product is submitted.

Why Are They Important?

As the use of automated online tools are increasingly adopted by schools and other educational agencies, teachers will want to know the degree to which they can or should rely on these tools.

What Do I Do?

◆ Know the limitations of the tool or service. For example, automated essay scoring is often more effective at evaluating usage and style matters than it is at evaluating content (compare Kellogg, Whiteford, & Quinlan, 2010).

◆ Teach students to use plagiarism and automated scoring tools to improve their writing. Students may wish to submit drafts of their work to these tools in order to ensure they have correctly cited sources, to help them make word choices thought-fully, and to attend to matters of style.

◆ Vary topics and prompts so that they are not easily copied from other sources or recycled from one class to another.

Additional Resource

http://www.delicious.com/TDWolsey/plagiarism

Publication

Cross-reference hashtag: #publication

> I wish we could change the world by creating powerful writers for forever instead of just indifferent writers for school.
> —MEM FOX (1993, p. 22)

We concur with Mem Fox (to hear her read her own work, such as *Koala Lou*, go to *http://www.memfox.net/mem-reads-aloud*) and with William Zinsser (1988) that "Writing is a form of thinking, whatever the subject" (p. vii). The ultimate aim of writing, whether scroll, book, or website, is communication through publication.

What Is It?

Publication of writing is defined in many ways. Tompkins (2003), in her description of the writing process, refers to it as "Stage 5" where students "Publish writing in an appropriate form. Share finished writing with an appropriate audience" (p. 7). Tompkins and others provide excellent suggestions for publication of students' writing. Spandel and Stiggins (1997) provide a two-page appendix in their book on outlets for student writing (places that publish student writing). Indeed, your authors coedited the California Reading Association's scholarly journal, *The California Reader*, which annually publishes the winning essays by students in its pages. But we would argue that audiences are often hypothetical (and in reality the teacher is the audience) and that publication is often putative, and little of it intended even for a bulletin board or a portfolio. Often, the audience is just the student. And perhaps that is enough.

Why Is It Important?

If we have something to say, we usually need someone to listen or read. But writing to learn (writing as thinking) needs corroboration and/or counterpoint in order to be more effective. The language arts are often conceptualized as two receptive processes—listening and reading—and two expressive processes—speaking and writing. When we have students engage in all four processes during the course of a lesson or unit, then we increase the chances that the learning will be deep enough to become part of our knowledge base (Marzano, 2004). Thus, two audiences are essential: the teacher and other students. While we want to encourage our students to publish more widely, day-to-day writing to learn means a smaller audience. What we have focused on is the gradual movement from knowledge telling to knowledge transformation (Bereiter & Scardamalia, 1987). Publishing students' writing means attending to an audience that is in the transformation of knowledge, not just reporting it.

How Will Technology Help?

Throughout this book we have provided many examples of technology assisting with writing instruction. Embedded in those examples are how technology can help. So we'd like to take you on a little tour of the publication possibilities that have already appeared in preceding techniques.

Part One

- ◆ Mrs. Gabriel's science students posted blog entries on the class webpage and published their answers and opinions to online surveys and polls.
- ◆ Students' work may be archived electronically as podcasts, vidcasts, or screencasts.
- ◆ Publish writing on the class homepage (for example, Mr. Coley).

Part Two

- ◆ Wikis and Google Docs.
- ◆ E-mails to the teacher's e-mail folder (see Mrs. Wozniak's writing assignment).
- ◆ Post to Blackboard, e-College, or Moodle (course management systems).
- ◆ Turn in student work to the class webpage or a cloud computing account (such as *Box.net*).
- ◆ Use and share social bookmarking resources.
- ◆ Ms. Nation's science students' use of PowerPoint (and other presentation software).

Part Three

- Ms. Kretschmar's use of Excel sheets for data mining of surveys and traditional print publication of shark information essays.
- Mr. Hemming's students' PowerPoint book reports, including multimedia.
- Tweeting in Ms. Obi's eighth-grade science class.
- Electronic entry or exit slips.
- Electronic journaling (Penzu Post, 1-minute papers, and Ms. Gabriel's humanities core).
- Blogs and classroom websites, such as Mr. Coley's.
- Online literature discussions and nonfiction text discussions.
- VoiceThreads for literature or vocabulary.
- Vocabulary video presentation (vocab vids).
- Collective or team writing to illustrate vocabulary words.
- Kristy Brown's language arts graffiti wall.
- Shared documents and website—Google Docs and TypeWithMe.
- Gina Girlando's online research paper in Wikispaces.
- Texting or tweeting in Ms. Cristobal's high school English class.

Part Four

- Ms. Nial's and Ms. Ondas's short writings on e-College on waves of water and waves of light (connecting and applying knowledge)—and building on electronic posts.
- Electronic summarizing and team inquiry in Mr. Boer's class (and website evaluation).
- RAFTdm (dm = digital media) in Mr. Hemming's class for memoirs on the Holocaust including VoiceThread.
- RAFTdm in Mr. Matica's middle school algebra class.
- Coach Kardio's assignment of a written analysis of three training regimens (threaded discussion, social networking, websources, quickwrites at computer stations, and publication on a wiki).
- Online tools for graphic organizers used by Coach Kardio (I-chart).
- Feedback, rubrics, and assessments using online tools (see sticky notes)—these are essential to students for audience awareness and publication.

Part Five

- Wikispaces for posting collaborative summaries and responses (LRCSummaries *Of Mice and Men* featuring 11th graders Laila, Nathan, and Lindsey).
- PBworks and Google Docs.
- Teen Ink for authentic student work and critiques.
- Podcasting at Kidcast for Teachers and having our students create them.
- Podbean for publishing podcasts.
- Pro/con "discussions" done electronically (Zwiers, 2008).

◆ Writing Haiku online and including multimedia.

◆ Having student portfolios (electronic) printed as keepsakes.

Part Six

◆ Stacy Miller's Power of One multimedia project.

◆ Mr. Coley's student-created podcasts.

To summarize, there are new outlets for publication of student work that are afforded by technology. Many of these are the same as the old forms (such as printed books, rather than photocopies of pencil-and-paper writing) but some are new and offer students a more compelling academic reason for social networking, such as Twitter and other types of electronic collaboration. We think the reasons for publication are the same as before. We wish to validate and congratulate our students for their thinking and learning. We know that most of our students will write in various genre (mostly practical) during their lives. Learning to write well means learning to think well, if we can believe our many writing mentors.

Teachers can begin to think about how their students' writing can be preserved. A student's portfolio of writings for their entire school career can be contained on a flash drive (backed up, of course!).

Common Core Content Standards for Writing, Grades 6–12

The following standards for grades 6–12 offer a focus for instruction each year to help ensure that students gain adequate mastery of a range of skills and applications. Each year in their writing, students should demonstrate increasing sophistication in all aspects of language use, from vocabulary and syntax to the development and organization of ideas, and they should address increasingly demanding content and sources. Students advancing through the grades are expected to meet each year's grade-specific standards and retain or further develop skills and understandings mastered in preceding grades. The expected growth in student writing ability is reflected both in the standards themselves and in the collection of annotated student writing samples.

Grade 6 Students	Grade 7 Students	Grade 8 Students
Text Types and Purposes		

1. Write arguments to support claims with clear reasons and relevant evidence.
   a. Introduce claim(s) and organize the reasons and evidence clearly.
   b. Support claim(s) with clear reasons and relevant evidence, using credible sources and demonstrating an understanding of the topic or text.
	1. Write arguments to support claims with clear reasons and relevant evidence.
	   a. Introduce claim(s), acknowledge alternate or opposing claims, and organize the reasons and evidence logically.
	   b. Support claim(s) with logical reasoning and relevant evidence, using accurate, credible sources and demonstrating an
		1. Write arguments to support claims with clear reasons and relevant evidence.
		   a. Introduce claim(s), acknowledge and distinguish the claim(s) from alternate or opposing claims, and organize the reasons and evidence logically.
		   b. Support claim(s) with logical reasoning and relevant evidence, using accurate, credible

Grade 6 Students	Grade 7 Students	Grade 8 Students
c. Use words, phrases, and clauses to clarify the relationships among claim(s) and reasons. **d.** Establish and maintain a formal style. **e.** Provide a concluding statement or section that follows from the argument presented.	understanding of the topic or text. **c.** Use words, phrases, and clauses to create cohesion and clarify the relationships among claim(s), reasons, and evidence. **d.** Establish and maintain a formal style. **e.** Provide a concluding statement or section that follows from and supports the argument presented.	sources and demonstrating an understanding of the topic or text. **c.** Use words, phrases, and clauses to create cohesion and clarify the relationships among claim(s), counterclaims, reasons, and evidence. **d.** Establish and maintain a formal style. **e.** Provide a concluding statement or section that follows from and supports the argument presented.

2. Write informative/explanatory texts to examine a topic and convey ideas, concepts, and information through the selection, organization, and analysis of relevant content.
    a. Introduce a topic; organize ideas, concepts, and information, using strategies such as definition, classification, comparison/contrast, and cause/effect; include formatting (e.g., headings), graphics (e.g., charts, tables), and multimedia when useful to aiding comprehension.
    b. Develop the topic with relevant facts, definitions, concrete details, quotations, or other information and examples.
    c. Use appropriate transitions to clarify the relationships among ideas and concepts.
    d. Use precise language and domain-specific vocabulary to inform about or explain the topic.
    e. Establish and maintain a formal style.
    f. Provide a concluding statement or section that follows from the information or explanation presented.
	2. Write informative/explanatory texts to examine a topic and convey ideas, concepts, and information through the selection, organization, and analysis of relevant content.
	    a. Introduce a topic clearly, previewing what is to follow; organize ideas, concepts, and information, using strategies such as definition, classification, comparison/contrast, and cause/effect; include formatting (e.g., headings), graphics (e.g., charts, tables), and multimedia when useful to aiding comprehension.
	    b. Develop the topic with relevant facts, definitions, concrete details, quotations, or other information and examples.
	    c. Use appropriate transitions to create cohesion and clarify the relationships among ideas and concepts.
	    d. Use precise language and domain-specific vocabulary to inform about or explain the topic.
	    e. Establish and maintain a formal style.
	    f. Provide a concluding statement or section that follows from and supports the information or explanation presented.
		2. Write informative/explanatory texts to examine a topic and convey ideas, concepts, and information through the selection, organization, and analysis of relevant content.
		    a. Introduce a topic clearly, previewing what is to follow; organize ideas, concepts, and information into broader categories; include formatting (e.g., headings), graphics (e.g., charts, tables), and multimedia when useful to aiding comprehension.
		    b. Develop the topic with relevant, well-chosen facts, definitions, concrete details, quotations, or other information and examples.
		    c. Use appropriate and varied transitions to create cohesion and clarify the relationships among ideas and concepts.
		    d. Use precise language and domain-specific vocabulary to inform about or explain the topic.
		    e. Establish and maintain a formal style.
		    f. Provide a concluding statement or section that follows from and supports the information or explanation presented.

Grade 6 Students	Grade 7 Students	Grade 8 Students
3. Write narratives to develop real or imagined experiences or events using effective technique, relevant descriptive details, and well-structured event sequences. 　**a.** Engage and orient the reader by establishing a context and introducing a narrator and/or characters; organize an event sequence that unfolds naturally and logically. 　**b.** Use narrative techniques, such as dialogue, pacing, and description, to develop experiences, events, and/or characters. 　**c.** Use a variety of transition words, phrases, and clauses to convey sequence and signal shifts from one time frame or setting to another. 　**d.** Use precise words and phrases, relevant descriptive details, and sensory language to convey experiences and events. 　**e.** Provide a conclusion that follows from the narrated experiences or events.	**3.** Write narratives to develop real or imagined experiences or events using effective technique, relevant descriptive details, and well-structured event sequences. 　**a.** Engage and orient the reader by establishing a context and point of view and introducing a narrator and/or characters; organize an event sequence that unfolds naturally and logically. 　**b.** Use narrative techniques, such as dialogue, pacing, and description, to develop experiences, events, and/or characters. 　**c.** Use a variety of transition words, phrases, and clauses to convey sequence and signal shifts from one time frame or setting to another. 　**d.** Use precise words and phrases, relevant descriptive details, and sensory language to capture the action and convey experiences and events. 　**e.** Provide a conclusion that follows from and reflects on the narrated experiences or events.	**3.** Write narratives to develop real or imagined experiences or events using effective technique, relevant descriptive details, and well-structured event sequences. 　**a.** Engage and orient the reader by establishing a context and point of view and introducing a narrator and/or characters; organize an event sequence that unfolds naturally and logically. 　**b.** Use narrative techniques, such as dialogue, pacing, and description, to develop experiences, events, and/or characters. 　**c.** Use a variety of transition words, phrases, and clauses to convey sequence, signal shifts from one time frame or setting to another, and show the relationships among experiences and events. 　**e.** Provide a conclusion that follows from and reflects on the narrated experiences or events.
4. Produce clear and coherent writing in which the development, organization, and style are appropriate to task, purpose, and audience. (Grade-specific expectations for writing types are defined in standards 1–3 above.)	**4.** Produce clear and coherent writing in which the development, organization, and style are appropriate to task, purpose, and audience. (Grade-specific expectations for writing types are defined in standards 1–3 above.)	**4.** Produce clear and coherent writing in which the development, organization, and style are appropriate to task, purpose, and audience. (Grade-specific expectations for writing types are defined in standards 1–3 above.)
5. With some guidance and support from peers and adults, develop and strengthen writing as needed by planning, revising, editing, rewriting, or trying a new approach. (Editing for conventions should demonstrate command of Language standards 1–3 up to and including grade 6.)	**5.** With some guidance and support from peers and adults, develop and strengthen writing as needed by planning, revising, editing, rewriting, or trying a new approach, focusing on how well purpose and audience have been addressed. (Editing for conventions should demonstrate command of Language standards 1–3 up to and including grade 7.)	**5.** With some guidance and support from peers and adults, develop and strengthen writing as needed by planning, revising, editing, rewriting, or trying a new approach, focusing on how well purpose and audience have been addressed. (Editing for conventions should demonstrate command of Language standards 1–3 up to and including grade 8.)

Grade 6 Students	Grade 7 Students	Grade 8 Students
6. Use technology, including the Internet, to produce and publish writing as well as to interact and collaborate with others; demonstrate sufficient command of keyboarding skills to type a minimum of three pages in a single sitting.	**6.** Use technology, including the Internet, to produce and publish writing and link to and cite sources as well as to interact and collaborate with others, including linking to and citing sources.	**6.** Use technology, including the Internet, to produce and publish writing and present the relationships between information and ideas efficiently as well as to interact and collaborate with others.
Research to Build and Present Knowledge		
7. Conduct short research projects to answer a question, drawing on several sources and refocusing the inquiry when appropriate.	**7.** Conduct short research projects to answer a question, drawing on several sources and generating additional related, focused questions for further research and investigation.	**7.** Conduct short research projects to answer a question (including a self-generated question), drawing on several sources and generating additional related, focused questions that allow for multiple avenues of exploration.
8. Gather relevant information from multiple print and digital sources; assess the credibility of each source; and quote or paraphrase the data and conclusions of others while avoiding plagiarism and providing basic bibliographic information for sources.	**8.** Gather relevant information from multiple print and digital sources, using search terms effectively; assess the credibility and accuracy of each source; and quote or paraphrase the data and conclusions of others while avoiding plagiarism and following a standard format for citation.	**8.** Gather relevant information from multiple print and digital sources, using search terms effectively; assess the credibility and accuracy of each source; and quote or paraphrase the data and conclusions of others while avoiding plagiarism and following a standard format for citation.
9. Draw evidence from literary or informational texts to support analysis, reflection, and research. **a.** Apply grade 6 Reading standards to literature (e.g., "Compare and contrast texts in different forms or genres [e.g., stories and poems; historical novels and fantasy stories] in terms of their approaches to similar themes and topics"). **b.** Apply grade 6 Reading standards to literary nonfiction (e.g., "Trace and evaluate the argument and specific claims in a text, distinguishing claims that are supported by reasons and evidence from claims that are not").	**9.** Draw evidence from literary or informational texts to support analysis, reflection, and research. **a.** Apply grade 7 Reading standards to literature (e.g., "Compare and contrast a fictional portrayal of a time, place, or character and a historical account of the same period as a means of understanding how authors of fiction use or alter history"). **b.** Apply grade 7 Reading standards to literary nonfiction (e.g., "Trace and evaluate the argument and specific claims in a text, assessing whether the reasoning is sound and the evidence is relevant and sufficient to support the claims").	**9.** Draw evidence from literary or informational texts to support analysis, reflection, and research. **a.** Apply grade 8 Reading standards to literature (e.g., "Analyze how a modern work of fiction draws on themes, patterns of events, or character types from myths, traditional stories, or religious works such as the Bible, including describing how the material is rendered new"). **b.** Apply grade 8 Reading standards to literary nonfiction (e.g., "Delineate and evaluate the argument and specific claims in a text, assessing whether the reasoning is sound and the evidence is relevant and sufficient; recognize when irrelevant evidence is introduced").

Grade 6 Students	Grade 7 Students	Grade 8 Students
Range of Writing		
10. Write routinely over extended time frames (time for research, reflection, and revision) and shorter time frames (a single sitting or a day or two) for a range of discipline-specific tasks, purposes, and audiences.	**10.** Write routinely over extended time frames (time for research, reflection, and revision) and shorter time frames (a single sitting or a day or two) for a range of discipline-specific tasks, purposes, and audiences.	**10.** Write routinely over extended time frames (time for research, reflection, and revision) and shorter time frames (a single sitting or a day or two) for a range of discipline-specific tasks, purposes, and audiences.

The CCR anchor standards and high school grade-specific standards work in tandem to define college and career readiness expectations—the former providing broad standards, the latter providing additional specificity.

Grades 9–10 Students	Grades 11–12 Students
Text Types and Purposes	
1. Write arguments to support claims in an analysis of substantive topics or texts, using valid reasoning and relevant and sufficient evidence. **a.** Introduce precise claim(s), distinguish the claim(s) from alternate or opposing claims, and create an organization that establishes clear relationships among claim(s), counterclaims, reasons, and evidence. **b.** Develop claim(s) and counterclaims fairly, supplying evidence for each while pointing out the strengths and limitations of both in a manner that anticipates the audience's knowledge level and concerns. **c.** Use words, phrases, and clauses to link the major sections of the text, create cohesion, and clarify the relationships between claim(s) and reasons, between reasons and evidence, and between claim(s) and counterclaims. **d.** Establish and maintain a formal style and objective tone while attending to the norms and conventions of the discipline in which they are writing. **e.** Provide a concluding statement or section that follows from and supports the argument presented.	**1.** Write arguments to support claims in an analysis of substantive topics or texts, using valid reasoning and relevant and sufficient evidence. **a.** Introduce precise, knowledgeable claim(s), establish the significance of the claim(s), distinguish the claim(s) from alternate or opposing claims, and create an organization that logically sequences claim(s), counterclaims, reasons, and evidence. **b.** Develop claim(s) and counterclaims fairly and thoroughly, supplying the most relevant evidence for each while pointing out the strengths and limitations of both in a manner that anticipates the audience's knowledge level, concerns, values, and possible biases. **c.** Use words, phrases, and clauses as well as varied syntax to link the major sections of the text, create cohesion, and clarify the relationships between claim(s) and reasons, between reasons and evidence, and between claim(s) and counterclaims. **d.** Establish and maintain a formal style and objective tone while attending to the norms and conventions of the discipline in which they are writing. **e.** Provide a concluding statement or section that follows from and supports the argument presented.
2. Write informative/explanatory texts to examine and convey complex ideas, concepts, and information clearly and accurately through the effective selection, organization, and analysis of content. **a.** Introduce a topic; organize complex ideas,	**2.** Write informative/explanatory texts to examine and convey complex ideas, concepts, and information clearly and accurately through the effective selection, organization, and analysis of content. **a.** Introduce a topic; organize complex ideas,

Grades 9–10 Students	Grades 11–12 Students
concepts, and information to make important connections and distinctions; include formatting (e.g., headings), graphics (e.g., figures, tables), and multimedia when useful to aiding comprehension. **b.** Develop the topic with well-chosen, relevant, and sufficient facts, extended definitions, concrete details, quotations, or other information and examples appropriate to the audience's knowledge of the topic. **c.** Use appropriate and varied transitions to link the major sections of the text, create cohesion, and clarify the relationships among complex ideas and concepts. **d.** Use precise language and domain-specific vocabulary to manage the complexity of the topic. **e.** Establish and maintain a formal style and objective tone while attending to the norms and conventions of the discipline in which they are writing. **f.** Provide a concluding statement or section that follows from and supports the information or explanation presented (e.g., articulating implications or the significance of the topic).	concepts, and information so that each new element builds on that which precedes it to create a unified whole; include formatting (e.g., headings), graphics (e.g., figures, tables), and multimedia when useful to aiding comprehension. **b.** Develop the topic thoroughly by selecting the most significant and relevant facts, extended definitions, concrete details, quotations, or other information and examples appropriate to the audience's knowledge of the topic. **c.** Use appropriate and varied transitions and syntax to link the major sections of the text, create cohesion, and clarify the relationships among complex ideas and concepts. **d.** Use precise language, domain-specific vocabulary, and techniques such as metaphor, simile, and analogy to manage the complexity of the topic. **e.** Establish and maintain a formal style and objective tone while attending to the norms and conventions of the discipline in which they are writing. **f.** Provide a concluding statement or section that follows from and supports the information or explanation presented (e.g., articulating implications or the significance of the topic).
3. Write narratives to develop real or imagined experiences or events using effective technique, well-chosen details, and well-structured event sequences. **a.** Engage and orient the reader by setting out a problem, situation, or observation, establishing one or multiple point(s) of view, and introducing a narrator and/or characters; create a smooth progression of experiences or events. **b.** Use narrative techniques, such as dialogue, pacing, description, reflection, and multiple plot lines, to develop experiences, events, and/or characters. **c.** Use a variety of techniques to sequence events so that they build on one another to create a coherent whole. **d.** Use precise words and phrases, telling details, and sensory language to convey a vivid picture of the experiences, events, setting, and/or characters. **e.** Provide a conclusion that follows from and reflects on what is experienced, observed, or resolved over the course of the narrative.	**3.** Write narratives to develop real or imagined experiences or events using effective technique, well-chosen details, and well-structured event sequences. **a.** Engage and orient the reader by setting out a problem, situation, or observation and its significance, establishing one or multiple point(s) of view, and introducing a narrator and/or characters; create a smooth progression of experiences or events. **b.** Use narrative techniques, such as dialogue, pacing, description, reflection, and multiple plot lines, to develop experiences, events, and/or characters. **c.** Use a variety of techniques to sequence events so that they build on one another to create a coherent whole and build toward a particular tone and outcome (e.g., a sense of mystery, suspense, growth, or resolution). **d.** Use precise words and phrases, telling details, and sensory language to convey a vivid picture of the experiences, events, setting, and/or characters. **e.** Provide a conclusion that follows from and reflects on what is experienced, observed, or resolved over the course of the narrative.

Grades 9–10 Students	Grades 11–12 Students
Production and Distribution of Writing	
4. Produce clear and coherent writing in which the development, organization, and style are appropriate to task, purpose, and audience. (Grade-specific expectations for writing types are defined in standards 1–3 above.)	**4.** Produce clear and coherent writing in which the development, organization, and style are appropriate to task, purpose, and audience. (Grade-specific expectations for writing types are defined in standards 1–3 above.)
5. Develop and strengthen writing as needed by planning, revising, editing, rewriting, or trying a new approach, focusing on addressing what is most significant for a specific purpose and audience. (Editing for conventions should demonstrate command of Language standards 1–3 up to and including grades 9–10.)	**5.** Develop and strengthen writing as needed by planning, revising, editing, rewriting, or trying a new approach, focusing on addressing what is most significant for a specific purpose and audience. (Editing for conventions should demonstrate command of Language standards 1–3 up to and including grades 11–12.)
6. Use technology, including the Internet, to produce, publish, and update individual or shared writing products, taking advantage of technology's capacity to link to other information and to display information flexibly and dynamically.	**6.** Use technology, including the Internet, to produce, publish, and update individual or shared writing products in response to ongoing feedback, including new arguments or information.
Research to Build and Present Knowledge	
7. Conduct short as well as more sustained research projects to answer a question (including a self-generated question) or solve a problem; narrow or broaden the inquiry when appropriate; synthesize multiple sources on the subject, demonstrating understanding of the subject under investigation.	**7.** Conduct short as well as more sustained research projects to answer a question (including a self-generated question) or solve a problem; narrow or broaden the inquiry when appropriate; synthesize multiple sources on the subject, demonstrating understanding of the subject under investigation.
8. Gather relevant information from multiple authoritative print and digital sources, using advanced searches effectively; assess the usefulness of each source in answering the research question; integrate information into the text selectively to maintain the flow of ideas, avoiding plagiarism and following a standard format for citation.	**8.** Gather relevant information from multiple authoritative print and digital sources, using advanced searches effectively; assess the strengths and limitations of each source in terms of the task, purpose, and audience; integrate information into the text selectively to maintain the flow of ideas, avoiding plagiarism and overreliance on any one source and following a standard format for citation.
9. Draw evidence from literary or informational texts to support analysis, reflection, and research. **a.** Apply grades 9–10 Reading standards to literature (e.g., "Analyze how an author draws on and transforms source material in a specific work [e.g., how Shakespeare treats a theme or topic from *Ovid* or the Bible or how a later author draws on a play by Shakespeare]"). **b.** Apply grades 9–10 Reading standards to literary nonfiction (e.g., "Delineate and evaluate the argument and specific claims in a text, assessing whether the reasoning is valid and the evidence is	**9.** Draw evidence from literary or informational texts to support analysis, reflection, and research. **a.** Apply grades 11–12 Reading standards to literature (e.g., "Demonstrate knowledge of eighteenth-, nineteenth-, and early twentieth-century foundational works of American literature, including how two or more texts from the same period treat similar themes or topics"). **b.** Apply grades 11–12 Reading standards to literary nonfiction (e.g., "Delineate and evaluate the reasoning in seminal U.S. texts, including the application of constitutional principles and use of

Grades 9–10 Students	Grades 11–12 Students
relevant and sufficient; identify false statements and fallacious reasoning").	legal reasoning [e.g., in U.S. Supreme Court case majority opinions and dissents] and the premises, purposes, and arguments in works of public advocacy [e.g., *The Federalist*, presidential addresses]").
Range of Writing	
10. Write routinely over extended time frames (time for research, reflection, and revision) and shorter time frames (a single sitting or a day or two) for a range of tasks, purposes, and audiences.	**10.** Write routinely over extended time frames (time for research, reflection, and revision) and shorter time frames (a single sitting or a day or two) for a range of tasks, purposes, and audiences.

Glossary

Academic writing: a form of academic discourse in written rather than oral form. It includes features found primarily in specific disciplines and content areas as well as features that cross academic disciplines (such as the Tier Two words identified by Coxhead, 2000).

Blog: short for "web log" and is usually a public-facing website on which a user posts commentary, photographs, or video in a journal-type format. Posts are archived in chronological order, but tags with keywords make specific entries easy to locate again. Teachers sometimes maintain a class blog on which students' work and class announcements are kept. Less often, students maintain their own blogs for academic purposes.

Collaborative writing: involves a single work composed by many students either working together in a classroom or other learning space or in an online environment using tools that allow synchronous (at the same time) or asynchronous (at different times) composing. Wikis, Google Docs, and other tools that permit sharing of a single file or document make this possible online.

Course management system (CMS) (sometimes called a learning management system): includes a suite of tools for classroom use including a place to upload work to be scored, threaded discussion groups, private journals, blogs, and means of delivering content via text, images, and video. Examples include eCollege and Moodle.

Eposter: an online advertisement, project explanation, or demonstration via text, images, and video. Glogster and Museum Box are tools with which students can create eposters.

Genre: a descriptive term for categories of works (in this case, referring to written text). What constitutes a genre is much debated and often in a state of flux. Classic genres include tragedy and comedy. Common references to genre today include the novel or poem, but the genre also refers to types of literature such as the western, science fiction, and young adult literature.

Knowledge transformation model: based on the work of Bereiter and Scardamalia (1987), informs many of the ideas contained in this book. Knowledge transformation suggests that writers consciously exercise control over the written work, especially when that writing presents a challenging problem. One implication of this model is that writers often learn as part of the composing process rather than just demonstrating what they already know.

Post: a message placed in an online environment for others to read. Posts can be found in threaded discussion groups, blog entries, wikis, and other message boards. The term "post" can be either a noun or a verb.

Short cues: writing tasks in short bursts such as a journal entry, threaded discussion post, or exit slip. They are typically intended to be shared with a teacher or peers, and they promote thinking about content or shaping ideas in many cases.

Social bookmarking: the use of an online tool to store and organize links to sites that are of interest to the user, but the tool also makes those links available to a social network of others who share the same interest. In this book, we have used *Delicious.com* to share some bookmarks with readers.

Social network: a group of individuals connected by a common interest or purpose. Social networks are not confined to online environments. Online social networks are created in a variety of ways including the popular online site Facebook. However, small, closed networks can be maintained for academic purposes using tools such as Ning, Nicenet, e-mail, or wikis.

Text structures: organizational patterns detectable in a given work (a text). Closely associated with text structure in the minds of many writing theorists and practitioners are overarching domains of writing types such as narration (primarily taking a storytelling approach), persuasion, and exposition (which is primarily intended to convey information). Common text structures are organizational in character and include such approaches as cause–effect, compare–contrast, problem solution, description, and so on. Note that written text often employs a number of organizational structures even though one structure may be more prominent.

Threaded discussion group (TDG): a group of individuals connected via an electronic network, such as through e-mail, listserv, a discussion forum, or a bulletin board service. Examples of bulletin board services include Yahoo! groups and Ning groups. Conversations are organized by topic with contributors posting messages by responding to each other in an asynchronous manner (one person might post in the evening, but another member of the group may choose to respond the next morning, for example). This allows members of the group to communicate about common interests asynchronously, in their own time and at their own pace.

Twitter (tweet): online social network in which participants post very short messages (called microblogging). Messages are typically 140 characters in length, but other tools make it possible to post a message on Twitter that exceed that length or contain other types of media. A tweet is a message posted on Twitter, whereas "to tweet" is a verb describing the action of posting on Twitter. Hashtags (preceded by "#") help organize tweets and make them easily searchable.

Web 2.0: sometimes referred to as the "read–write web," is the evolution of social media (wikis, blogs, and other participatory digital tools) that permit the user to add content to the web rather than simply retrieving information places on the web by those with sophisticated programming expertise.

Wiki: includes the most popular of websites, Wikipedia (with a capital letter), in which users all over the world are invited to contribute to the site. However, a wiki (with a lower case letter) is a form of social media and a tool that foregrounds group collaboration to create a website including a class or small group of students working on a project.

References

American Association of Colleges for Teacher Education and the Partnership for 21st Century Skills (AACTE & P21). (2010). *21st century knowledge and skills in educator preparation.* Retrieved from *http://aacte.org/index.php?/Research-Policy/Recent-Reports-on-Educator-Preparation/aacte-and-p21–release-paper-on-21st-century-knowledge-and-skills-in-educator-preparation.html*

Adler, M. J. (1982). *The Paideia proposal: An education manifesto.* New York: Macmillan.

Alderson, J. C., & Wall, D. (1993). Does washback exist? *Applied Linguistics, 14*(2), 115–129.

American Psychological Association. (2010). *Publication manual of the American Psychological Association* (6th ed.). Washington, DC: Author.

Anderson, L. W., & Krathwohl, D. R. (Eds.). (2001). *A taxonomy for learning, teaching, and assessing: Revision of Bloom's taxonomy of educational objectives.* New York: Longman.

Apple, Inc. (2012). Voiceover [software]. Retrieved from *http://www.apple.com/accessibility/voiceover.*

Applebee, A. N. (1981). *Writing in the secondary school: English and the content areas.* Urbana, IL: National Council of Teachers of English.

Applebee, A. N. (1984). *Contexts for learning to write: Studies of secondary school instruction.* Urbana, IL: National Council of Teachers of English.

Atwell, N. (1987). *In the middle: Writing, reading, and learning with adolescents.* Portsmouth, NH: Heinemann.

Atwell, N. (2002). *Lessons that change writers.* Portsmouth, NH: Heinemann.

Baird, R. (2006, November/December). Model showcase: A bare-bones guide to persuasive writing. *Writing (Weekly Reader),* 16–18.

Barone, D. (2011). Practicing persuasion. *The California Reader, 45*(1), 15–20.

Barthes, R. (1953/1967). *Writing degree zero* (A. Lavers & C. Smith, Trans.). New York: Hill and Wang. (Original work published 1953)

Beach, R., & Friedrich, T. (2006). Response to writing. In C. A. MacArthur, S. Graham, & J. Fitzgerald (eds), *Handbook of writing research* (pp. 222–234). New York: Guilford Press.

Beck, I. L., McKeown, M. G., & Kucan, L. (2002). *Bringing words to life: Robust vocabulary instruction.* New York: Guilford Press.

Beck, S. W., & Jeffery, J. W. (2007). Genres of high-stakes writing assessments and the construct of writing competence. *Assessing Writing, 12*(1), 60–79.

Beckenstein, W., & Staunton, M. (1998). *The effects of computer location on first graders' usage and enjoyment of computers.* Retrieved from ERIC database. (ED419523)

Benjamin, A. (1999). *Writing in the content areas.* Larchmont, NY: Eye on Education.

Bereiter, C., & Scardamalia, M. (1987). *The psychology of written composition.* Hillsdale, NJ: Erlbaum.

Berninger, V. W., & Richards, T. L. (2002). *Brain literacy for educators and psychologists.* Boston: Academic Press.

Berry, K. S. (1985). Talking to learn subject matter/learning subject matter talk. *Language Arts, 62*(1), 34–42.

Blamey, K. L., Meyer, C. K., & Walpole, S. (2009). Middle and high school literacy coaches: A national survey. *Journal of Adolescent and Adult Literacy, 52*(4), 310–323.

Bourgeois, M. (n.d.). Managing your classroom computer center. *Scholastic.* Retrieved from *http://www2.scholastic.com/browse/article.jsp?id=6752.*

Bowers-Campbell, J. (2011, May). Take it out of class: Exploring virtual literature circles. *Journal of Adult and Adolescent Literacy, 54*(8), 557–567.

Bradbury, R. (1974). Just this side of Byzantium: An introduction. In *Dandelion wine* (pp. vii–xii). New York: Bantam Books. (Original work published 1957)

Bravo, M. A., & Cervetti, G. N. (2008). Teaching vocabulary through text and experience in content areas. In A. E. Farstrup & S. J. Samuels (Eds.), *What research has to say about vocabulary instruction* (pp. 130–149). Newark, DE: International Reading Association.

Britton, J. (1992). *Language and learning: The importance of speech in children's development, new edition.* London: Penguin Books.

Brown, A. L., Campione, J. C., & Day, J. D. (1981). Learning to learn: On training students to learn from texts. *Educational Researcher, 10*(2), 14–21.

Bruce, B. C. (Ed.). (2003). *Literacy in the information age: Inquiries into meaning making with new technologies.* Newark, DE: International Reading Association.

Bruner, J. (1978). The role of dialogue in language acquisition. In A. Sinclair, R. J. Jarvelle, & W. J. M. Levelt (Eds.), *The child's concept of language* (pp. 241–256). New York: Springer-Verlag.

Cahill, T. (2003). *Sailing the wine-dark sea: Why the Greeks matter.* New York: Doubleday.

California Department of Education. (2007). *English/language arts framework.* Sacramento, CA: Author. Retrieved from *http://www.cde.ca.gov/ci/rl/cf.*

California Department of Education. (2010). *California high school exit examination—CalEdFacts.* Retrieved from *http://www.cde.ca.gov/ta/tg/hs/cefcahsee.asp.*

Calkins, L. M. (1994). *The art of teaching writing.* Portsmouth, NH: Heinemann.

Campbell, C. (2009). Middle years students' use of self-regulating strategies in an online journaling environment. *EducationalTechnology and Society, 12*(3), 98–106.

Cappello, M. (2006). Under construction: Voice and identity development in writing workshop. *Language Arts, 83*(6), 482–491.

CAST. (2011). *Universal design for learning guidelines version 2.0.* Wakefield, MA: Author. Retrieved from *http://www.udlcenter.org/aboutudl/udlguidelines.*

Castek, J., Dalton, B., & Grisham, D. L. (2012). Using multimedia to support generative vocabulary learning. In E. J. Kame'enui & J. F. Baumann (Eds.), *Vocabulary instruction: Research to practice* (2nd ed.). New York: Guilford Press.

Caverly, D. C. (2010). Techtalk: Assistive technology for writing. *Journal of Developmental Education, 31*(3), 36–37.

Cazden, C. B. (2001). *Classroom discourse: The language of teaching and learning* (2nd ed.). Portsmouth, NH: Heinemann.

Cernohous, S., Wolsey, T. D., & Grisham, D. L. (2010). Editors' introduction: Contemporary technological innovations in teaching and learning and teacher education. *Teacher Education Quarterly, Special Online Edition.* Retrieved from *http://teqjournal.org/editors.html.*

Chandler, M. (1977). Social cognition: A select review in current research. In W. Overton & J. McCarthy Gallagher (Eds.), *Knowledge and development* (pp. 93–148). New York: Plenum Press.

Chapman, C., & King, R. (2009). *Differentiated instructional strategies for reading in the content areas* (2nd ed.). Thousand Oaks, CA: Corwin.

Clarke, L. W., & Besnoy, K. D. (2010). Connecting the old to the new: What technology-crazed adolescents tell us about teaching content area literacy. *Journal of Media Literacy Education, 2*(1), 47–56.

Cobern, W. W., Schuster, D., Adams, B., Applegate, B., Skjold, B., Undreiu, A., et al. (2010). Experimental comparison of inquiry and direct instruction in science. *Research in Science and Technological Education, 28*(1), 81–96.

Common[T1] Core Standards Initiative. (2010). Common core state standards for English language arts & literacy in history/social studies, science, and technical subjects. Council of Chief State School Officers and the National Governors Association. Retrieved from *http://www.corestandards.org/assets/CCSSI_ELA%20Standards.pdf.*

Covill, A. E. (2011). College students' perceptions of the traditional lecture method. *College Student Journal, 45*(1), 92–101.

Coxhead, A. (2000). A new academic word list. *TESOL Quarterly, 34*(2), 213–238.

Crick, F. (1988). *What mad pursuit: A personal view of scientific discovery.* New York: Basic Books.

Csikszentmihalyi, M. (1996). *Flow and the psychology of discovery and invention* [Electronic version]. New York: HarperCollins e-books.

Daines, D. (1986). Are teachers asking higher level questions? *Education, 106,* 368–374.

Dalton, B., & Grisham, D. L. (2011). E-voc strategies: Ten ways to improve vocabulary teaching using technology. *The Reading Teacher, 64*(5), 306–317.

Dalton, B., & Strangman, N. (2006). Improving struggling readers' comprehension through scaffolded hypertexts and other computer-based literacy programs. In D. Reinking, M. C. McKenna, L. D. Labbo, & R. D. Keiffer (Eds.), *Handbook of literacy and technology* (2nd ed., pp. 75–92). Mahwah, NJ: Erlbaum.

Daniels, H. (2002). *Literature circles: Voice and choice in book clubs and reading groups.* Portland, ME: Stenhouse.

Daniels, H., Zemelman, S., & Steineke, N. (2007). *Content-area writing: Every teacher's guide.* Portsmouth, NH: Heinemann.

Davis, A., & McGrail, E. (2009). "Proof-revising" with podcasting: Keeping readers in mind as students listen to and rethink their writing. *The Reading Teacher, 62*(6), 522–529.

Day, A. G. (1947). Writer's magic. *American Association of University Professors Bulletin, 33,* 269–278.

Dejoy, N. C. (1999). I was a process-model baby. In J. Kent (Ed.), *Beyond the writing process paradigm: Post-process theory* (pp. 163–178). Carbondale: Southern Illinois University Press.

Dewey, J. (1900). *The school and society and the child and the curriculum.* Chicago: University of Chicago Press.

Don Johnston, Inc. (2008). Don Johnston Assistive Technology. Retrieved from *http://www.donjohnston.com.*

Dornan, R. W., Rosen, L. M., & Wilson, M. (2003). *Within and beyond the writing process in the secondary English classroom.* Boston: Pearson Education Group.

Drabick, D. A. G., Weisberg, R., Paul, L., & Bubier, J. L. (2007). Keeping it short and sweet: Brief, ungraded writing assignments facilitate learning. *Teaching of Psychology, 34*(3), 172–176.

DuFour, R., & Eaker, R. (1998). *Professional learning communities at work: Best practices for enhancing student achievement.* Bloomington, IA: National Education Service.

Duke, C. R. (2001). Student writing: Response as assessment. In C. R. Duke & R. Sanchez (Eds.), *Assessing writing across the curriculum* (pp. 31–48). Durham, NC: Carolina Academic Press.

Durkin, D. (1990). Dolores Durkin speaks on instruction. *The Reading Teacher, 43*(7), 472–726.

Dutro, S., & Moran, C. (2003). Rethinking English language instruction: An architectural approach. In G. G. Garcia (Ed.), *English learners: Researching the highest levels of English literacy* (pp. 227–258). Newark, DE: International Reading Association.

Eagleton, M. B., & Dobler, E. (2007). *Reading the web: Strategies for Internet inquiry.* New York: Guilford Press.

Einstein, A. (1961). *Relativity: The special and the general theory, a clear explanation anyone can understand.* New York: Crown.

Emig, J. (1971). *The composing processes of twelfth graders.* Urbana, IL: National Council of Teachers of English.

English, C. (2007, September). Finding a voice in a threaded discussion group: Talking about literature online. *English Journal, 97*(1), 56–61.

Entrepreneur. (2010). Podcast. Retrieved from *http://www.entrepreneur.com/encyclopedia/term/159122.html.*

Erikson, E. H. (1968). *Identity: Youth and crisis.* New York: Norton.

eSchool News. (2010, June 4). *Kentucky offers cloud-based software to 700,000 school users.* Retrieved from *http://www.eschoolnews.com/2010/06/04/kentucky-offers-cloud-based-software-to-700000–school-users/?ast=40.*

Fang, Z., & Schleppegrell, M. J. (2010). Disciplinary literacies across content areas: Supporting secondary reading through functional language analysis. *Journal of Adolescent and Adult Literacy, 53*(7), 587–597.

Fang, Z., Schleppegrell, M. J., & Cox, B. E. (2006). Understanding the language demands of schooling: Nouns in academic registers. *Journal of Literacy Research, 38*, 247–273.

Farnan, N., & Fearn, L. (2008). Writing in the disciplines: More than writing across the curriculum. In D. Lapp, J. Flood, & N. Farnan (Eds.), *Content area reading and learning: Instructional strategies* (3rd ed., pp. 403–423). New York: Erlbaum.

Fearn, L., & Farnan, N. (2001). *Interactions: Teaching writing and the language arts.* Boston: Allyn & Bacon.

Fisher, D., & Frey, N. (2004). *Improving adolescent literacy: Strategies at work.* Upper Saddle River, NJ: Pearson, Merrill, Prentice Hall.

Fisher, D., & Frey, N. (2008). Do the right thing. *English Journal, 97*(6), 38–42. Retrieved from *http://www.fisherandfrey.com/wp-content/uploads/2010/01/ej-technology.pdf.*

Fox, M. (1993). *Radical reflections.* New York: Harcourt Brace.

Frey, N., Fisher, D., & Gonzalez, A. (2010). *Literacy 2.0: Reading and writing in 21st century classrooms.* Bloomington, IN: Solution Tree Press.

Frost, R. L. (Estate of). (2006). *The notebooks of Robert Frost.* Cambridge, MA: Harvard University Press.

Gallagher, K. (2006). *Teaching adolescent writers.* Portland, ME: Stenhouse.

Gardner, H. (1983). *Frames of mind: The theory of multiple intelligences.* New York: Basic Books.

Gardner, H. (1993). *Creating minds: An anatomy of creativity seen through the lives of Freud, Einstein, Picasso, Stravinsky, Eliot, Graham, and Gandhi.* New York: Basic Books.

Gere, A., Christenbury, L., & Sassi, K. (2005). *Writing on demand: Best practices and strategies for success.* Portsmouth NH: Heinemann.

Glasser, W. (1986). *Control theory in the classroom.* New York: Harper & Row.

Goldberg, N. (2000). *Thunder and lightning: Cracking open the writer's craft.* New York: Bantam Books.

Google. (2011). Google apps for education edition. Retrieved from *http://www.google.com/educators/p_apps.html.*

Gorham, J. (1988, January). The relationship between verbal teacher immediacy behaviors and student learning. *Communication Education, 37*(1), 40–53.

Graham, S., & Perrin, D. (2007). *Writing next: Effective strategies to improve writing of adolescents in middle and high school.* NY: Carnegie Corporation.

Grisham, D. L. (1989). How I discovered team writing: Its benefits and drawbacks. *California English, 25*(5), 6–9.

Grisham, D. L. (1997). Ways to increase student engagement in reading. *Northwest Journal of Reading, 6,* 15–21.

Grisham, D. L., Bicais, J., & Crosby, S. (2012, April 14). *A portrait of the teacher as an artist.* Paper presented at the annual meeting of the American Educational Research Association, Vancouver, British Columbia.

Grisham, D. L., & Molinelli, P. (1995). *Professional's guide: Cooperative learning.* Westminster, CA: Teacher Created Materials.

Grisham, D. L., & Smetana, L. (2011). Generative technology for teacher educators. *Journal of Reading Education, 36*(3), 12–18.

Grisham, D. L., & Wolsey, T. D. (2006). Recentering the middle school classroom as a vibrant learning community: Students, literacy, and technology intersect. *Journal of Adult and Adolescent Literacy, 49*(8), 648–660.

Grisham, D. L., & Wolsey, T. D. (2005). Assessing writing: Comparing the responses of 8th graders, preservice teachers, and experienced teachers in a graduate reading program. *Reading and Writing Quarterly, 21*(4), 315–330.

Grisham, D. L., & Wolsey, T. D. (with Soto, G.). (2011). An interview with Gary Soto. *The California Reader, 44*(2), 37–39.

Grisham, D. L., Wozniak, C., & Wolsey, T. D. (2010). Going beyond opinion: Teaching elementary students to write persuasively. In B. Moss & D. Lapp (Eds.), *Teaching new literacies in grades 2–4: Resources for 21st-century classrooms* (pp. 97–111). New York: Guilford Press.

Hacker, D. (2004). Self-regulated comprehension during normal reading. In R. B. Ruddell & N. Unrau (Eds.), *Theoretical models and processes of reading* (5th ed., pp. 755–779). Newark, DE: International Reading Association.

Hall, T., Strangman, N., & Meyer, A. (2003). *Differentiated instruction and implications for UDL implementation.* Retrieved from *http://aim.cast.org/learn/historyarchive/ backgroundpapers/differentiated_instruction_udl.*

Hattie, J. & Timperley, H. (2007). The power of feedback. *Review of Educational Research, 77,* 81–112.

Hawking, S. (1988). *A brief history of time* (updated and expanded ed.). New York: Bantam Books.

Hayakawa, S. I., & Hayakawa, A. R. (1990). *Language in thought and action* (5th ed.). San Diego: Harcourt.

Hillocks, G. (1986). *Research on written composition: New directions for teaching.* Urbana, IL: ERIC Clearinghouse on Reading and Communication Skills.

Hillocks, G. (2002). *The testing trap: How state writing assessments control learning.* New York: Teachers College Press.

Hoffman, J. V. (1992). Critical reading/thinking across the curriculum: Using I-charts to support learning. *Language Arts, 69,* 121–127.

Hornik, S. (1999). Implications of the electronic one-minute paper. In B. Collis & R. Oliver (Eds.), *Proceedings of world conference on educational multimedia, hypermedia and telecommunications 1999* (pp. 1223–1224). Chesapeake, VA: Association for the Advancement of Computing in Education.

Hunter, M. (1982). *Mastery teaching: Increasing instructional effectiveness in elementary, secondary schools, colleges, and universities.* Thousand Oaks, CA: Corwin Press.

Hyland, K., & Tse, P. (2004). Metadiscourse in academic writing: A reappraisal. *Applied Linguistics, 25*(2), 156–177.

Hynd-Shanahan, C., Holschuh, J. P., & Hubbard, B. P. (2004). Thinking like an historian: College students' reading of multiple historical documents. *Journal of Literacy Research, 36,* 141–176.

Inspiration Software, Inc. (2011). Inspiration. Beaverton, OR: Author.

International Reading Association. (2009). *New literacies and 21st century technologies: A position statement of the International Reading Association.* Retrieved from *http://www.reading.org/General/AboutIRA/PositionStatements/21stCenturyLiteracies.aspx.*

Johnson, D. (2010). Teaching with authors' blogs: Connection, collaboration, creativity. *Journal of Adult and Adolescent Literacy, 54, 3,* 172–180.

Johnson, D. W., Johnson, R. T., & Holubec, E. J. (1994). *The new circles of learning: Cooperation in the classroom and school.* Alexandria, VA: Association for Supervision andCurriculum Development.

Jones, F. (2007). *Tools for teaching* (2nd ed.). Santa Cruz, CA: Jones & Associates.

Karchmer-Klein, R. (2007). Best practices in using the Internet to support writing. In S. Graham, C. A. MacArthur, & J. Fitzgerald (Eds.), *Best practices in writing* (pp. 222–241). New York: Guilford Press.

Karchmer-Klein, R., MacArthur, C., & Najera, K. (2008, December). *The effects of electronic concept mapping software on fifth grade students' writing.* Paper presented at the 58th annual meeting of the National Reading Conference, Orlando, FL.

Kellogg, R. T., & Whiteford, A. P. (2009). Training advanced writing skills: The case for deliberate practice. *Educational Psychologist, 44*(4), 250–266.

Kellogg, R. T., Whiteford, A. P., & Quinlan, T. (2010). Does automated feedback help students learn to write?. *Journal of Educational Computing Research, 42*(2), 173–196.

Killion, J. (1999). Journaling. *Journal of Staff Development, 20*(3). Retrieved from *http://www.learningforward.org/news/jsd/killion203.cfm.*

King, F. B., & LaRocco, D. J. (2006, February). E-journaling: A strategy to support student reflection and understanding. *Current Issues in Education, 9*(4). Available at *http://cie.ed.asu.edu/volume9/number4.*

King-Sears, M. E., Swanson, C., & Mainzer, L. (2011). TECHnology and literacy for adolescents with disabilities. *Journal of Adolescent and Adult Literacy, 54*(8), 569–578.

Klein, P. D., & Rose, M. A. (2010). Teaching argument and explanation to prepare junior students for writing to learn. *Reading Research Quarterly, 45*(4), 433–461.

Krathwohl, D. R. (2002). A revision of Bloom's taxonomy: An overview. *Theory into Practice, 41*(4), 212–218.

Lapp, D., Fisher, D., & Wolsey, T. D. (2009). *Literacy growth for every child: Differentiated small-group instruction K–6.* New York: Guilford Press.

Lapp, D., Shea, A., & Wolsey, T. D. (2011). Blogging and audience awareness. *Journal of Education, 191*(191)(1), 33–44.

Lee, C. D. (2006). Every good-bye ain't gone: Analyzing the cultural underpinnings of classroom talk. *International Journal of Qualitative Studies in Education, 19*(3), 305–327.

Lee, H. S. (2008). *A case study of cross-cultural and cross-age online literature discussion.* Retrieved from *https://mospace.umsystem.edu/xmlui/handle/10355/9103.*

Lemke, J. L. (1989). Making text talk. *Theory-into-practice, 28*(2), 136–141.

Lenski, S., & Verbruggen, F. (2010). *Writing instruction and assessment for English language learners, K–8.* New York: Guilford Press.

Leu, D. J., Jr. (2000). Literacy and technology: Deictic consequences for literacy education in an information age. In M. L. Kamil, P. Mosenthal, P. D. Pearson, & R. Barr (Eds.), *Handbook of reading research, Volume III* (pp. 743–770). Mahwah, NJ: Erlbaum.

Leu, D. J., Kinzer, C. K., Coiro, J., & Cammack. D. W. (2004). Toward a theory of new literacies emerging from the Internet and other information and communication technologies. In R. B. Ruddell & N. Unrau (Eds.), *Theoretical models and processes of reading* (5th ed., pp. 1570–1613). Newark, DE: International Reading Association.

Leu, D. J., Leu, D. D., & Coiro, J. (2004). *Teaching with the Internet K–12: New literacies for new times* (4th ed.). Norwood, MA: Christopher-Gordon.

Lewis, C., & Fabos, B. (2005). Instant messaging, literacies, and social identities. *Reading Research Quarterly, 40*(4), 470–501.

Lyle, S. (1993). An investigation into ways in which children talk themselves into meaning. *Language and Education, 7*(3), 181–187.

MacArthur, C. (2006). Assistive technology for writing: Tools for struggling writers. In L. Van Waes, M. Leijten, & C. M. Neuwirth (Eds.), *Writing and digital media* (pp. 11–29). Amsterdam: Elsevier.

Macbeth, K. P. (2010). Deliberate false provisions: The use and usefulness of models in learning academic writing. *Journal of Second Language Writing, 19*(1), 33–48.

MacOn, J., Bewell, D., & Vogt, M. (1991). *Responses to literature.* Newark, DE: International Reading Association.

Maine Department of Education. (2009). *About MLTI.* Retrieved from *http://www.maine.gov/mlti/about/index.shtml.*

Marzano, R. J. (2004). *Building background knowledge for academic achievement.* Alexandria, VA: Association for Supervision and Curriculum Development.

Marzano, R. J., Pickering, D. J., & Pollock, J. E. (2001). *Classroom instruction that works: Research-based strategies for increasing student achievement.* Alexandria, VA: Association for Supervision and Curriculum Development.

McIntosh, M. E. (1991). No time for writing in your class? *The Mathematics Teacher, 84*(6), 423–433.

Mehan, H. (1979). *Learning lessons: Social organization in the classroom.* Cambridge MA: Harvard University Press.

Merritt, S. P. (2003). *Writing across the curriculum: High school teacher handbook.* Retrieved from *http://www.ncpublicschools.org/docs/curriculum/languagearts/secondary/writing/writinghandbook.pdf.*

Microsoft, Inc. (2011). Word 2010 [software]. Retrieved from *http://office.microsoft.com/en-us/word.*

Modern Language Association. (2009). *MLA handbook for writers of research papers* (7th ed.). New York: Author.

Moje, E. B. (2008). Foregrounding the disciplines in secondary literacy teaching and learning: A call for change. *Journal of Adult and Adolescent Literacy, 52,* 96–107.

Moje, E. B., Young, J. P., Readence, J. E., & Moore, D. W. (2000). Reinventing adolescent literacy for new times: Perennial and millennial issues. *Journal of Adolescent and Adult Literacy, 43*(5), 400–410.

Montelongo, J., Berber-Jiminez, L., Hernandez, A. C., & Hosking, D. (2006). Teaching expository text structures. *The Science Teacher, 73*(2), 28–31.

Montgomery, K. (2000). Classroom rubrics: Systematizing what teachers do naturally. *Clearing House, 73*(6), 324–328.

Murray, D. (2005). *Write to learn* (8th ed.). Boston: Thomson Wadsworth.

National Education Technology Panel. (2010). *Transforming American education: Learning powered by technology.* Washington, DC: United States Department of Education.

New London Group. (1996). A pedagogy of multiliteracies: Designing social futures. *Harvard Educational Review, 66*(1), 60–92.

November, A. (2008). *Web literacy for educators.* Thousand Oaks, CA: Corwin Press.

Ogle, D. (1986). K-W-L: A teaching model that develops active reading of expository text. *The Reading Teacher, 39,* 564–570.

Palincsar, A. S., & Brown. A. L. (1984). Reciprocal teaching of comprehension-fostering and comprehension-monitoring activities. *Cognition and Instruction, 1,* 117–175.

Pew Internet and American Life Project. (2010). *Generations online.* Retrieved from *http://www.pewinternet.org/Reports/2010/Generations-2010/Overview.aspx.*

Pimple, K. D. (2002). *Using short writing assessments in teaching research ethics.* Retrieved from *http://poynter.indiana.edu/tre/kdp-writing.pdf.*

Pintrich, P. R. (2002). The role of metacognitive knowledge in learning, teaching, and assessing. *Theory Into Practice, 41*(4), 220–225.

Popham, W. J. (1997). What's wrong—and what's right—with rubrics [Electronic version]. *Educational Leadership, 55*(2), 72–75.

Prensky, M. (2001). Digital natives, digital immigrants [Electronic version]. *On the Horizon, 9*(5), 1–6. Available at *http://www.marcprensky.com/writing/Prensky%20–%20Digital%20Natives,%20Digital%20Immigrants%20–%20Part1.pdf.*

Price, J. J. (1989). Learning mathematics through writing: Some guidelines. *College Mathematics Journal, 20*(5), 393–401.

Rose, D., & Meyer, A. (2002). *Teaching every student in the digital age: Universal design for learning.* Alexandria, VA: Association for Supervision and Curriculum Development. Retrieved from *http://www.cast.org/teachingeverystudent/ideas/tes/index.cfm.*

Rosen, L. D. (2010). *Rewired: Understanding the iGeneration and the way they learn.* New York: Palgrave-MacMillan.

Rowlands, K. D. (2007). Check it out! Using checklists to support student learning. *English Journal, 96*(6), 61–66.

Ruiling, L., & Overbaugh, R. C. (2009). School environment and technology implementation in K–12 classrooms. *Computers in the Schools, 26*(2), 89–106.

Rupley, W. H., Nichols, W. D., & Blair, T. R. (2008). Language and culture in literacy instruction: Where have they gone? *The Teacher Educator, 43*(3), 238–248.

Santa, C. M. (1988). *Content reading including study systems: Reading, writing and studying across the curriculum.* Dubuque, IA: Kendall/Hunt.

Scarcella, R. (2003). *Accelerating academic English: A focus on the English learner.* Oakland, CA: Regents of the University of California.

Schrock, K. (2009). *Critical evaluation of a website: Secondary school level.* Retrieved from *http://school.discoveryeducation.com/schrockguide/eval.html.*

Shanahan, T., & Shanahan, C. (2008). Teaching disciplinary literacy to adolescents: Rethinking content-area literacy. *Harvard Educational Review, 78*(1), 40–59.

Shellard, E., & Protheroe, N. (2004). *Writing across the curriculum to increase student learning in middle and high school.* Arlington, VA: Educational Research Service.

Smetana, L., & Grisham, D. L. (2011). Generative technology for teacher educators. *Journal of Reading Education, 36*(3), 12–18.

Smetana, L. D., Odelson, D., Burns, H., & Grisham, D. L. (2009, November). Using graphic novels in the high school classroom: Engaging deaf students with a new genre. *Journal of Adult and Adolescent Literacy, 53*(3), 228–240.

Software and Information Industry Association. (2011, August 1). Results of the spring 2010 SIIA vision K–20 survey. Retrieved from *http://www.siia.net/visionk20/pages/progress.html.*

Spandel, V. (2009). *Creating writers through 6-trait writing assessment and instruction* (5th ed.). Boston: Allyn & Bacon.

Spandel, V., & Stiggins, R. J. (1997). *Creating writers: Linking writing assessment and instruction.* New York: Longman.

Starr, L. (2004). Managing technology: Tips from the experts. *Education World.* Available at *http://www.educationworld.com/a_tech/tech/tech116.shtml.*

Steinbeck, J. (1952). *East of Eden.* New York: Viking.

Steinbeck, J. (1969). *Journal of a novel: The east of Eden letters.* New York: Penguin Books.

Stiggins, R. (2005). *Student-involved assessment for learning* (4th ed.). Upper Saddle River, NJ: Pearson, Merrill, Prentice Hall.

Strauss, W., & Howe, N. (1991). *Generations: The history of America's future, 1584–2069.* New York: Quill, Morrow.

Strunk, W., & White, E. B. (2000). *The elements of style* (4th ed.). New York: Longman.

Techpudding. (2011, February 13). Flip your classroom = no more lectures! (+ free resource list). *Techpudding: Spoonfuls of Educational Technology.* Retrieved from *http://techpudding.com/2011/02/13/flip-your-classroom-no-more-lectures-free-resource-list.*

Tchudi, S. (1986). *Teaching writing in the content areas: College level.* Washington, DC: National Education Association.

Thinkmap, Inc. (2011) The visual thesaurus®. Retrieved from *http://www.visualthesaurus.com.*

Tibbs, K. (2010, March). *Cell phones R 4 more than texting.* Presentation at the Mid-America Association for Computers in Education (MACE), New York.

Thomas, A. (2007). *Youth online: Identity and literacy in the digital age.* New York: Lang.

Tomlinson, C. A. (2001). *How to differentiate instruction in mixed-ability classrooms* (2nd ed.) Alexandria, VA: Association for Supervision and Curriculum Development.

Tomlinson, C. A. (2008). Learning to love assessment. *Educational Leadership, 65*(4), 8–13. Retrieved from *http://www.ascd.org/publications/educational-leadership/ dec07/vol65/num04/Learning-to-Love-Assessment.aspx.*

Tomlinson, C. A., & Allan, S. D. (2000). *Leadership for differentiating schools and classrooms.* Alexandria, VA: Association for Supervision and Curriculum Development. Available at *http://www.ascd.org/publications/books/100216.aspx.*

Tompkins, G. (2003). *Literacy for the 21st century* (3rd ed.). New York: Merrill Prentice Hall.

Ullman, E. (2011, February). School CIO: The new one-to-one. *Tech and Learning, 31*(7), 54–57.

Viscovich, S., Eschenauer, R., Sinatra, R., & Beasley, T. M. (2008). Connecting critical thinking, organizational structures, and report writing. *Journal of School Connections, 1*(1), 63–86.

WHS Style Guide Committee. (2011, August 1). *WHS style guide.* Retrieved from *http:// www.wayzata.k12.mn.us/whs/index.php?option=com_content&view=article&id=1 252:introduction-whs-style-guide&catid=100:whs-style-guide&Itemid=2020.*

Wiggins, G. (2007, November 15). *What is an essential question?* Retrieved from *http:// www.authenticeducation.org/bigideas/article.lasso?artId=53.*

Wiggins, G., & McTighe, J. (2005). *Understanding by design* (expanded 2nd ed.). Alexandria, VA: Association for Supervision and Curriculum Development.

Williams, B. T. (2008, May). Tomorrow will not be like today: Literacy and identity in a world of multiliteracies. *Journal of Adult and Adolescent Literacy, 51*(8), 682–686.

Wold, L. S., Elish-Piper, L., & Schultz, B. (2010). Engaging high school students in reading and understanding the canon through the use of linked text sets. In S. Szabo, M. B. Sampson, M. M. Foote, & F. Falk-Ross (Eds.), *Mentoring literacy professionals: Continuing the spirit of CRA/ALER after 50 years* (pp. 391–401). Commerce: Texas A&M University–Commerce.

Wolsey, T. D. (2004, January/February). Literature discussion in cyberspace: Young adolescents using threaded discussion groups to talk about books. *Reading Online, 7*(4). Available at *http://www.readingonline.org/articles/art_index.asp?HREF=wolsey/ index.html.*

Wolsey, T. D. (2010). Complexity in student writing: The relationship between the task and vocabulary uptake. *Literacy Research and Instruction, 49*(2), 194–208.

Wolsey, T. D., & Bostick, P. (2008). The C in ICT: Communication at the heart of literacy learning. *The California Reader, 41*(2), 33–39.

Wolsey, T. D., & Fisher, D., with Burns, A. (2009). *Learning to predict and predicting to learn: How thinking about what might happen next helps students learn.* Boston: Allyn & Bacon, Pearson.

Wurster, S. (2011). *The big 6: About.* Retrieved from *http://www.big6.com/about.*

Yoder, K. K. (2005). *Student talk during the writing process from sixth-graders' perspectives.* Unpublished doctoral dissertation, University of San Francisco, San Francisco, CA.

Zandvliet, D. B. (2006). *Education is not rocket science: The case for deconstructing computer labs in schools.* Rotterdam, The Netherlands: Sense.

Zinsser, W. (1980). *On writing well: An informal guide to writing nonfiction* (2nd ed.). New York: Harper & Row.

Zinsser, W. (1988). *Writing to learn: How to write—and think—clearly about any subject at all*. New York: Harper & Row.

Zwiers, J. (2008). *Building academic language: Essential practices for content classrooms*. Newark, DE: International Reading Association.

Children and Young Adults' Literature Cited

Anderson, L. H. (2000). *Fever, 1793*. New York: Simon & Schuster.

Burnett, F. H. (1911). *The secret garden*. New York: Stokes.

Deedy, C. A. (2007). *Martina, the beautiful cockroach: A Cuban folktale*. Atlanta: Peachtree.

Forster, E. M. (1908). *A room with a view*. London: Edward Arnold.

Hurst, J. (1960, July). The scarlet ibis. *The Atlantic Monthly*, pp. 48–53.

Meyer, S. (2005). *Twilight*. New York: Little, Brown.

Munsch, R. (1986). *Love you forever*. Scarborough, ON: Firefly Books.

Namioka, L. (1999). *Ties that bind, ties that break*. New York: Random House.

Pelzer, D. (1995). *A child called "It."* Deerfield Beach, FL: Heath Communications.

Portman, R. (2000). Bagger and Hardy measure the course at night. On *The legend of Bagger Vance: Music from the motion picture*. [MP3]. Santa Monica, CA: Chapter III Records.

Spiegelman, A. (1986). *Maus I: A survivor's tale*. New York: Pantheon.

Steinbeck, J. (1965). *Of mice and men*. New York: Bantam.

Wiesel, E. (1960). *Night*. New York: Bantam Books.

Index

Page numbers <u>**underlined and in bold**</u> indicate entries found in the Glossary.